ACKNOWLEDGEMENT

We wish to thank The Ford Motor Co. Ltd. for their co-operation and also for supplying data and illustrations. Considerable assistance has also been given by owners, who have discussed their cars in detail, and we would like to express our gratitude for this invaluable advice and help.

ACKNOWLEDGEMENTS

This book is to be returned on or before
the last date stamped below.

Capri 2600, 2800, 1972-76 Autobook

By Kenneth Ball

and the Autobooks Team of Technical Writers

Ford Capri 2600 V6 1972-73
Ford Capri 2800 V6 1974-76

Autobooks Ltd. Golden Lane Brighton BN1 2QJ England

The AUTOBOOK series of Workshop Manuals is the largest in the world and covers the majority of British and Continental motor cars, as well as all major Japanese and Australian models. For a full list see the back of this manual.

CONTENTS

Acknowledgement

Introduction

ISBN 0 85147 645 7

First Edition   1975
Second Edition, fully revised   1976

© Autobooks Ltd 1976

754

Printed and bound in Brighton England for Autobooks Ltd by G. Beard & Son Ltd
B

INTRODUCTION

This do-it-yourself Workshop Manual has been specially written for the owner who wishes to maintain his car in first class condition and to carry out his own servicing and repairs. Considerable savings on garage charges can be made, and one can drive in safety and confidence knowing the work has been done properly.

Comprehensive step-by-step instructions and illustrations are given on all dismantling, overhauling and assembling operations. Certain assemblies require the use of expensive special tools, the purchase of which would be unjustified. In these cases information is included but the reader is recommended to hand the unit to the agent for attention.

Throughout the Manual hints and tips are included which will be found invaluable, and there is an easy to follow fault diagnosis at the end of each chapter.

Whilst every care has been taken to ensure correctness of information it is obviously not possible to guarantee complete freedom from errors or to accept liability arising from such errors or omissions.

Instructions may refer to the righthand or lefthand sides of the vehicle or the components. These are the same as the righthand or lefthand of an observer standing behind the car and looking forward.

CHAPTER 1

THE ENGINE

1:1 Description

The engine used in these cars is a six cylinder water cooled unit arranged in a V formation having overhead valves operated by pushrods and a single camshaft in the angle of the V and driven by helical gears from the crankshaft. See **FIG 1:1**.

Up to and including 1973 models the engine capacity was 2600 cc (155 cu inch) using bore and stroke dimensions of 3.545 and 2.630 inch respectively. For 1974 these dimensions were increased to 3.66 and 2.70 inch for a capacity of 2800 cc (170.8 cu inch). Servicing procedures are not affected, but any variations will be mentioned as applicable and detailed specifications are given in **Technical Data** at the end of the manual.

The cylinder block is of cast iron construction and with the cylinders at an angle of 60 degrees is very rigid and compact. Four main bearings carry the crankshaft in replaceable copper alloy shells and the connecting rod big-ends are also lined with copper/lead inserts.

The overhead valves run in guides which are an integral part of the cylinder head and are actuated by steel push-rods through solid lifters and rocker arms. Valve clearances are set by self locking screws in the rocker arms which pivot on a shaft, drilled as necessary to provide oilways for lubricating the valve gear.

The aluminium inlet manifold has individual passages to the ports in the cylinder head and includes water passages for the engine coolant which is discharged through a connection at the front. The coolant also provides the heat necessary to ensure fuel vaporisation in the inlet ducts without the need for a hot-spot.

A rotor type oil pump is driven by a shaft off the distributor drive at the rear end of the camshaft. A non-adjustable spring loaded relief valve limits the pressure in the system to approximately 50 lb/sq inch and a full flow filter on the right cylinder bank filters the entire output from the pump before it passes into the engine. The lubrication system is shown in **FIG 1:2**.

Crankcase ventilation is obtained by connecting a hose with a regulator valve from the lefthand rocker cover to the intake where it mixes with the fuel/air mixture in the carburetter.

1:2 Maintenance

Under normal conditions very little maintenance should be required on these engines apart from topping up or changing the engine oil at the specified intervals. Adjustments to the fuel and ignition systems, fan belt adjustment, attention to the valve gear and decarbonising the

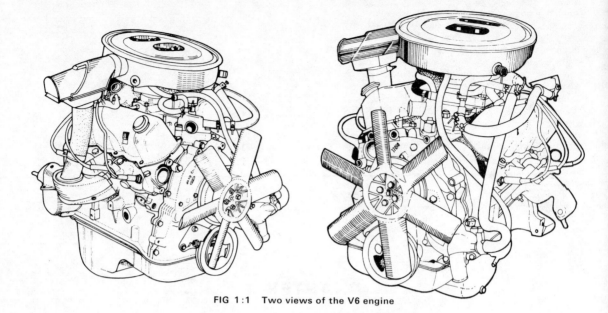

FIG 1:1   Two views of the V6 engine

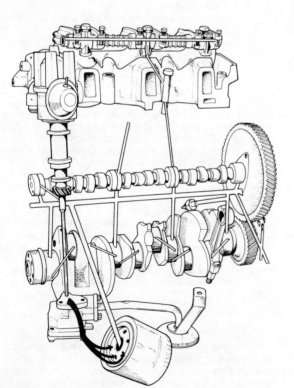

FIG 1:2   The engine lubrication system

cylinder head etc. are all dealt with in their respective places in this book.

Many of the servicing operations which the owner/ driver may wish to do for himself can be carried out without removing the engine from the car, but as these may also be part of a more general overhaul, it will be convenient to describe first the procedure for removing the engine and then the individual components in the order in which they may be serviced.

The section 'Hints on maintenance and overhaul' at the end of this manual contains much information which will be of assistance to the less experienced owners who decide to do their own repairs and they are advised to study them as by doing so they may avoid a great deal of time wasting and trouble.

1:3 Removing the engine

Raise and remove the hood, disconnect the battery and drain the cooling system, collecting the coolant if it contains fresh anti-freeze.

Remove the carburetter air cleaner assembly. Disconnect the upper and lower hoses from the radiator.

Remove the bolts attaching the fan shroud and remove the radiator and shroud together after removing the transmission oil cooler pipes if applicable.

Disconnect the alternator and remove it from the engine. Disconnect the ground wires from the cylinder block and the heater hoses at the block and water pump.

Disconnect and plug the fuel supply pipe at the fuel pump. Disconnect the accelerator linkage at the carburetter and inlet manifold. Disconnect the downshift linkage on automatic models.

Disconnect the engine wire loom at the ignition coil and also the brake booster vacuum line.

Jack-up the car and support it securely on stands.

Disconnect the exhaust pipes at the manifolds. Disconnect and remove the starter.

Remove the engine front support bolts.

On automatic transmission models remove the inspection cover from the converter and disconnect the flywheel. Remove the downshift rod. Remove the bolts securing the converter housing to the engine block and the bolt between the housing and the adaptor plate.

On manual transmission models, remove the clutch linkage and the bolts securing the bell housing to the engine.

Lower the car and attach suitable lifting tackle to lifting brackets at the exhaust manifolds.

Place a jack under the transmission, raise the engine slightly and carefully pull it from the transmission, taking great care not to allow any load to strain the main drive shaft.

Carefully raise the engine from the car and transfer it to an engine stand or bench.

When the Thermactor system of emission control, using an air pump, is fitted it may be necessary to remove certain pipes and components to provide adequate clearance for engine removal. If applicable, remove the power steering pump.

When air conditioning is fitted to the car it will be necessary to have the system evacuated by a qualified service station before attempting to disconnect any components in the system. **Failure to do this can result in serious personal injury.**

Installation:

Prepare the engine on its lifting gear for lowering into its compartment.

On manual transmission models, check the concentric position of the clutch disc using a centralising tool such as T72C-7137 as shown in **FIG 1:3** and fit the rear plate pilot studs and rear plate as in **FIG 1:4**.

Carefully lower the engine, making sure that the exhaust manifolds line up with the exhaust pipes.

Ease the main drive shaft into the clutch disc noting that it may be necessary to rotate the crankshaft slightly until the splines in the two parts are able to mesh.

On automatic models, start the converter pilot into the crankshaft.

Fit the bell housing or converter housing upper securing bolts, taking care to see that the locating pegs in the engine engage the flywheel housing. Remove the jack from under the transmission and also the engine lifting sling.

Position the downshift rod on an automatic transmission and engine.

Raise the car and support it on stands.

On automatic models, position the linkage bracket and fit the remaining converter housing bolts. Fit the bolt between the housing and adaptor plate. Bolt on the flywheel and fit the inspection cover. Connect the downshift rod on the transmission.

On manual transmissions, remove the pilot studs and fit the bolts on the lower part of the bell housing. Connect the clutch linkage.

Fit the starter and connect the cable. Secure the exhaust pipes to the manifolds. Fit the engine front support bolts. Lower the car to the ground.

Install the ground cable and the engine wire loom, connecting it to the ignition coil. Fit the water temperature and oil pressure sending units. Connect the brake servo vacuum line.

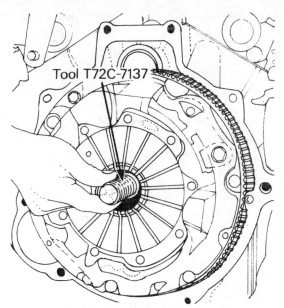

FIG 1:3   Centralising the clutch

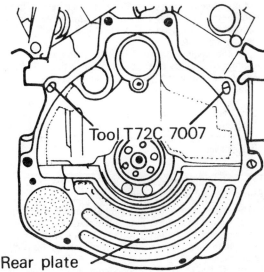

Rear plate

FIG 1:4   Showing the rear plate and pilot studs installed

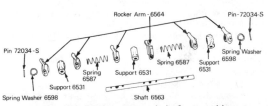

FIG 1:5   Rocker arm and shaft assembly

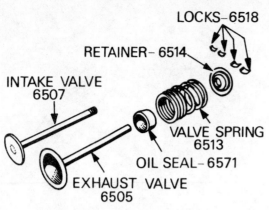

LOCKS—6518

RETAINER—6514

INTAKE VALVE
6507

VALVE SPRING
6513

OIL SEAL—6571

EXHAUST VALVE
6505

FIG 1:6   Valve assemblies

Fit the throttle linkage and the downshift rod on automatic models. Connect the vacuum pipes and the fuel supply pipe to the pump. Fit the heater hoses to the pump and cylinder block.

Refit the alternator and its bracket, adjusting the tension on the belt as described in **Chapter 4**.

Place the fan shroud in position, install the radiator and the two hoses and then fit the shroud attaching bolts.

If an air pump or air conditioning equipment is to be refitted, this must be installed as applicable and, if appropriate, arrangements made for refilling the air conditioning system.

Fill the cooling system. Fill the crankcase with a recommended grade of engine oil. Adjust the downshift linkage on automatic models. Reconnect the battery cables.

Start the engine and allow it to run at a fast idle to warm it up while checking all hoses and joints for leaks. Make any necessary adjustments to the ignition timing or slow running speed as described in **Chapters 2** and **3** respectively.

1:4 Servicing the cylinder head and valves

Removing a cylinder head:

This is one of the many servicing operations which can be carried out with the engine still in the car.

Disconnect the battery and drain the cooling system. Remove the air cleaner and control linkage from the carburetter.

Lift off the spark plug connectors and remove the distributor cap complete with cables. Disconnect the vacuum line and remove the distributor.

Disconnect all heater and water hoses and also the fuel supply pipe. Remove the valve gear cover.

Unscrew the manifold nuts evenly and remove the carburetter and the inlet manifold.

Remove the rocker arm shaft and oil retainer plates. Withdraw the pushrods and place them on one side in sequence so as to ensure replacement in their original position.

Remove the exhaust manifold.

Remove the cylinder head securing bolts and lift off the head and gasket.

Valve rocker arm shaft:

This is removed from the cylinder head by unscrewing the bolts in the three mounting supports and is disassembled by driving out the locating sleeve from the shaft with a drift or mandrel, then removing the spring washer and the remaining components in the order shown in **FIG 1:5**.

When reassembling, first see that the oil supply bores in the rocker shaft are pointed downwards towards the cylinder head in the fitted position. This position can be verified by a notch cut in the front face of the shaft.

Drive one locating sleeve into the shaft and assemble the parts in the order shown in the illustration, the rocker supports with the oil exit passage must be so fitted that this is to the rear on the righthand side and to the front on the left.

Disassembly:

Before removing the valves from the head, remove all carbon deposits from the combustion chambers and valve heads with a scraper and wire brush. This will avoid damage to the valve seats, but be careful not to scratch the head gasket surfaces.

With a suitable compressor compress the valve springs so that the retainer locks can be removed. Lift off the retainers, springs and oil seals (see **FIG 1:6**). The seals should be discarded in favour of new seals, but the valves must be identified for correct refitting.

Thoroughly clean and inspect all parts.

Servicing the valves:

If, after cleaning, a valve has an excessive clearance in its guide, it will be necessary to ream the guide to one of the standard oversizes and an oversize valve fitted.

The valve seats are all at an angle of 45 deg. and should make a clean gas-tight contact all around the valve head. This can usually be obtained by grinding in with a carborundum paste, but if the wear or pitting is excessive it may be necessary to have the valves re-faced and the seats re-cut. This is usually an operation best entrusted to a service station.

Grinding can be done at home using a simple suction tool on the valve head and using a to and fro rotary motion with a smear of grinding paste on the two seating surfaces until the two seats have an even grey matt finish. A seat width of $\frac{1}{16}$ to $\frac{3}{32}$ inch is acceptable, but if the edge of the valve head is less than $\frac{1}{32}$ inch after grinding, the valve must be replaced. Clean off all traces of paste when finished.

Valve springs:

These should be checked for condition by comparison with a new spring and any that have compressed or lost their tension should be renewed.

Note that the coils at one end of the spring are closer than at the other, the close end is fitted next to the cylinder head.

Assembling the cylinder head:

When all the parts have passed inspection or been renewed reassembly can begin.

Lubricate lightly each valve stem and guide and fit each valve into its original guide or to which it has been fitted in the case of new parts. Fit new stem oil seals.

Fit the spring and spring retaining collar, compress the spring and fit the retainer locks.

Re-installing the cylinder head:

Place new gaskets in position on the cylinder block, noting that left and righthand gaskets are not interchangeable. Each gasket is marked FRONT and TOP for correct fitting.

Lower the head carefully, guiding it over the positioning studs and then tighten the eight bolts in the sequence shown in **FIG 1 : 7** and in three stages: first to a torque of 30-40 lb ft, then to 40-50 lb ft and finally to 65-80 lb ft.

Apply a smear of sealing compound to the mating surfaces and place the inlet manifold in position, making sure that the tube on the right bank cylinder head fits into the cut-out in the manifold gasket. Apply a little sealer to the retaining bolt bosses and lower the inlet manifold into position.

Fit the manifold securing bolts finger tight only and then tighten in the sequence shown in **FIG 1 : 8** and in two stages: first to 2-6 lb ft and finally to 15-18 lb ft.

Lubricate the push rods with engine oil and insert into the tappets, taking care to restore them to their original positions.

Fit the exhaust manifolds, noting that no gasket is used but the mating surfaces should be smeared with graphite grease. After fitting the righthand manifold, refit the shroud if one is used.

Before commencing to install the valve rocker shaft assembly slacken off the valve lash adjusting screws a few turns and apply some engine oil all over to provide the initial lubrication.

Fit the assembly on to the cylinder block, guiding the ball ends of the adjusting screws into the recesses in the push rod ends. Fit and tighten the bolts in the support stands to a torque of 35 lb ft.

Adjust the valve clearances as described in **Section 1 : 5**.

Fit the distributor and set the timing as described in **Chapter 3**. Fit the spark plugs and tighten to 20-25 lb ft.

Fit the valve gear covers using new gaskets. Fit the distributor cap and spark plug cables.

Fit the carburetter with a new gasket and check the operation of the linkage. Fit the fuel supply pipe.

1 : 5 Adjusting valve clearances or lash

Valve clearances are adjusted by the rotation of self-locking screws at the push rod end of each valve rocker arm and the correct clearances with a cold engine are: Inlet .014 inch. Exhaust .016 inch.

Most operators have their own method of valve adjustment and there is probably no reason to depart from this. The following is the procedure recommended by the makers.

The valve lash is adjusted by positioning each piston in turn at TDC on the compression stroke in the firing order of 1-4-2-5-3-6.

Rotate the crankshaft (clockwise) until No. 1 is at TDC on the compression stroke and both valves fully closed.

Using a step-type feeler gauge (GO and NO GO) and a ring spanner on the hexagon head of the adjuster, set the clearances to specification.

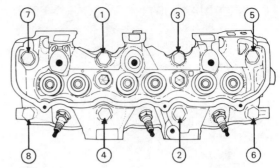

FIG 1 : 7 Sequence for tightening the cylinder head bolts

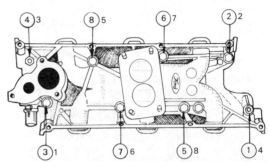

FIG 1 : 8 Sequence for tightening the inlet manifold nuts and bolts. The numbers in circles refer to 2600 cc engines, those without circles to the 2800 cc engines .

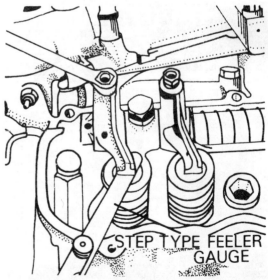

FIG 1 : 9 Adjusting valve lash

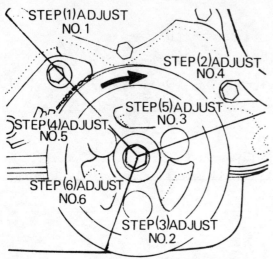

FIG 1:10 Six positions of the crankshaft for lash adjustment

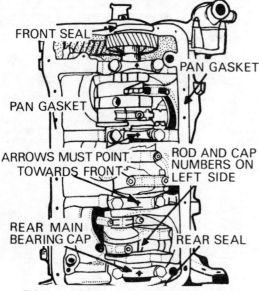

FIG 1:11 Oil pan gaskets and seals installed

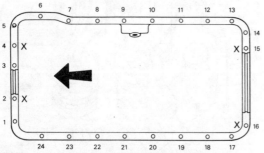

FIG 1:12 Sequence for tightening the oil pan bolts on 2800 cc engines. The four bolts marked X should be inserted first

Adjust the valves in the remaining cylinders following the firing order sequence. This can most easily be accomplished by rotating the engine in increments of one third of a revolution (120 deg.). This will be made clear by reference to **FIGS 1:9** and **1:10**. After two complete revolutions all the pistons will have been at their TDC positions for adjustment.

1:6 The oil pan

If necessary, the oil pan can be removed with only a slight adjustment of the engine in the car.

Remove the oil level dipstick. Remove the fan shroud attachment bolts and move it over the fan. Disconnect the battery and loosen the alternator mounting bolts and bracket.

Raise the car on to some stands and drain the oil from the engine.

Remove the splash shield and the starter. Remove the nuts from the engine front support.

Raise the engine sufficiently to give clearance and place wood blocks between the engine front supports and the chassis brackets.

Remove the clutch or converter housing cover as appropriate.

Undo the retaining bolts and drop the oil pan.

Refitting:

Clean the gasket surfaces of both cylinder block and oil pan and coat with sealer. Make sure that the oil pump pick up tube and filter are clean.

Place the two piece gasket in position on the cylinder block. See **FIG 1:11**.

The oil pan front seal goes on the cylinder front cover with the tabs on the seal over the pan gasket.

The pan rear seal is placed on the rear main bearing cap with the tabs over the pan gasket.

Hold the pan up against the cylinder block and hold it in place with a bolt on either side. Fit the remaining bolts and tighten them from the centre outwards in two stages: first to 2–4 lb ft and second to 5–8 lb ft. On 2800 cc engines the sequence recommended is shown in **FIG 1:12**.

The remainder of the refitting procedure is the reverse of removal.

1:7 The oil pump

To gain access to the oil pump, first remove the oil pan as described in **Section 1:6**, then remove the bolt securing the pick-up screen to the main bearing cap.

Remove the attachment bolts and lift off the pump and withdraw the pump drive shaft.

Dismantling:

Remove the pick-up tube and screen assembly from the pump housing.

Remove the pump cover and lift out the two piece rotor assembly, marking the units for later assembly.

If further dismantling is needed, a small hole must be drilled in the centre of the pressure relief valve plug, a screw threaded in the hole and the plug pulled out.

Remove the relief valve spring and valve.

Inspection:

After cleaning all the parts and inspecting for damage, check for wear as follows.

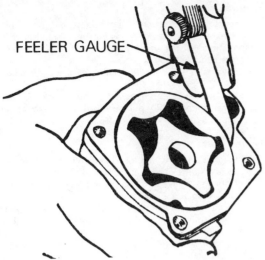

FIG 1:13 Checking clearance between outer race and housing

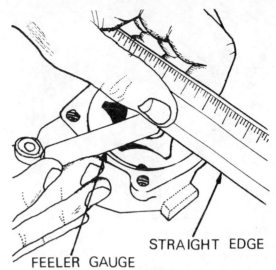

FIG 1:14 Checking rotor end play

Refer to **FIG 1:13** and measure the clearance between the outer race and the housing. This should be between .006 and .012 inch.

Refer to **FIG 1:14**. Place a straight edge across the pump as shown and measure the clearance (rotor end play) between the straight edge and the rotor and outer race. This should be between .0012 and .004 inch.

If the clearances are outside these limits either a new rotor assembly or a new pump housing or both will have to be obtained. Note that the two rotors are a matched pair and the outer race, rotor and shaft are replaced only as an assembly.

Check the relief valve piston for damage and movement in its bore, see also that the spring is not worn or damaged.

Assembly:

Dip the relief valve and spring into some clean engine oil and fit into the housing.

The new retaining plug is fitted by pushing it into the housing, with the flat side outwards, until it bottoms and then spread in the housing, by hammering on a $\frac{1}{2}$ inch diameter drift, to prevent its accidental removal.

Fit the two rotors in the housing with the dot marks upwards and lubricated with engine oil. Place the cover in position and tighten the retaining screws.

Fit the drive shaft into the rotors and check for free rotation.

Refit the pick-up tube with a new gasket.

Refitting the pump:

Prime the oil pump by pouring some clean engine oil in one of the ports and rotate the pump shaft to distribute the oil.

Insert the pump drive shaft into its recess with the pointed end inwards. Using a new gasket, fit the pump and tighten the securing screws.

Fit the screws attaching the pick-up tube to the main bearing and install the oil pan as described earlier.

1:8 Front cover and timing gear

Removing the cover:

Remove the oil pan as described in **Section 1:6**. Remove the radiator (**Chapter 4**) and the alternator.

Remove the water hoses, unbolt the water pump and lift it off together with its seal. Remove the fan and the crankshaft pulley, also the air pump when fitted.

Unscrew the timing cover bolts and lift the cover from the front engine flange, if necessary tapping lightly with a mallet to break the seal. See **FIG 1:15**.

If necessary the two guide sleeves (**FIG 1:16**) can be removed at this time and if the front cover plate gasket needs renewing, remove two screws and lift off the cover plate.

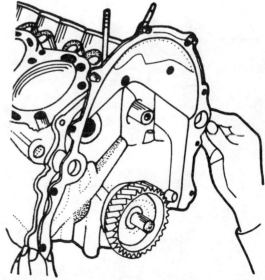

FIG 1:15 The front cover plate

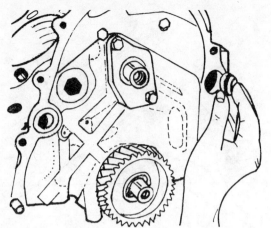

FIG 1:16 Fitting or removing front cover guide sleeves

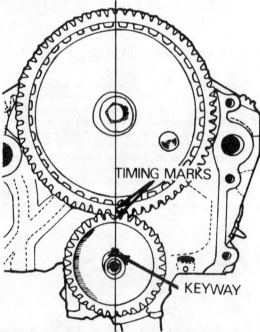

TIMING MARKS

KEYWAY

FIG 1:17 Correct installation of the two timing wheels

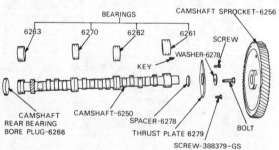

BEARINGS

CAMSHAFT SPROCKET-6256

6263   6270   6262   6261

SCREW

WASHER-6278

KEY

CAMSHAFT-6250

SPACER-6278

CAMSHAFT
REAR BEARING
BORE PLUG-6266

THRUST PLATE 6279

BOLT

SCREW-388379-GS

FIG 1:18 The camshaft and related components

Front oil seal:

Support the front cover to avoid damage if the seal is to be removed after the cover has been removed from the engine. Drive out the seal using tool No. T72C-6150 or any other suitable tube.

A new seal is fitted in the front cover using the same tool.

The front seal can be removed without removing the front cover if required by pulling it out with a claw type extractor such as tool No. 1175-AB.

Timing gears:

The timing gears, which may be seen in their installation position in **FIG 1:17**, are removed as follows:

Pull out the crankshaft gear with a two legged claw puller and remove the key from the shaft.

The camshaft gear can be pulled off by hand, or assisted by some gentle levering, after removing the central retaining bolt.

Unscrew the two retaining bolts and lift off the camshaft thrust plate, key and spacer ring. The camshaft is now ready for removal, but see **Section 1:9**.

Reassembly:

This will be a reversal of the removal procedure with attention to the following points:

If either the crankshaft or the camshaft has been moved in the slightest degree since the removal of their gear wheels, it will be necessary to re-time them as detailed under **Camshaft** in **Section 1:9**.

Apply some sealing compound to the gasket surfaces of the cylinder block and front cover plate and place the gasket and cover plate in position on the block, holding them temporarily by four front cover screws. Fit and tighten the two cover plate retaining bolts and remove the temporary fastenings.

Fit new seal rings to the guide sleeves and insert them, with no sealer, into the block with their chamfered side outwards.

Apply some sealer to the front cover gasket and place it in position. Fit the front cover and all the retaining screws loosely and then centralise the cover by inserting tool No. T72C-6150 in the oil seal. Tighten the retaining screws to a torque of 9-12 lb ft.

1:9 The camshaft

The camshaft and its related parts are shown in **FIG 1:18**.

Removal:

If this is to be carried out with the engine in position the procedure is as follows:

Remove the radiator and hoses.

Remove the distributor, alternator, carburetter and inlet manifold.

Take off the overhead valve gear covers and remove the rocker arm and shaft assemblies. Lift out the push rods and place them in sequence so that they may be restored later to their original positions.

Remove the oil pan. Remove the front cover as described in **Section 1:8** and pull off the camshaft gear and thrust plate.

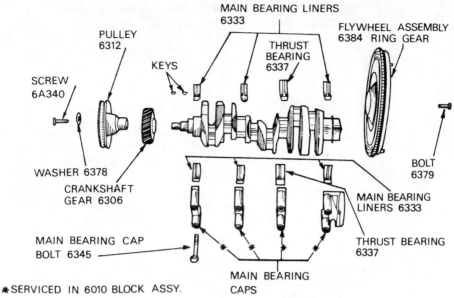

MAIN BEARING LINERS
6333

PULLEY
6312

KEYS

THRUST
BEARING
6337

FLYWHEEL ASSEMBLY
6384 RING GEAR

SCREW
6A340

WASHER 6378

CRANKSHAFT
GEAR 6306

BOLT
6379

MAIN BEARING
LINERS 6333

MAIN BEARING CAP
BOLT 6345

THRUST BEARING
6337

MAIN BEARING
CAPS

★SERVICED IN 6010 BLOCK ASSY.

FIG 1:19   The crankshaft and related components

Use a magnet to extract the valve lifters from their bores and be sure to identify them so that they may be refitted in the same positions.

Very carefully pull out the camshaft to avoid damage to the bearings.

Installation:

Smear the whole shaft with engine oil and very carefully insert it into the block, the bearing surfaces may easily be damaged.

Fit the spacer ring with its chamfered side inwards, insert the key and fit the thrust plate, making sure that it covers the main oil gallery.

Measure the camshaft end play. This should be between .001 and .004 inch and a selection of spacer ring and thrust plate thicknesses is available to obtain this.

Rotate the crankshaft and camshaft as necessary to bring the timing dots on the two wheels in the position shown in **FIG 1:17**, then fit the gear wheel with its washer and tighten the retaining bolt to a torque of 32-36 lb ft.

Replace the valve lifters and push rods in their original locations and all other components in the reverse order of removal.

Adjust the valve clearances as described in **Section 1:5** and the distributor timing according to the instructions in **Chapter 3**.

1:10 The flywheel

Before the flywheel can be unbolted the transmission must be removed together with the clutch or fluid converter as appropriate. These operations are described in **Chapters 5** and **7**.

Remove the six securing bolts and lift off the flywheel and ring gear after marking it to ensure correct replacement.

Ring gear:

If the ring gear shows signs of excessive wear or damage it should be removed and a new gear fitted.

Heat the ring gear with a blow torch on the engine side and knock it off the flywheel, being most careful not to hit the flywheel in the process.

The new ring gear must be heated evenly all over, but not higher than 500°F or the temper will be impaired. This temperature can be distinguished by a light straw colour. Slip the ring onto the flywheel ensuring that it is seated properly against the shoulder and allow to cool.

Checking the run-out:

After the flywheel has been re-fixed onto the crankshaft flange, check the run-out by means of a dial indicator mounted so that its stylus bears on the face of the flywheel.

Turn the flywheel through a complete rotation, holding it fully forward or backward so that any crankshaft end play will not be included in the run-out measurement.

If the clutch face run-out exceeds .007 inch, remove the flywheel and check for burrs or other irregularities on the mating faces. Check also on the run-out of the crankshaft flange. If these points are in order a new flywheel should be fitted.

On automatic transmission models the stylus of the dial indicator should rest on the face of the ring gear adjacent to the gear teeth for taking the run-out measurements.

1:11 The crankshaft

For this the engine must be removed from the car and transferred to the bench or an engine stand with the flywheel, oil pan, and front cover removed. If the pistons are to be removed, the cylinder heads also will have to be removed.

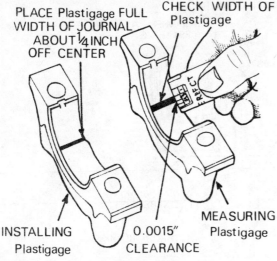

PLACE Plastigage FULL WIDTH OF JOURNAL ABOUT ¼ INCH OFF CENTER

CHECK WIDTH OF Plastigage

INSTALLING Plastigage

0.0015" CLEARANCE

MEASURING Plastigage

FIG 1:20   Measuring bearing clearance with Plastigage

With the engine inverted, confirm first that all main and connecting rod bearing caps are marked as it is most important that they are refitted in their original locations.

Remove the crankshaft gear wheel and then, one rod at a time, remove the connecting rod bearing nuts, lift off the bearing caps and inserts and carefully push the piston and rod down in the cylinder.

Remove the main bearing bolts and lift off the caps and inserts. Discard the rear oil seal.

Lift out the crankshaft and remove the bearing inserts, identifying them for later re-assembly. See **FIG 1:19**.

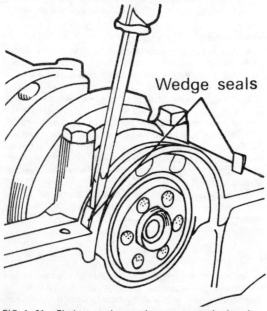

Wedge seals

FIG 1:21   Fitting wedge seals to rear main bearing cap

Main and connecting rod bearings:

Check that the crankshaft journals are free from scoring and are not excessively worn. Light blemishes on the journals may be dressed with an oil stone or the shaft ground to the next undersize bearing. Heavy markings or wear which cannot be cleaned up to the maximum undersize bearing will necessitate a new crankshaft.

Having cleaned all journals and bearings, the clearance at each bearing should be measured with Plastigage as follows:

Refer to **FIG 1:20**. Place a strip of the Plastigage across the full width of the bearing surface and about $\frac{1}{4}$ inch off centre. Replace the crankshaft journal in the bearing, fit the cap and tighten the bolts. In the case of a main bearing a support should be placed under the crankshaft in order that its weight will not compress the strip and give an erroneous reading. Do not turn the shaft while the strip is in place.

Remove the cap and compare the width of the strip with the scale provided. If this is done at the widest and narrowest parts, the difference in widths will give the taper of the journal.

If the clearance exceeds the specified limits it is permissible to try .001 or .002 inch half bearings in combination with the standard bearing. If this is done on more than one main bearing, be sure that the undersizes are all fitted on the cylinder block side of the bearing. If the combination of standard and .002 undersize bearings does not bring the clearance within the specified limits, the journal will have to be ground and undersize bearings fitted.

Repeat this procedure on all the bearings and when all have been found satisfactory or suitably adjusted the crankshaft can be refitted.

Installing the crankshaft:

Make sure that all is spotlessly clean, then assemble all the main bearing inserts in their correct locations in the block or bearing caps. Check the alignment of the oil holes in the inserts with those in the block.

Coat all running surfaces with engine oil and carefully lower the crankshaft into position.

Apply a thin coating of sealing compound to the rear sealing surface of the rear main bearing cap and fit all the main bearing caps in their correct locations. Note that the arrows on the front and centre caps must point to the front.

Fit all the main bearing bolts finger tight only and then all, except the centre thrust bearing, to the specified torque of 65-75 lb ft progressively in rotation.

Align the thrust bearing surfaces by levering the crankshaft towards the front and the thrust bearing cap towards the rear and, holding in this position, tighten the bolts to the specified torque.

Coat the sealing lip of a new crankshaft oil seal with engine oil, slide it over the end of the shaft and drive it into position, making sure that it seats firmly in the bottom of the groove.

Refer to **FIG 1:21**, and push the two wedge shaped seals between the cylinder block and the rear main bearing cap with a large blunt screwdriver. The round side of the seals should face the bearing.

Coat liberally with engine oil and refit the connecting rod bearings and caps, ensuring that they are all in their correct positions. Tighten the cap nuts to 22-26 lb ft.

Refit the oil pump and all remaining parts in the reverse order of dismantling.

1:12 Servicing connecting rods and pistons

As the pistons have to be taken out at the top end of the engine it is necessary for this operation to remove the cylinder head and also the oil pan in accordance with the details given earlier in this chapter.

It may be found that a ridge of carbon has formed around the top lip of each cylinder bore and this should be removed carefully before pushing the pistons out.

Make sure that all the connecting rod caps are marked so that they can be re-installed in their original positions.

Rotate the crankshaft until the piston/rod assembly to be removed is at the bottom of its stroke to remove the connecting rod nuts and cap.

Push the assembly out of the top of the cylinder using the wooden handle of a hammer and taking care not to scratch the journal or bore surfaces in the process.

Loosely fit the cap back on to its rod before proceeding to the next cylinder.

Piston pins:

Before commencing to separate the piston pins from their pistons, make sure that all the pistons, pins and connecting rods are identified so that they will be re-fitted into their original cylinder bores.

The piston pin is pressed out of the piston using the tool shown in **FIG 1:22** in an arbor press.

When refitting a piston pin, remember that the numbered side of the connecting rod bearing and cap is towards the left of the engine and the notch in the piston crown is towards the front.

Smear with oil and start the piston pin in the piston and connecting rod, tapping lightly with a mallet if necessary, then in the press, press the pin fully home until it is centred in the piston.

Piston rings:

These should always be removed from the piston upwards, being careful not to scratch the piston. After removal, clean the rings and carefully scrape any carbon out of their grooves.

Before refitting a ring to its piston it should be checked for correct gap in its cylinder bore. This is done by pushing it squarely into its bore, using the head of a piston to ensure correct positioning. See **FIG 1:23**.

Measure the gap between the two ring ends and compare it with the specifications given in Technical Data. If the gap is too wide another ring must be used, if it is too narrow either find another ring of the correct size or file the ends down to size.

Check also the ring side clearance in its groove by sliding the correct size feeler gauge round the piston between the ring and its lower land. There should be no binding at any point nor any high steps where wear has occurred.

DRIVER DETAIL A.7

INSERT THIS END FOR INSTALLATION

REVERSIBLE LOCATOR DETAIL A-5

INSERT THIS END FOR PIN REMOVAL

Tool T72C-6135

Tool T68P-6135-A

CUP DETAIL A.1

FIG 1:22 Fitting or removing piston pin

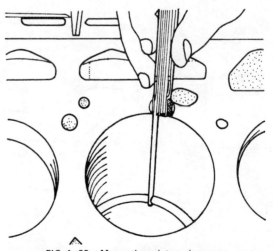

FIG 1:23 Measuring piston ring gap

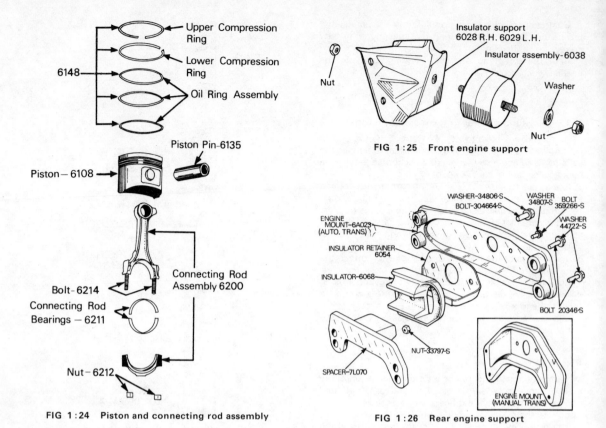

Upper Compression Ring

Lower Compression Ring

6148

Oil Ring Assembly

Piston Pin-6135

Piston — 6108

Bolt-6214

Connecting Rod Bearings — 6211

Connecting Rod Assembly 6200

Nut — 6212

FIG 1:24 Piston and connecting rod assembly

Insulator support 6028 R.H. 6029 L.H.

Insulator assembly-6038

Nut

Washer

Nut

FIG 1:25 Front engine support

WASHER-34806-S

BOLT-304664-S

WASHER 34807-S

BOLT 359266-S

WASHER 44722-S

ENGINE MOUNT-6A023 (AUTO. TRANS)

INSULATOR RETAINER 6054

INSULATOR-6068

BOLT 20346-S

NUT-33797-S

SPACER-7L070

ENGINE MOUNT (MANUAL TRANS)

FIG 1:26 Rear engine support

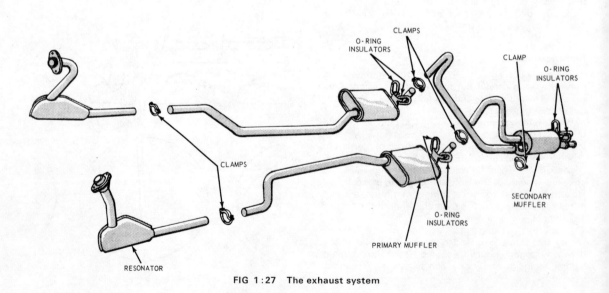

CLAMPS

O-RING INSULATORS

CLAMP

O-RING INSULATORS

CLAMPS

SECONDARY MUFFLER

O-RING INSULATORS

PRIMARY MUFFLER

RESONATOR

FIG 1:27 The exhaust system

Pistons:

After cleaning off any deposits from the piston surfaces—use a solvent but not a caustic or wire brush—inspect the piston for excessive wear or damage. The outside diameter of the piston should be measured at piston pin height and at right angles to the bore axis.

Measure also the cylinder bore and ensure that the piston will have the proper clearance of .001 to .003 inch. If a new piston of the same grade size but slightly larger or smaller cannot be fitted, the bore will have to be refinished to provide the correct clearance or bored out to take one of the two standard oversizes of + .020 or .040 inch.

The component parts of a complete piston assembly are shown in **FIG 1 : 24**. Fit the piston rings in their grooves and arrange the ring gaps equally around the piston circumference and install the piston pin.

The connecting rods and bearing caps are numbered from 1 to 3 in the right bank and from 4 to 6 in the left bank beginning at the front of the engine and these numbers must all be on the same (left) side when installed.

Fit a ring compressor over the piston and push the assembly down into its bore, guiding the connecting rod to avoid damage to the bore or the crankshaft journal.

Check the clearance of each bearing as described in **Section 1 : 11**, apply a light coat of engine oil and fit the bearing cap with the piston at the bottom of its stroke, tightening the nuts to a torque of 22-26 lb ft.

After the bearings have all been installed, check the side clearance between the rods on each crankshaft journal.

1 : 13 Engine mountings

Front:

The engine front mountings—see **FIG 1 : 25**—are located on each side of the cylinder block. Removal is effected as follows:

Raise the engine sufficiently to remove the insulator assembly.

Remove the support bracket attachment screws and lift off the bracket.

Refitting is carried out in the reverse order.

Rear:

Support the transmission by placing a jack underneath it and then remove the bolt retaining the insulator to the extension housing. See **FIG 1 : 26**.

Remove the four bolts holding the support bracket to the body and take off the rear support assembly.

Remove two bolts attaching the insulator to the support bracket.

Reverse the above procedure to refit the support.

1 : 14 Crankcase ventilation system

This requires very little attention provided that the crankcase emission filter element in the air cleaner is replaced every 6000 miles and the oil filler breather cap is cleaned.

Remove the filler cap and oil separator and wash in a petroleum based solvent. Just shake the cap dry and refit.

The ventilation system connections on the carburetter spacer or intake manifold may be cleaned by careful probing with a flexible wire or bottle brush. Hoses may be washed in a solvent and allowed to dry.

Removal:

Remove the inlet hose from the air cleaner and disconnect the carbon canister hose. Remove the air cleaner.

Hold the crankcase vent hose near the carburetter spacer and unscrew the regulator valve from the spacer.

Remove the regulator valve from the vent hose and the vent hose from the hose fitting.

Reassemble in the reverse order and run the engine while testing for leaks.

1 : 15 The exhaust system

The system of exhaust pipes and expansion chambers or mufflers is shown in **FIG 1 : 27** which should enable any maintenance required to be easily carried out.

From each bank of cylinders a short pipe connects the exhaust manifold with a small resonator box from the rear of which another pipe projects and is secured by means of a clamp to the inlet pipe of the primary muffler.

The primary mufflers are supported on two rubber O rings which, in addition to providing a flexible mounting, assist in insulating the car from the exhaust vibrations.

From the primary mufflers two pipes lead to a secondary muffler mounted again on two rubber O rings, at the lefthand rear of the car.

When installing an exhaust system, fit all the parts but do not fully tighten until the alignment is correct. The muffler clamps are tightened to a torque of 25-35 lb ft and the nuts on the pipe flanges to 17-25 lb ft. The brackets for the O rings are tightened to 9 lb ft.

1 : 16 Fault diagnosis

(a) Engine will not start

1 Defective coil
2 Faulty distributor capacitor (condenser)
3 Dirty, pitted or incorrectly set contact breaker points
4 Ignition wires loose, insulation faulty
5 Water on sparking plug leads
6 Battery discharged, terminals corroded
7 Faulty or jammed starter
8 Plug leads wrongly connected
9 Vapour lock in fuel pipes due to heat
10 Defective fuel pump
11 Overchoking or underchoking of carburetter
12 Blocked petrol filter or carburetter jets
13 Leaking valves
14 Sticking valves
15 Valve timing incorrect
16 Ignition timing incorrect

(b) Engine stalls

1 Check 1, 2, 3, 4, 5, 10, 11, 12, 13 and 14 in (a)
2 Sparking plugs defective or gaps incorrect
3 Retarded ignition
4 Mixture too weak
5 Water in fuel system
6 Petrol tank vent blocked
7 Incorrect valve clearances

(c) Engine idles badly

1 Check 2 and 7 in (b)
2 Air leak at manifold joints
3 Carburetter jet settings wrong
4 Air leak in carburetter
5 Over-rich mixture ·
6 Worn piston rings
7 Worn valve stems or guide bores
8 Weak exhaust valve springs

(d) Engine misfires

1 Check 1, 2, 3, 4, 5, 8, 10, 12, 13, 14, 15 and 16 in (a) and 2, 3, 4 and 7 in (b)
2 Weak or broken valve springs

(e) Compression low

1 Check 13 and 14 in (a), 6 and 7 in (c), and 2 in (d)
2 Worn piston ring grooves
3 Scored or worn cylinder bores

(f) Engine lacks power

1 Check 3, 10, 11, 12, 13, 14, 15 and 16 in (a), 2, 3, 4, and 7 in (b), 6 and 7 in (c), and 2 in (d). Also check (e)
2 Leaking joint washers
3 Fouled sparking plugs
4 Automatic advance not operating

(g) Burnt valves or seats

1 Check 13 and 14 in (a), 7 in (b), and 2 in (d)
2 Excessive carbon round valve seats and head

(h) Sticking valves

1 Check 2 in (d)
2 Bent valve stem
3 Scored valve stem or guide bore
4 Incorrect valve clearance

(j) Excessive cylinder wear

1 Check 11 in (a) and see **Chapter 4**
2 Lack of oil
3 Dirty oil
4 Piston rings gummed up or broken
5 Badly fitting piston rings, gaps too small
6 Bent connecting rod

(k) Excessive oil consumption

1 Check 6 and 7 in (c) and check (j)
2 Ring gaps too wide
3 Oil return holes in piston choked with carbon
4 Scored cylinders
5 Oil level too high
6 External oil leaks, seals defective
7 Ineffective valve stem oil seals

(l) Crankshaft and connecting rod bearing failure

1 Check 2 in (j)
2 Restricted oilways
3 Worn journals or crankpins
4 Loose bearing caps
5 Extremely low oil pressure
6 Bent connecting rod

(m) Engine vibration

1 Loose alternator mounting
2 Engine mountings loose or defective
3 Exhaust pipe mountings defective
4 Fan out of balance, blades broken
5 Misfiring due to mixture, ignition or mechanical faults

CHAPTER 2

THE FUEL SYSTEM

2:1 General description

The fuel tank on these cars, which holds 12 gallons ($9\frac{3}{4}$ gallons Imperial) of fuel is located in the luggage compartment and has a vacuum and pressure sensitive filler cap in the righthand quarter panel.

A fuel evaporative emission system is incorporated which is designed to limit the emission of fuel vapours into the atmosphere or the escape of raw fuel from the tank. The system is shown diagrammatically in **FIG 2:1** and comprises four main components: fuel tank, pressure and vacuum sensitive cap, a .040 inch restrictor in the vapour line and an absorbent charcoal canister.

From the tank the fuel is pumped to the carburetter by a single action fuel pump mounted on the lefthand side of the engine and driven by a rod which is given a reciprocating movement by an eccentric on the camshaft.

Before entering the carburetter the fuel passes through an in-line filter which is a sealed unit and requires no attention. Servicing the filter is not possible and it must be renewed at the specified intervals or earlier if necessary.

A double barrelled down-draught carburetter is used, with a fully automatic choke or mixture enrichment device. The two throttle plates are coupled together so that differential operation is obtained.

2:2 The fuel tank and evaporative emission system

The filler neck of the tank has a double sealing and by using a twin tube construction performs the dual function of venting air through a secondary concentric chamber and sensing the level of the fuel in the tank.

There are two valves in the filler cap, one to release any excess pressure inside the tank in the event of a blockage in the vapour line and the other, a vacuum relief, to admit air as the fuel is consumed.

When the fuel level covers the fill control tube, vapours can no longer escape and the filler tube will start to fill up. So a vapour lock is formed by the .040 inch restrictor and there is no flow through the vapour line to the charcoal canister.

In this way the fuel level in the tank is controlled and the fill control tube is so positioned as to maintain an expansion area of approximately 10 per cent of the tank capacity.

Under normal conditions of expansion in the tank vapour is forced through the restrictor to be absorbed by the charcoal in the canister mounted in the engine compartment. With one end open to atmosphere and the other connected by a hose to the carburetter air cleaner, any vapours absorbed by the charcoal are extracted and passed to the inlet duct when the engine is running. If a

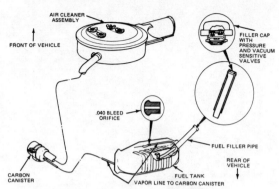

FIG 2:1   Fuel evaporative emission system

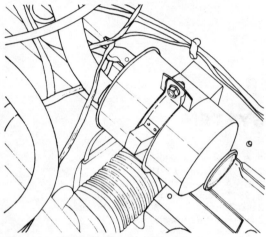

FIG 2:2   The charcoal canister

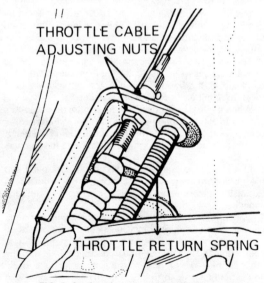

FIG 2:3   Accelerator cable adjustment

blockage occurs here, causing the vapour pressure to reach .7 to 1.5 lb sq inch the pressure relief valve in the fuel filler cap opens and provides an escape route to atmosphere.

Removing the fuel tank:

Drain off any fuel in the tank, loosen the lower clamp securing the hose to the neck of the tank and disconnect the fuel and vapour lines.

Remove the four bolts holding the tank and lower the tank sufficiently to permit the removal of the cable to the gauge sender unit. Remove the tank.

If repairs involving the use of heat are to be made to the tank, it should be taken to a service station for professional attention as the precautions necessary are beyond the scope of most home operators.

Refit the fuel tank in the reverse order carefully checking for leaks and the operation of the gauge. Note that this takes about thirty seconds to give a true reading.

Removing the charcoal canister:

This is shown in **FIG 2:2** and is secured by a centre clamp.

Remove the clip and the large air hose from the canister. Remove the spring clip retaining the vapour line hose and disconnect the hose.

Remove the centre clamp bolt and lift off the canister.

Refit by reversing the above, tightening the clamp bolt to 15-18 lb ft.

2:3 The fuel pump

Low fuel pump pressure will cause a weak mixture to be provided by the carburetter, accompanied by starvation at high engine speeds. Excessive pressure from the pump will be shown in flooding and high fuel consumption. Insufficient delivery volume will cause fuel starvation at speed.

Testing the pump is normally carried out with the pump in situ and the engine running, using special connector pieces, pressure gauges and graduated containers. These are not likely to be available to most home operators, so if the hoses, unions and filler are in order it will be advisable to seek the assistance of the service station or fit a replacement pump as no servicing is possible.

Removing the pump:

Being careful to catch any spillage, disconnect the inlet and delivery pipes at the pump.

Remove the two mounting screws and lift off the pump. Discard the gasket as a new one should be used when refitting.

When refitting, make sure that all old sealing material is removed from the joint faces, apply a suitable oil resistant sealer to both sides of the new gasket and fit the pump. Make sure that the pump operating rod is riding correctly on the camshaft eccentric.

Install the mounting screws and tighten them evenly to 12-15 lb ft.

Connect the two hose pipes using new clamps if possible to ensure a leak proof joint.

Start the engine and check for leaks.

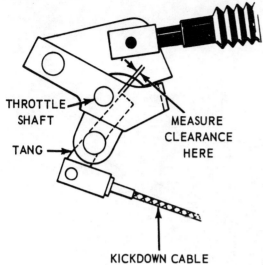

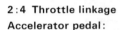

THROTTLE SHAFT

TANG

MEASURE CLEARANCE HERE

KICKDOWN CABLE

FIG 2:4   Adjusting the kick-down linkage

2:4 Throttle linkage

Accelerator pedal:

Remove the clip and disconnect the throttle cable from the lever on the pedal shaft.

Disconnect the return spring from the pedal and remove the retaining pins from each side of the righthand bush.

Withdraw the pedal and shaft assembly from the mounting bracket.

To refit insert the pedal shaft into the bushes with enough pressure to spring the lefthand bush into its locating groove and then fit the retaining pins on either side of the righthand bush.

Connect the pedal return spring. Connect the operating cable to the lever and secure with the clip. Adjust the pedal as follows:

Manual transmission:

Place a .015 inch feeler gauge between the return stop and the pedal arm and adjust the stop until the front face of the accelerator pedal pad is $4\frac{1}{2}$ inches from the floor pan.

Adjust the throttle cable as necessary with the adjusting nuts shown in **FIG 2:3**.

Automatic transmission:

With the cable disconnected from the bell crank ball joint adjust the pedal height to $4\frac{1}{2}$ inches between the top face of the pad and the floor pan by turning the stop bolt located underneath the instrument panel.

Set the engine to idle at the specified speed and adjust the accelerator cable until the cable just slides onto the bell crank ball joint. Connect the cable to the ball joint.

Carry out a check to ensure that the throttle plates are correctly moved into the full open and idle positions when the accelerator pedal is depressed or released.

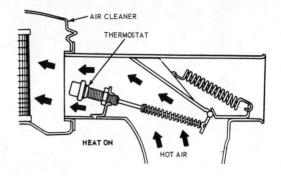

AIR CLEANER

THERMOSTAT

HEAT ON

HOT AIR

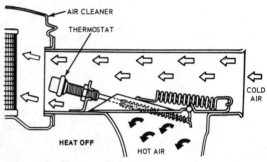

AIR CLEANER

THERMOSTAT

HEAT OFF

HOT AIR

COLD AIR

FIG 2:5   Air duct and thermostatic valve assembly. Above, hot air admitted. Below, cold air admitted

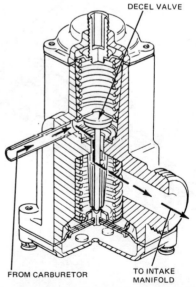

DECEL VALVE

FROM CARBURETOR

TO INTAKE MANIFOLD

FIG 2:6   The decel valve, shown in the open position

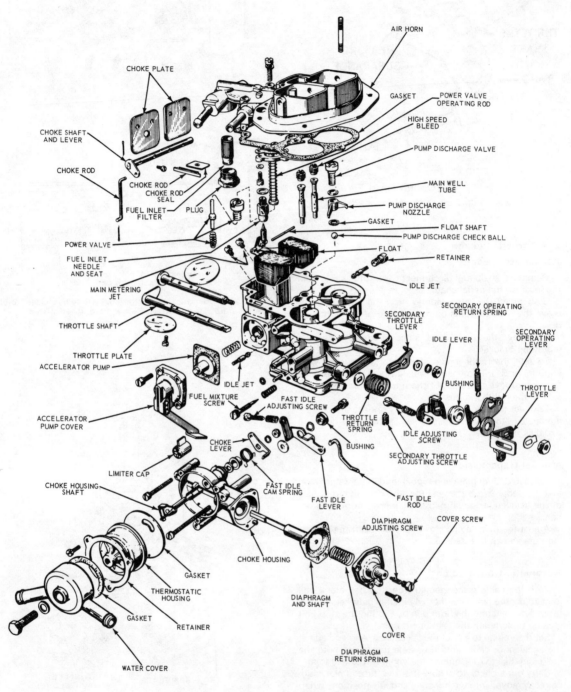

CHOKE PLATE

AIR HORN

CHOKE SHAFT
AND LEVER

GASKET

POWER VALVE
OPERATING ROD

CHOKE ROD

HIGH SPEED
BLEED

PUMP DISCHARGE VALVE

CHOKE ROD
SEAL

CHOKE ROD

FUEL INLET
FILTER

PLUG

MAIN WELL
TUBE

PUMP DISCHARGE
NOZZLE

GASKET

FLOAT SHAFT

PUMP DISCHARGE CHECK BALL

POWER VALVE

FUEL INLET
NEEDLE
AND SEAT

FLOAT

RETAINER

IDLE JET

MAIN METERING
JET

THROTTLE SHAFT

SECONDARY
THROTTLE
LEVER

SECONDARY OPERATING
RETURN SPRING

IDLE LEVER

SECONDARY
OPERATING
LEVER

THROTTLE PLATE

ACCELERATOR PUMP

IDLE JET

FUEL MIXTURE
SCREW

FAST IDLE
ADJUSTING SCREW

BUSHING

THROTTLE
LEVER

ACCELERATOR
PUMP COVER

THROTTLE
RETURN
SPRING

IDLE ADJUSTING
SCREW

BUSHING

SECONDARY THROTTLE
ADJUSTING SCREW

CHOKE
LEVER

LIMITER CAP

CHOKE HOUSING
SHAFT

FAST IDLE
CAM SPRING

FAST IDLE
LEVER

FAST IDLE
ROD

DIAPHRAGM
ADJUSTING SCREW

COVER SCREW

CHOKE HOUSING

GASKET

THERMOSTATIC
HOUSING

DIAPHRAGM
AND SHAFT

COVER

GASKET

RETAINER

DIAPHRAGM
RETURN SPRING

WATER COVER

FIG 2:7   The components of the Motorcraft 2-V carburetter

Kickdown linkage (Refer to **FIG 2:4**):

Move the throttle to the fully open position and position the kickdown cable so that the tang, dotted in the illustration just makes contact with the throttle shaft.

If any adjustment is required, loosen the two adjusting nuts at the bracket, move the cable as necessary and retighten the nuts.

2:5 Air cleaner and duct system

This, as will be seen from reference to **FIG 2:5**, includes a spring loaded flap valve which controls the proportions of hot and cold air passing to the carburetter in order to maintain an intake temperature of 90°-100°F during normal operating conditions.

This control is obtained by the action of the thermostatically controlled link which responds to the temperature of the air stream and opens or closes the flap as necessary.

Testing:

With the assembly in situ on a cold engine and the temperature in the engine compartment less than 100°F, the valve flap should be in the HEAT ON position as shown in the upper illustration. If it is not, check to see that there is no binding or mechanical interference to prevent its free movement.

Remove the assembly from the car and immerse it fully in a suitable container of water and raise the water temperature to 100°F. After five minutes the temperature will be stabilised and flap should still be in the HEAT ON position.

Increase the water temperature to 135°F allow five minutes and observe the position of the flap. It should now be in the HEAT OFF position as in the lower illustration.

If these conditions are not obtained and there is no interference to free movement, the complete duct and valve assembly must be renewed.

Removal:

Unscrew the two hexagon headed cap screws securing the air intake duct to the air cleaner and lift the complete assembly from the engine.

Detach the valve plate tension spring from the valve plate with a pair of long nose pliers.

Loosen the thermostat locknut and unscrew the thermostat from its bracket. Pull the valve plate out of the duct.

Assembly and installation are carried out in the reverse order not forgetting to check the operation of the valve as described above.

2:6 The decel valve

This device, shown in **FIG 2:6** is another feature of the emission control system. It is mounted on the intake manifold adjacent to the carburetter and its function is to meter to the engine an additional supply of fuel and air during engine deceleration periods. This permits a more complete combustion at these times and therefore a lower level of exhaust emission.

During periods of deceleration, manifold depression forces the diaphragm assembly against the spring which in turn raises the valve to the open position shown in the diagram. With the valve in this position the vacuum in the manifold is able to pull a metered amount of mixture from the carburetter and through the valve assembly for a period of $1\frac{1}{2}$ to $3\frac{1}{2}$ seconds, according to the valve setting.

Adjustment:

If the idle speed after releasing the throttle, remains high or if the idle speed is obtained immediately the throttle is released, the timing of the decel valve may be incorrect.

Connect a tachometer to the engine and, using a T piece, connect a vacuum gauge in the fuel/air line from the decel valve to the carburetter.

Run the engine at idle to ensure that it is fully warmed up and then increase the speed to 3000 rev/min for about two seconds. The gear selector should be in Park when automatic transmission is fitted.

Release the throttle and note the time interval until the vacuum gauge registers zero. This should be between $1\frac{1}{2}$ to 3 seconds.

If the decel valve requires adjustment—this may be made with a $\frac{3}{8}$ inch allen key through the top aperture—pull off the coloured cap (when fitted) and insert the tool into the nylon adjuster.

To increase the valve timing the adjuster must be unscrewed, one turn increasing the time interval by approximately $\frac{1}{2}$ second. Screwing the adjuster in will decrease the timing. When the adjuster is flush with the threaded collar top, the maximum permissible adjustment is one turn inward or nine turns outward.

If the operation time cannot be set within the specified limits, fit a new decel valve.

A rough idle may be caused by a leak in the decel valve. This may be checked by using the following procedure.

Run the engine at idling speed and disconnect the hose from the decel valve to the carburetter. Note any difference in the quality of the idling.

If the idle is now correct, a fault in the decel valve is indicated, so replace the hose and check the tightness of the screws securing the diaphragm assembly.

If these are found to be in order, remove the valve from the engine and plug the hole in the manifold. If the idling is now corrected fit a new decel valve and adjust to specification.

2:7 Motorcraft 2-V carburetter

This is a downdraught two-stage, two venturi type, in which the secondary throttle commences to open when the primary throttle has completed about the first 60 deg. of its travel. Both throttles reach the fully open position together.

The primary stage which is a little smaller than the secondary, includes an idle, idle transfer, accelerator pump, main metering and power enrichment systems. The secondary stage includes a transfer, main metering and power enrichment systems. Both stages draw their fuel supply from a common float chamber.

A fully automatic strangler type choke for cold starting is included, which is thermostatically controlled by the temperature of the cooling water circulating through the choke outer casing. On later cars a ceramic positive temperature coefficient (PTC) heater is fitted in place of the gasket between the choke housing and the water

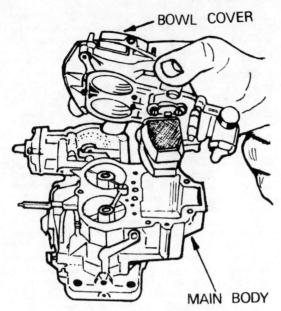

FIG 2:8   Removing the float chamber cover assembly

cover. At temperatures below about 60°F the built-in bi-metal switch is open and the heater is not energised and normal thermostatic spring choking occurs. Above 60°F the switch closes and energises the heater which opens the choke after one to two minutes. There is also a hot idle compensator located in the carburetter spacer, which increases the idle speed during prolonged periods of idling when the engine temperature rises.

The carburetter is calibrated to conform with existing Federal exhaust emission requirements and incorporates tamper proof slow running volume control screws to limit the range of adjustment and prevent an excessively rich setting.

The component parts of the carburetter are shown in FIG 2:7, and dismantling is carried out as follows:

Removing:

Remove the air cleaner and disconnect the fuel supply line, the vacuum pipes and the decel valve pipe at the carburetter. Uncouple the throttle control lever.

Partially drain the cooling system to below the level of the automatic choke water cover and detach the two water hoses. Disconnect the throttle solenoid and electric choke if fitted.

Remove the carburetter securing nuts and washers, lift off the carburetter and clean the joint faces. Discard the gasket as a new one should be used when re-fitting.

Bowl cover:

Remove the inlet filter plug and withdraw the filter. Remove the bowl cover screws and washers, also the retaining clips from the choke rod. Carefully lift off the bowl cover, FIG 2:8.

Remove the choke rod seal plug and seal, the float pivot pin, float and inlet needle. Remove the three screws and washers securing the vacuum diaphragm and lift it away.

Automatic choke:

Withdraw the centre screw and remove the water cover and gasket. Note the index mark setting on the two mating flanges then withdraw the three retaining screws and remove the retaining ring, thermostatic housing and gasket or ceramic heater unit.

Remove the three screws, noting the location of the long screw, separate the choke housing from the main body, FIG 2:9, and disengage the fast idle rod. Remove the O-ring from the vacuum passage.

Remove the choke shaft nut and lock washer, noting the position of the fast idle cam spring.

Remove the spring loop and then the choke lever and spring and spring retainer. Remove the choke shaft washer, shaft, lever and teflon bearing.

Remove the fast idle rod, shaft retaining screw, bush and spring washer. Remove the fast idle lever and spacer, adjusting screw and spring.

Remove the three retaining screws and lift off the choke diaphragm cover assembly, return spring and diaphragm and shaft assembly. Remove the diaphragm plug and adjusting screw from the cover.

Accelerator pump:

Withdraw the four retaining screws and remove the pump cover, diaphragm assembly and pump return spring.

Remove the pump discharge valve assembly, nozzle and two gaskets. Remove the pump channel plug screws.

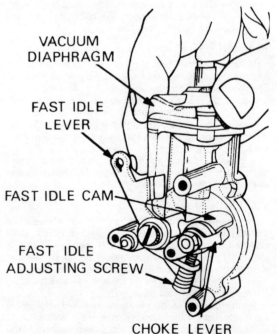

FIG 2:9   Removing the automatic choke

Main body, see FIG 2:10:

Remove the primary and secondary main well air bleed plugs, main well tubes and metering jets. Note carefully the sizes and locations so that they will be refitted correctly. Remove the power valve and gasket, both idle jet retainer plugs and jets which are located on the sides of the carburetter body.

Turn the idle limiter cap in to the stop and remove it. Count and record the turns (to the nearest $\frac{1}{16}$th of a turn) required to lightly seat the idle fuel adjustment needle then remove the needle and spring.

Remove the secondary operating lever return spring, the primary throttle lever nut and lockwasher then the lever and flat washer. Remove the secondary operating lever assembly and bushing.

Remove the idle adjusting lever spring and shaft washer, **noting how the primary throttle return spring is hooked over the idle adjusting lever and the carburetter body.**

Remove the idle speed screw and spring from the idle adjusting lever. Remove the secondary throttle lever nut, back washer, flat washer and secondary throttle lever. Remove the secondary idle adjusting screw.

Assembling the carburetter:

This is a reversal of the disassembly procedure, but note the following points:

When fitting the idle fuel adjustment needle and spring, turn it fully in and then back off by the number of turns counted when dismantling.

Fit a new limiter cap with the stop tab against the lean side of the stop on the carburetter body.

Fit the choke thermostatic housing in its original position as noted earlier.

Check, and if necessary adjust, the float setting before assembling the fuel bowl cover and float assembly. This is described in **Section 2:8.**

2:8 Adjusting the carburetter

Idle speed and fuel mixture:

A plastic limiter cap is fitted on the head of the idle fuel mixture adjusting screw as shown in **FIG 2:11** and any adjustment **must** be within the range of this limiter.

Before starting to adjust the idle speed, ensure that all engine services are correctly adjusted and that normal operating temperature has been stabilised.

Disconnect the decel valve hose at the decel valve and then plug the decel valve fitting.

On cars equipped with automatic transmission the idle speed must be set with the selector in Drive range, except when using an exhaust gas analyser. The air cleaner must be in place.

Using the curb idle adjusting screw, shown in **FIG 2:12**, adjust the idle speed to the specified figure and then turn the idle mixture adjusting screw inward to obtain the smoothest idle possible within the range of the idle limiter.

Fast-idle cam clearance:

Insert the shank of a $\frac{5}{32}$ inch drill between the lower edge of the choke plate and the side of the carburetter bore. Hold the fast idle screw on the second step of the fast idle cam and check that the clearance between the

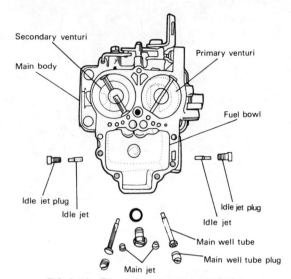

FIG 2:10   The main metering and idle jets

tang of the choke lever and the arm of the fast-idle cam is .010 inch. If necessary, the choke lever tang must be bent up or down to obtain the dimension.

Choke plate vacuum pull-down:

It will be necessary to remove the air cleaner in order to gain access to remove the three hexagon headed screws which attach the thermostatic spring cover. Do NOT remove the screw from the centre of the water cover.

Pull the water cover and spring cover assembly out of the way and set the fast idle cam on the top step.

Use a screwdriver to push the diaphragm stem back against its stop as shown in **FIG 2:13**, and insert a rod or drill between the lower edge of the choke plate and the wall of the carburetter bore of .236 inch gauge. Take up any play in the choke linkage by applying finger pressure to the top edge of the choke plate.

Adjust the choke plate to side wall clearance by removing the plug from the diaphragm and turning the adjustment screw in or out as required.

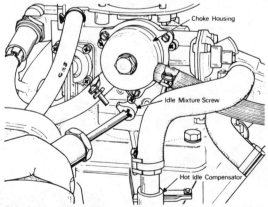

FIG 2:11   Idle mixture adjustment screw showing limiter

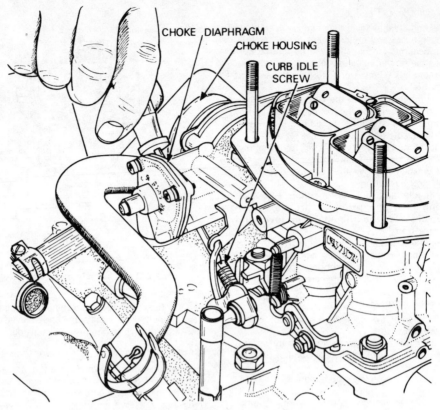

CHOKE DIAPHRAGM
CHOKE HOUSING
CURB IDLE SCREW

FIG 2:12   Setting the slow-running

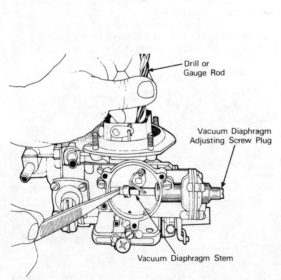

Drill or Gauge Rod

Vacuum Diaphragm Adjusting Screw Plug

Vacuum Diaphragm Stem

FIG 2:13   Measuring the choke plate pulldown

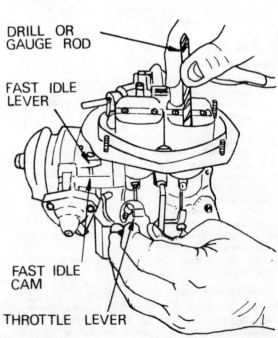

DRILL OR GAUGE ROD

FAST IDLE LEVER

FAST IDLE CAM

THROTTLE LEVER

FIG 2:14   Adjusting the dechoke setting

Dechoke clearance:

With the air cleaner removed, hold the throttle lever in the fully open position and take up any play in the choke linkage by pressing against the top edge of the choke plate.

The clearance between the lower edge of the choke plate and the side wall should be .256 inch. Adjust to this clearance by bending the tab on the fast idle lever where it touches the fast idle cam. See **FIG 2:14**.

Fast idle speed adjustment:

With the engine at normal operating temperature and the fast idle screw positioned on the second step of the fast idle cam against the shoulder of the first step, the engine speed should be approximately 1500 rev/min.

Any adjustment necessary to obtain this speed is made by turning the fast idle adjustment screw against the fast idle lever in or out as appropriate.

Secondary throttle stop:

Slacken off the secondary throttle stop adjusting screw until the secondary throttle seats fully in its bore.

Turn the screw inwards until it just touches the tab on the secondary throttle lever and then a further quarter of a turn.

Float adjustment:

With the float chamber cover assembly held in an inverted position and the float tang resting lightly on the spring loaded fuel inlet needle it should be just possible to insert a .40 inch drill between the edge of the float and the bowl cover as shown in **FIG 2:15**.

To adjust this clearance, bend the float tang up or down as required. Do not scratch or damage the tang, and see that both floats are adjusted equally.

At the same time measure between the float bumper spring and the float drop tang. This should be between .010 and .025 inch. Adjust if necessary by bending the tang as required.

Choke thermostatic spring housing:

If this has been removed for any reason, or if the operation or setting is suspect, loosen the three cover retaining screws when the cover can be rotated without disturbing the water cover.

The correct position for the cover is $\frac{1}{8}$ inch in an anti-clockwise direction (lean) from the index mark. Tighten the cover screws and replace the air cleaner.

2:9 Emission control systems

In order to comply with Federal emission regulations a number of devices and systems have been introduced, but very little can be or should be attempted by way of home servicing. Some of these systems are described briefly here and from 1974 a plate is attached to each car giving details of equipment fitted and the appropriate settings.

Spark delay valve (SDV):

This is connected in the vacuum supply line to the advance side of the distributor and has the effect of delaying the spark advance during periods of accleration.

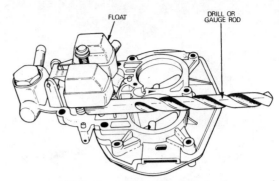

FIG 2:15 Adjusting the float level

Exhaust Gas Recirculation (EGR) system:

In this system a metered quantity of exhaust gas is transferred from the exhaust pipe to the inlet manifold through the EGR valve fitted to the carburetter/manifold joint, the valve being actuated by a vacuum picked up from the carburetter.

In addition to controlling the amount of exhaust gas transferred by carburetter depression, arrangements are also made to effect control by engine temperature and road speed. By these means the EGR valve is closed until the engine has warmed up sufficiently or when full power is required for acceleration.

Decel valve:

Some engines are fitted with a second deceleration valve (see **Section 2:6**) designed for control from a temperature sensitive ported vacuum switch (PVS).

Thermactor system:

In this system a pump is driven by a belt at the front of the engine and pumps air into the exhaust ports for mixing with and detoxing the exhaust gases before passing into the atmosphere through the exhaust pipes. Suitable devices are included to by-pass the pumped air to atmosphere on the over-run or to prevent the reverse flow from the exhaust in the event of a leak or pump failure.

2:10 Motorcraft 2150 2-V carburetter

This type of carburetter is fitted to 1976 models and an exploded view of the components is given in **FIG 2:16**.

In operation this carburetter is similar to that described earlier, including the electrically assisted choke mechanism. It also has a solenoid dashpot throttle positioner, to reduce emission on the over-run by delaying the complete closure of the throttle plate, and a thermostatically controlled hot idle compensator, by means of which extra air is added to the mixture to prevent over-rich mixtures at high under-bonnet temperatures.

Most of the adjustable settings are set at the factory and the owner/driver is not encouraged to interfere with them as in every case there is the likelihood of infringing emission regulations if special equipment is not available.

The following guide to adjusting the idling speeds is given in order to assist where professional help is not

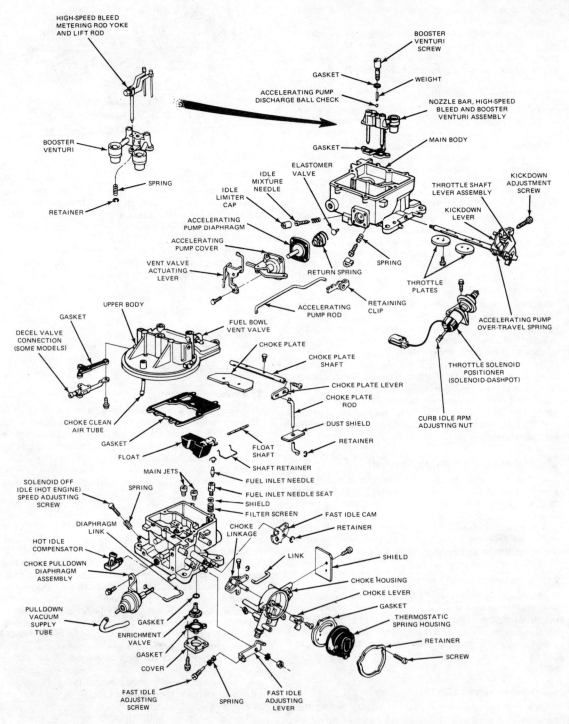

HIGH-SPEED BLEED
METERING ROD YOKE
AND LIFT ROD

BOOSTER
VENTURI
SCREW

GASKET

WEIGHT

ACCELERATING PUMP
DISCHARGE BALL CHECK

NOZZLE BAR, HIGH-SPEED
BLEED AND BOOSTER
VENTURI ASSEMBLY

BOOSTER
VENTURI

GASKET

MAIN BODY

SPRING

RETAINER

ELASTOMER
VALVE

THROTTLE SHAFT
LEVER ASSEMBLY

KICKDOWN
ADJUSTMENT
SCREW

IDLE
MIXTURE
NEEDLE

IDLE
LIMITER
CAP

KICKDOWN
LEVER

ACCELERATING
PUMP DIAPHRAGM

ACCELERATING
PUMP COVER

SPRING

VENT VALVE
ACTUATING
LEVER

RETURN SPRING

THROTTLE
PLATES

UPPER BODY

ACCELERATING
PUMP ROD

RETAINING
CLIP

ACCELERATING PUMP
OVER-TRAVEL SPRING

GASKET

FUEL BOWL
VENT VALVE

DECEL VALVE
CONNECTION
(SOME MODELS)

CHOKE PLATE

CHOKE PLATE
SHAFT

THROTTLE SOLENOID
POSITIONER
(SOLENOID-DASHPOT)

CHOKE PLATE LEVER

CHOKE PLATE
ROD

CHOKE CLEAN
AIR TUBE

DUST SHIELD

CURB IDLE RPM
ADJUSTING NUT

GASKET

RETAINER

FLOAT

FLOAT
SHAFT

MAIN JETS

SHAFT RETAINER

SOLENOID OFF
IDLE (HOT ENGINE)
SPEED ADJUSTING
SCREW

SPRING

FUEL INLET NEEDLE

FUEL INLET NEEDLE SEAT

SHIELD

FILTER SCREEN

FAST IDLE CAM

DIAPHRAGM
LINK

CHOKE
LINKAGE

RETAINER

HOT IDLE
COMPENSATOR

LINK

SHIELD

CHOKE PULLDOWN
DIAPHRAGM
ASSEMBLY

CHOKE HOUSING

CHOKE LEVER

PULLDOWN
VACUUM
SUPPLY
TUBE

GASKET

GASKET

ENRICHMENT
VALVE

THERMOSTATIC
SPRING HOUSING

GASKET

RETAINER

COVER

SCREW

FAST IDLE
ADJUSTING
SCREW

SPRING

FAST IDLE
ADJUSTING
LEVER

FIG 2:16   Exploded view of the 2150 2-V carburetter components available. It is assumed that all engine services are in order and that the engine is at normal working temperature. Details of idle speed, etc., will be found on the data specification decal in the engine compartment of each vehicle.

Adjusting the idle:

Remove the vacuum line to the exhaust gas recirculation valve and the air cleaner and plug both vacuum lines.

Remove the spark delay valve, when fitted, and connect the part throttle vacuum line direct to the advance side of the distributor. When a dual diaphragm is fitted, the line from the inlet manifold to the retard side must be left in place.

Set the throttle to the kick-down step on the choke cam with the adjusting screw against the shoulder of the step and use the screw to obtain the specified engine speed. Kick the throttle off the step and allow the engine to return to idle.

Repeat this last operation until the specified fast-idle speed is regularly obtained; this is usually 1600 rev/min.

Accelerate to about 2000 rev/min for 10 seconds and then return to idle. Press the throttle linkage hard against the stem of the solenoid to collapse the plunger.

With N selected on an automatic transmission, use the throttle lever adjusting screw on the carburetter body to obtain the lower TSP (Throttle Solenoid Positioner) — off idle speed 550 rev/min. Again accelerate to 2000 rev/min for 10 seconds and wait, if applicable, for five seconds to check the curb idle speed.

Select D on an automatic and turn the hexagon head on the TSP plunger to obtain the specified curb idle speed. If adjustment is necessary, speed up the engine again and repeat the last operation until the correct speed is regularly obtained. See **FIG 2:17**.

Refit any components removed and connect the vacuum lines to their proper unions.

If the engine does not idle evenly and it is considered that a slight adjustment of the mixture might rectify the fault, the idle mixture screws may be used but only within the limits imposed by the limiter caps. For further adjustment a CO meter is essential.

2:11 Fault diagnosis

(a) Insufficient fuel delivered

1 Vented tank cap defective
2 Fuel line blocked or restricted
3 Air leak between tank and pump
4 Filter blocked or restricted

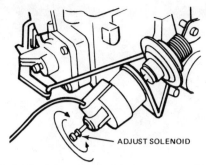

FIG 2:17 Adjusting the idle speed on the TSP

5 Pump pressure low
6 Pump capacity low
7 Fuel vaporising in line due to heat

(b) Excessive fuel consumption

1 Carburetter requires adjustment
2 Fuel leakage
3 Automatic choke defective
4 Float level too high
5 Pump pressure high
6 Decel valve defective
7 Idling speed too high
8 Excessive engine temperature
9 Brakes binding
10 Tyres under-inflated

(c) Idling speed too high

1 Incorrect adjustment
2 Sticking throttle linkage
3 Worn throttle plate(s)

(d) Rough idling

1 Check 1 in (c)
2 Crankcase ventilation system faulty
3 Dirty air cleaner element

(e) No fuel delivery

1 Check 1, 2, 3 and 4 in (a)
2 Float needle stuck
3 Pump defective

NOTES

CHAPTER 3

THE IGNITION SYSTEM

3:1 Description

The ignition system comprises the coil, a Bosch distributor and the spark plugs. To promote longer life for the components and to ensure easier starting under cold conditions, the actual running voltage of the system is reduced by means of a resistance wire in the circuit between the ignition switch and the coil. This resistance is by-passed when the starter is operated, thus applying full battery voltage at this time.

The distributor is mounted at the righthand rear of the inlet manifold and is driven from the camshaft by an extension of the shaft which also drives the oil pump.

Ignition timing is controlled automatically by a combination of centrifugal weights and a dual diaphragm vacuum unit. As the engine speed increases, these weights which may be seen in the exploded diagram of the distributor in **FIG 3:1**, move outwards and turn the cams relative to the drive shaft and cause the points to open earlier and advance the ignition.

The vacuum unit consists of two independently operating diaphragms of which the outer, or primary, diaphragm uses carburetter depression to advance the timing while the inner, secondary, diaphragm is actuated by the inlet manifold depression to retard the spark during periods of closed throttle idling and so assisting in the reduction of exhaust emissions.

3:2 Routine maintenance

Very little attention is needed beyond ensuring that all parts of the system are kept clean and dry. At intervals of 6000 miles the spark plugs should be taken out for inspection and cleaned and adjusted if necessary. At 10,000 miles the plugs should be renewed.

Also at 6000 miles the contact breaker should be examined and the points cleaned and the gap checked. A couple of drops of oil should be applied to the felt wick in the recess under the rotor arm and a smear of grease on the cams. Do not overlubricate as the lubricant may easily find its way on to the points and cause difficult starting and irregular running. A drop of oil may also be applied to the weight pivots and the moving contact pivot.

Clean inside the distributor cap and check for signs of cracks or tracking which would indicate sparking across the segments or to earth. In this case a new cap must be fitted. Check also the central spring contact.

3:3 Servicing the contact breaker

Remove the distributor cap and the rotor, then rotate the crankshaft slowly until the contact breaker rubbing block is on the high point of a cam and the points fully open. If the contact surfaces are only slightly discoloured or pitted they may be cleaned up with a little denatured alcohol and a stiff brush.

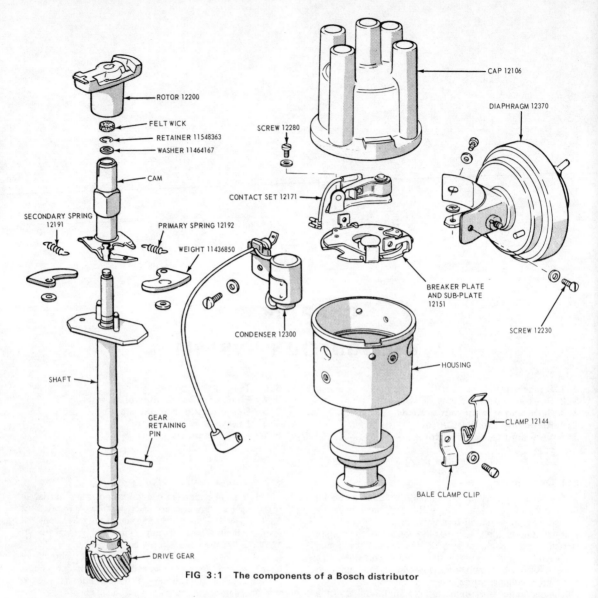

ROTOR 12200

FELT WICK

RETAINER 11548363

WASHER 11464167

CAP 12106

SCREW 12280

DIAPHRAGM 12370

CAM

CONTACT SET 12171

SECONDARY SPRING 12191

PRIMARY SPRING 12192

WEIGHT 11436850

BREAKER PLATE AND SUB-PLATE 12151

SCREW 12230

CONDENSER 12300

HOUSING

SHAFT

GEAR RETAINING PIN

CLAMP 12144

BALE CLAMP CLIP

DRIVE GEAR

FIG 3:1   The components of a Bosch distributor

In normal use there will be some transference of metal from one point to the other, causing a pip on one contact and a corresponding crater in the other. If it is decided to rub this down with a fine file, make sure that the surfaces remain square to each other and remove all traces of dust when completed.

If the metal transference approaches the contact breaker gap, the assembly should be removed and renewed.

See **FIG 3:2**. Disconnect the wire from the condenser and coil. Remove the single retaining screw and lift off the breaker point assembly.

If the condenser is to be renewed also, remove the screw attaching it to the distributor body, ease the grommet out of the body and disconnect the wire at the coil.

To install, fit the breaker point wire into the distributor, replace the screw securing the condenser and reconnect the wire to the coil.

Place the points assembly in position as shown and secure with the screw.

Reconnect the breaker point wire to the condenser and coil terminal. Adjust the points as follows:

Adjusting the breaker points:

Ensure that the rubbing block is on the top of a cam and then loosen the points attaching screw slightly.

Insert the clean blade of the correct feeler gauge (.025 inch or .64 mm) between the points and adjust the points by inserting a screwdriver between the bosses on the advance plate and the notch in the base plate as shown in **FIG 3 : 3**. When the feeler blade is a sliding fit tighten the mounting screw.

If possible, this operation should be followed by a check on the ignition timing as described later in this chapter.

3 : 4 Removing the distributor

Remove the distributor cap and disconnect the vacuum pipes from the advance capsule.

It will assist reinstallation if the engine is turned to the firing point for No. 1 cylinder before removing the distributor. This is with No. 1 piston at 12 deg. BTDC on the compression stroke, i.e. with both valves closed (see **FIG 3 : 4**).

Unscrew the distributor securing bolt and lift out the complete unit.

Installation:

Ensure first that the crankshaft has not been moved from the position noted above, then insert the distributor drive shaft into its recess.

Make sure that the pump drive shaft is fully seated and that the rotor lines up with the No. 1 mark on the distributor body when fully engaged and then refit the clamp bolt.

Refit the vacuum pipes and the distributor cap. A timing check may be made, but if the engine was not moved this should not be necessary.

3 : 5 Servicing the distributor

Refer to **FIG 3 : 1**. Disconnect the condenser lead from the contact breaker, remove the securing screw, ease the grommet from the housing and lift out the condenser assembly.

Release the diaphragm rod from the breaker plate by removing the C clip, take out the two screws and lift away the diaphragm assembly.

Remove the securing screw and lift off the contact breaker assembly.

Remove the two screws for the clips holding down the distributor cap, noting that they also retain the breaker plate assembly which can now be lifted out assisted, if necessary, by a screwdriver inserted through the diaphragm rod opening.

Carefully detach the two springs from the centrifugal weights and note that they are not both the same.

The cam assembly can be levered over its retaining ring by using a screwdriver inserted through the vacuum rod opening and lifting up the lower edge of the cam. Lift off the cam together with the retaining ring and the felt pad.

Pull out the pad and the retainer, lift off the advance weights.

Inspection:

Carefully clean and dry all the parts, using a mild solvent if necessary. Do not use a wire brush or harsh abrasive.

If any of the cam lobes are scored or worn the cam assembly should be renewed.

Check the contact breaker plate for damage or distortion and renew if defective. Check also for damage or cracks in the distributor housing.

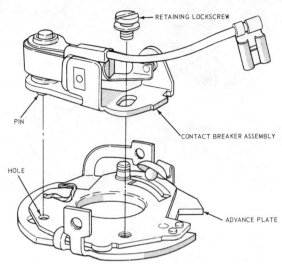

FIG 3 : 2   The contact breaker mechanism

Test the vacuum capsule for leaks and see that the bracket and rod are not damaged or bent.

Inspect the cap for cracks, excessively burnt contacts and a broken central contact button. Renew the cap if in any way defective.

Reassembly:

Fit the weights after smearing grease over their pivot pins, then lubricate the shaft and position the cam assembly. Secure with the retaining ring and insert the lubricated felt wick.

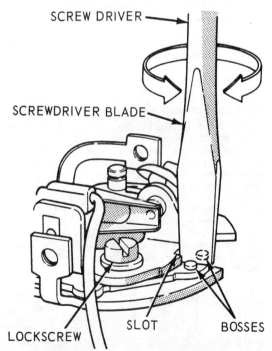

FIG 3 : 3   Adjusting the contact breaker points

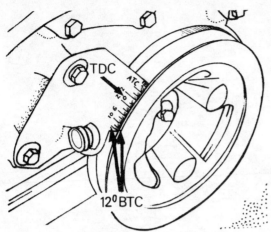

FIG 3:4 The timing marks on crankshaft pulley and front cover

See that the two springs are sound and refit them in their original positions on the advance mechanism.

Place the breaker plate in position and secure with the clamp clips and screws.

Push the condenser lead and grommet through the aperture in the housing and secure the condenser with its screw.

Position the breaker assembly and secure with the screw.

Hook the diaphragm rod over the pin on the breaker plate and fit the two screws attaching the capsule to the distributor body. Replace the C clip retaining the rod on its pin.

Adjust the contact breaker points to the correct gap as described in **Section 3:3** and connect the lead to the terminal.

Fit the distributor cap and re-install the distributor as described in **Section 3:4**, noting that the vacuum unit will be facing outwards at approximately 90 deg. to the crankshaft axis. Reset the timing as described in **Section 3:6**.

3:6 Timing the ignition

Ensure first that the contact breaker gap is correct (.025 inch) then rotate the crankshaft until No. 1 piston is almost at TDC on the compression stroke and the notch in the rim of the crankshaft pulley is in line with the specified timing mark (12 deg.) on the front engine cover. This is shown in **FIG 3:4**.

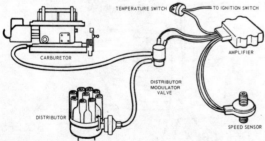

FIG 3:5 Components of the Electronic Spark Control System

Later cars have a graduated scale marked on the rim of the crankshaft vibration damper, instead of a single notch, and a timing pointer mounted on the front of the block. They also have alignment marks on the distributor body and rotor.

Loosen the distributor clamping bolt and very carefully rotate the distributor body as necessary until the points are just opening and the rotor is in line with the segment for No. 1 in the distributor cap. Tighten the clamp bolt.

A more accurate method of determining the exact moment at which the points break is to wire a 12-volt bulb between the low tension terminal on the distributor and a good earthing point then, with the ignition switched on, the bulb will light up as the points open.

The setting may be checked by rotating the engine and observing that the points break again at the moment the 12 deg. mark comes opposite the notch in the pulley.

Stroboscopic timing:

This will give the most accurate setting for the ignition if the equipment is available.

Clean the two appropriate timing marks and apply a spot of white paint to make them clearly visible.

Disconnect and plug the vacuum pipes.

Connect the stroboscopic timing lamp to No. 1 spark plug according to the maker's instructions. Connect an engine speed tachometer (rev counter).

Start the engine and reduce the idle speed to 600 rev/min to ensure that the centrifugal advance mechanism does not upset the calibrations.

Aim the timing lamp at the timing marks and if they do not appear in line, slacken off the distributor clamp bolt and rotate the body until the two marks coincide. It will be noted that turning the distributor clockwise advances the timing. Tighten the clamp bolt.

If the engine speed is now slowly increased, the notch on the pulley should appear to move in an anticlockwise direction and vice versa when speed is reduced. This indicates that the centrifugal advance is functioning correctly.

3:7 Electronic spark control system

This system, referred to as ESC, is used in the United States and Canada to control exhaust emissions by delaying the vacuum application to the distributor advance unit as required.

The system consists of a speed sensor located in the engine compartment and connected in series with a two-piece speedometer drive cable, an ambient air temperature switch in the door pillar, distributor modulator valve (solenoid) and an electronic amplifier which functions as a switch board to pass on signals to regulate the modulator valve. These components are shown diagrammatically in **FIG 3:5**.

The testing and servicing of these items is best entrusted to a qualified service station, but it may be of interest to describe briefly what their functions are.

The modulator valve, inserted in the vacuum line between the distributor and carburetter, is normally open, but when energised by signals from the amplifier it closes, cuts off the vacuum supply and prevents vacuum advance.

Outside air temperature is sensed by the air temperature switch mounted in the righthand door pillar, and at temperatures below 49°F this switch is open and permits normal vacuum advance to occur. At 65°F the switch closes and causes the vacuum to be cut off and the ignition is therefore retarded.

The speed sensor consists of a magnet rotating within a stationary winding and creates a voltage frequency proportional to the speed of the vehicle. As the speed reaches the operating limit of 37 or 40 mile/hour, depending on application, the modulator valve is triggered to allow full vacuum advance, but when the vehicle speed drops to about 18 mile/hour signals from the speed sensor cause the modulator valve to close and cut off the vacuum. From that speed and below, therefore, no vacuum is applied and the ignition is retarded.

It should be noted that this latter control of the ignition timing occurs only when an ambient temperature of 65°F or above has closed the contacts of the air temperature switch.

3:8 Sparking plugs and leads

The spark plug type recommended for use on early cars is the Autolite AG22 and the gap specified is .025 inch. For later cars Autolite AGRF-52 plugs are specified with a gap of .032 inch, but see the vehicle data plate in the engine compartment where several specifications for the individual vehicle are quoted. It is recommended that the plugs should be taken out for inspection, and regapping if necessary, every 6000 miles.

Remove the cable from each plug by twisting and pulling the moulded cap only. Do not pull on the wire or the connection may be broken and the weathersealing damaged.

Loosen each plug by one or two turns and then blow out all accumulated dirt in the recess before removing the plug. Sand blasting is a most effective way of cleaning dirty plugs, after which the electrodes should be dressed with a flat file until the surfaces are parallel and bright.

Examine the plugs carefully for cracked or broken insulators or excessively worn electrodes and renew if necessary. Adjust the gap by bending the earthed electrode only.

The ceramic insulator should be wiped clean and dry, the circular gaskets renewed if they have been excessively flattened and the screw threads cleaned up by means of a wire brush.

Replace the plugs, tightening to a torque of 22 to 28 ft lb and reconnect the HT cables, making sure that the caps are pressed fully onto the plug connectors.

Sparking plug condition:

An examination of the firing points of a plug can give a very good indication of the condition of the engine and its auxiliaries. Normally the deposit will be a light grey or tan on the firing surfaces and this can be cleaned up very easily.

Wet black deposits are usually due to oil entering the combustion chamber past worn pistons and rings or down valve guides with excessive clearances. A hotter plug may be used with advantage under these conditions, but an engine overhaul may be the real solution.

Dry, fluffy, black deposits may be due to running with an over-rich mixture or incomplete combustion due to defective ignition. This may be cleaned off, but the appropriate services should be checked.

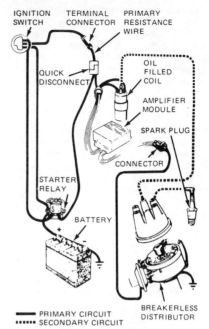

PRIMARY CIRCUIT
SECONDARY CIRCUIT

FIG 3:6   The ignition wiring circuit for a breakerless system

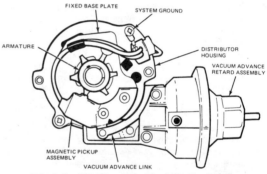

FIG 3:7   The Bosch breakerless distributor

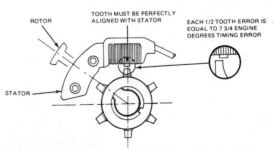

FIG 3:8   Showing the correct position of the distributor for static timing

Overheating is usually indicated by a whitish blistered appearance and perhaps heavy erosion. The cause may be weak mixture, poor cooling, incorrect ignition timing or over loading the engine. A new plug should be fitted and the engine services checked.

It is false economy to continue with defective plugs and they should be renewed if at all doubtful, certainly after 10,000-12,000 miles.

HT cables:

It should be noted that the high tension cables employed with these engines are of the suppressor type and they are carefully calibrated for length and resistance. It is important, therefore, when replacing cables that the same type should be used. The cables fitted as standard have a resistance of 5000-9000 ohms per foot.

3:9 Breakerless distributor

For 1976 models a Bosch breakerless distributor is used which dispenses with the conventional contact breaker and has in its place a magnetic pick up and armature assembly coupled to an electronic amplifier module. Otherwise the system is very similar to that described previously.

Principle of operation:

Refer to **FIG 3:6**. When the ignition is switched on, the primary circuit is live and the coil energised. Current flows through the coil primary windings and amplifier module to earth.

As each of the six spokes on the rotating armature in the distributor comes close to the magnetic pick-up, see **FIG 3:7**, a voltage is induced which causes the amplifier to switch off the primary current and the magnetic field in the coil collapses. This induces a high voltage in the coil secondary winding which flows through the distributor to the appropriate sparking plug. A timing circuit in the amplifier turns the current on again after the coil field has collapsed in readiness for firing the next sparking plug.

Removing the distributor:

In the event of a fault in this type of distributor the only items which can be serviced are the rotor arm and cap. A breakdown in any other part requires the renewal of the complete assembly.

Remove the carburetter air cleaner assembly and disconnect the distributor wiring connector from the harness. Disconnect the vacuum lines, lift off the cap and tie it out of the way.

Make suitable alignment marks to ensure correct positioning of the rotor and the body in the block when refitting. Unscrew the distributor mounting bolt and lift it out. Do not turn the engine or the timing will have to be reset.

Refitting:

Provided that the engine has not been moved, this is simply a matter of lining up the marks made earlier and fitting the distributor in place and securing the mounting bolt.

If the engine has been moved, proceed as follows:

Rotate the engine to TDC for No. 1 after the compression stroke with both valves closed and align the correct initial timing mark on the crankshaft damper rim with the pointer on the front of the cylinder block. It should be noted that the initial timing is specified on the engine data plate in each car. The plate also includes the requisite data for stroboscopic timing which should preferably follow the static setting.

Fit the distributor into the engine with one of the armature segments in the exact position shown in **FIG 3:8** and the rotor at No. 1 firing position.

It is important to ensure that the distributor shaft is correctly engaged with the oil pump drive and that the armature tooth is accurately aligned. This can be effected by rotating the distributor as necessary before finally securing the clamp.

Refit the items disconnected on removal and check the timing with a stroboscopic lamp if available.

3:10 Fault diagnosis

(a) Engine will not fire

1 Battery discharged
2 Contact breaker points dirty, pitted or wrongly adjusted
3 Distributor cap dirty, cracked or 'tracking'
4 Rotor arm not making contact with cap electrode
5 Faulty cable or loose connection in low tension circuit.
6 Distributor rotor arm cracked or 'tracking'
7 Faulty ignition coil
8 Broken contact breaker spring
9 Contact points stuck open
10 Defective ignition switch
11 Plug leads wrongly connected

(b) Engine misfires

1 Check 2, 3, 5 and 7 in (a)
2 Weak contact breaker spring
3 High tension plug or coil leads wet, cracked or perished
4 Sparking plug(s) loose
5 Sparking plug insulation cracked
6 Sparking plug gap incorrectly set
7 Ignition timing too far advanced
8 Excessive wear of distributor spindles and bushes

(c) Engine lacks power

1 Check 2 and 3 in (a) and check (b)
2 Ignition timing retarded
3 Defective centrifugal or vacuum units in distributor
4 Vacuum unit suction pipe detached or leaking
5 Sparking plugs worn out
6 One plug lead detached

CHAPTER 4

THE COOLING SYSTEM

4:1 Description

The cooling system employed with these engines is a little different from conventional practice in that the thermostat, which controls the coolant flow around the engine and radiator, is located in the lower lefthand corner of the cylinder block front cover. With this location, the thermostat controls the flow of coolant from the radiator rather than into it as with the more common top location.

A centrifugal type water pump is used and the system has three operating stages according to the position of the thermostat. The layout of the system and details of water circulation are shown in **FIGS 4 : 1** and **4 : 2**.

From the top of the engine block the coolant enters the top of the radiator and passes downwards through the tubes and is then drawn from the bottom by the action of the water pump under working conditions and passed through the water passages in the cylinder block.

It will be seen that water for the car's heating system is taken from an outlet on the inlet manifold and returned for re-heating by way of the return hose connected to the thermostat housing.

A smaller hose is also connected to the inlet manifold for the purpose of supplying the heated water for the automatic choke in the carburetter. This is a continuous circuit with water returning to the heater return hose for recirculation.

To ensure that the engine reaches its working temperature quickly, there is a by-pass circuit through which the coolant flows directly from the cylinder head position down to the inlet housing on the front cover. In this way the radiator is by-passed and a quick warm up is achieved.

Reference to **FIG 4 : 2** shows the three operating stages of the system. They are as follows:

In Stage one, when the engine is cold, the front end of the thermostat is closed and there is no passage from the radiator to the water pump. The back of the thermostat is open and all other circuits are open allowing full circulation around the engine and heater assemblies.

Stage two comes into operation when the engine reaches working temperature between 180° and 198°F, when the thermostat opens at both ends and all the circuits are open to provide a blended coolant mixture.

Should extreme temperatures be reached, 203° to 223°F, Stage three comes into operation when the back of the thermostat closes and the bypass is shut off and all the coolant flow is directed through the radiator for maximum cooling effect.

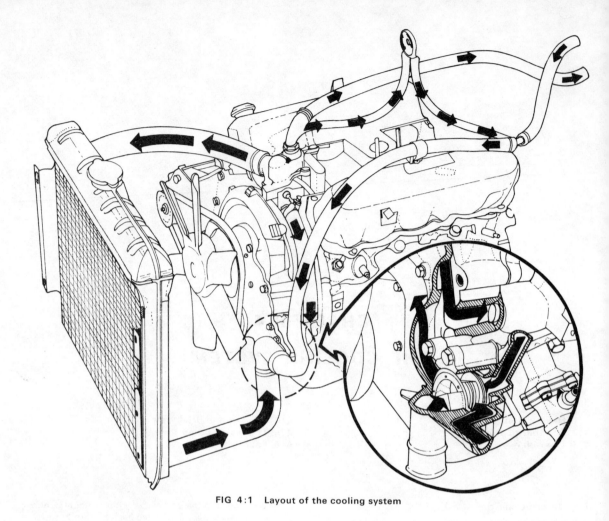

FIG 4:1   Layout of the cooling system

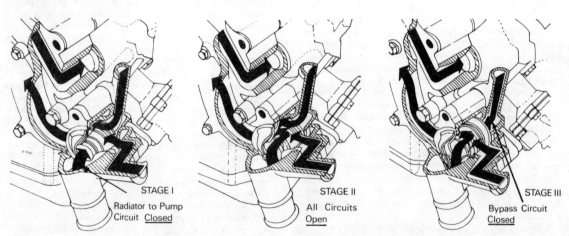

STAGE I

Radiator to Pump
Circuit <u>Closed</u>

STAGE II

All Circuits
<u>Open</u>

STAGE III

Bypass Circuit
<u>Closed</u>

FIG 4:2   The three stages of thermostat operation

4:2 The thermostat

Since the satisfactory operation of the cooling system depends on the thermostat, it is important to ensure that it functions correctly. If faulty working is suspected, remove and test it as follows:

Drain off the coolant into a suitable container, retaining the fluid for further use if it is not more than 12 months old or dirty. There are three draining points, one at the bottom of the radiator and one on each side of the engine block.

Disconnect the top and bottom radiator hoses.

Remove the three screws securing the thermostat housing cover to the water pump and pull the housing cover away from the water pump and lift out the thermostat.

Test the thermostat by suspending it freely in a container of water together with an accurate thermometer.

Slowly heat the water and observe the temperature and the action of the thermostat valves. It is important that neither instrument should be in contact with the sides or bottom of the container.

The thermostat should commence to open at 185° to 192°F (85° to 89°C) and be fully open at 210° to 216°F (99° to 102°C). If it does not open as stated, or if it does not close at comparable temperatures when the temperature is lowered, the unit must be discarded as no adjustment is possible.

Clean the housing cover and pump gasket surfaces before refitting and use a new gasket.

Place the thermostat carefully in the water pump and fit the housing cover, noting that the cover will not seat correctly in the housing cover if incorrectly installed. Fit the three securing screws.

Replace the two radiator hoses and refill the system, using either the coolant drained off earlier or with a recommended mixture of antifreeze and water.

To bleed the system of air, disconnect the heater hose from the coolant outlet on the inlet manifold and hold the hose at the same height as the elbow. Pour coolant into the radiator filler orifice until it starts to discharge from both elbow and hose. Reconnect the hose and run the engine up to full operating temperature. Check the level and top up as necessary.

4:3 The radiator

Removal:

Raise the engine hood and place protective sheets over the fenders. Remove the radiator upper splash shield. Place a suitable receptacle underneath the car and open the drain plugs. See FIG 4:3. Draining will be facilitated if the radiator cap is removed. As longlife antifreeze is used the coolant should be retained for further use.

Loosen the hose clamps and remove the top and bottom hoses from the radiator. Disconnect the hoses for the automatic transmission cooler when fitted.

If applicable, remove the four screws retaining the shroud and slide it to the rear over the fan. Remove the four bolts and spring washers securing the radiator and lift it away.

Cleaning:

Periodically the radiator should be flushed out using a hose pipe inserted in the filler and all the drain

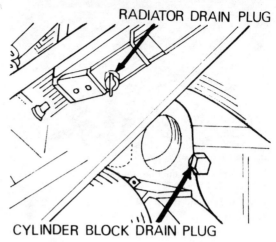

RADIATOR DRAIN PLUG

CYLINDER BLOCK DRAIN PLUG

FIG 4:3   Typical coolant drain plugs

cocks open. Allow the water to flow through the system until all loose sediment has been flushed out and the water is running clear. It is also advisable to flush or blow through the cooling fins to remove dirt or insects which may have accumulated in the crevices.

As it is not always convenient to do this with the radiator installed, the opportunity should be taken while the radiator is off the car. Sometimes it may be found that larger accumulations will not flow through this way and the answer is to reverse-flush by attaching the hose pipe to the drain hole and allowing the water to discharge from the filler aperture.

Refitting:

This is a reversal of the removal procedure, after which the system should be refilled and bled as described in **Section 4:2**.

Radiator filler cap:

The filler cap contains two concentric valves of which the outer valve seals the system until the heating of the coolant causes a pressure of 13 lb/sq inch to develop. At this pressure the valve lifts and vents surplus air or water through the overflow pipe. By pressurising the system in this manner the boiling point of the coolant is raised and the engine is able to run hotter and more efficiently.

Because of this raised boiling point under pressure, the filler cap should never be removed when the engine is hot without first releasing the pressure. To achieve this the cap has a double releasing action whereby the first part of the release turning movement takes it to a detent position at which the pressure can be released without lifting the cap completely off. Even with this safety device, care must be taken as there may be a considerable blow-off of steam with a hot engine.

The second valve in the filler cap is fitted in order to allow air to enter the system and prevent a vacuum when the coolant cools down.

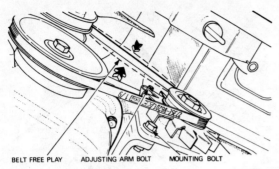

BELT FREE PLAY   ADJUSTING ARM BOLT   MOUNTING BOLT

FIG 4:4   Adjusting the fan belt tension

4:4 The fan and drive belt

Removal:

Slacken off the alternator adjusting and mounting bolts and push the alternator in towards the engine to loosen the belt tension.

Lift the belt over the alternator pulley and then detach if from the crankshaft, pump and fan pulleys.

The fan and pulley may be detached by removing the four securing bolts and washers.

When refitting the fan and pulley, torque the securing screws to 7 to 9 lb ft.

Later cars have the fan blade assembly attached to the water pump spindle through a viscous coupling; this is designed to slip at high speeds and so reduce fan speed and noise.

To remove this fan assembly it is first necessary to remove the radiator, as described in **Section 4:3**, and then unscrew the centre retaining bolt. The fan is secured to the coupling by four bolts.

Refitting and adjusting the belt:

The belt is refitted by reversing the removal procedure, after which the tension must be adjusted.

With the alternator mounting and adjusting bolts only fingertight move the alternator in or out as required until the belt can be moved up and down a total of $\frac{1}{2}$ inch at a point midway between the water pump and alternator pulleys as shown in **FIG 4:4** when finger pressure is applied. Tighten the mounting bolts and re-check.

4:5 The water pump

Removal:

Drain and collect the coolant as described earlier then detach the lower radiator hose and the heater return hose from the water inlet housing.

Loosen the alternator mounting bolts and remove the fan belt as described in **Section 4:4**. Remove the fan and pulley.

Unscrew the bolts securing the water pump assembly and remove complete with inlet housing and thermostat from the front cover.

Installation:

First clean off all traces of jointing material from the mating surfaces, then apply a little sealer to both sides of a new gasket and place the gasket on the pump.

Place the pump assembly in position and insert two bolts fingertight to hold it on the front cover.

Clean the joint surfaces of the water inlet housing, apply sealer to both sides of a new gasket and position the gasket on the pump assembly.

Place the thermostat in position and fit the rubber gasket. Position the water inlet housing and screw it together with the by-pass flange to the water pump. Tighten up all the securing bolts.

Fit the fan and pulley. Fit and adjust the belt. Reconnect the hoses and tighten their securing clamps. Fill the system as described in **Section 4:2**. Run the engine and examine for leaks.

4:6 Fault diagnosis

(a) Internal water leakage

1 Cracked cylinder wall
2 Loose cylinder head bolts
3 Cracked cylinder head
4 Faulty head gasket
5 Distorted head

(b) Poor circulation

1 Radiator core blocked
2 Engine water passages restricted
3 Low level of coolant
4 Loose fan belt
5 Defective thermostat
6 Perished or collapsed hoses
7 Air lock in system

(c) Corrosion

1 Impurities in water
2 Infrequent draining and flushing

(d) Overheating

1 Check (b)
2 Sludge in crankcase
3 Faulty ignition timing
4 Low oil level in sump
5 Tight engine, perhaps after rebore
6 Choked exhaust system
7 Binding brakes
8 Slipping clutch
9 Incorrect valve timing
10 Retarded ignition
11 Mixture too weak

CHAPTER 5

THE CLUTCH

5:1 Description

The clutch employed on these cars is the single dry plate type with a spring cushioned hub. A diaphragm spring is used to provide the necessary pressure and operation of the release mechanism is by means of a cable linkage.

The components of the clutch and its associated parts are shown in FIG 5:1 the clutch pressure plate assembly is bolted to the rear face of the flywheel and consists of a pressed steel cover housing a pressure plate and the diaphragm spring.

The driven plate, or clutch disc is held by the pressure of the spring between the pressure plate and the flywheel and is carried on splines machined on the main drive shaft into the gearbox. Thus, when engaged, the drive is transmitted from the flywheel and pressure plate face to the clutch disc and to the gearbox.

Pressure on the clutch pedal is transmitted to the release bearing by the cable and release lever, which deflects the diaphragm spring and relieves the pressure on the pressure plate, the clutch disc is no longer held and so slows down and stops and disconnects the engine from the gearbox.

5:2 Routine maintenance

The only item to be mentioned under this heading is a regular inspection to ensure that the clutch pedal free travel is as specified. This should also be checked if the clutch should fail to disengage correctly or whenever new clutch parts are fitted. Correct adjustment here is most important as failure to maintain the clearance frequently results in complete clutch failure.

Pull off the rubber boot over the release lever and see that the ball end of the operating cable is well greased.

2600 models:

Loosen the locknut FIG 5:2 and with the clutch pedal pressed up against its stop on the pedal bracket, turn the adjusting nut as necessary to obtain a clearance of between .138 and .144 inch between the nut and the clutch housing as shown in FIG 5:3 this setting corresponds to free travel at the clutch pedal of .5 to .75 inch.

Tighten the locknut and check that the pedal end of the cable is also well lubricated.

2800 models:

Wedge the clutch pedal up against its back stop with a block of wood or other suitable means under the pedal.

Pull the cable casing forward until the adjusting nut is pulled out of its recess in the bushing. Holding the nut out, pull the cable forward sufficiently to take up any free play in the release lever. Turn the nut until it just touches the hexagonal recess then release the cable, causing the nut to enter the shaped recess in the bushing.

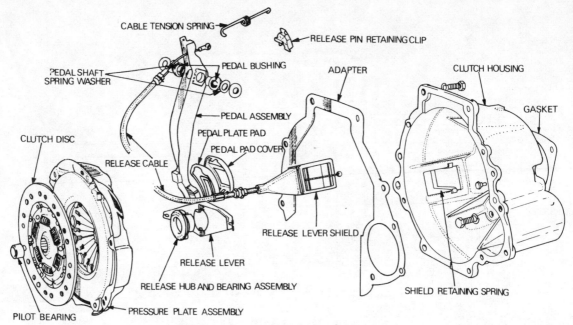

FIG 5:1   Components of a clutch mechanism

CABLE TENSION SPRING

RELEASE PIN RETAINING CLIP

PEDAL SHAFT
SPRING WASHER

PEDAL BUSHING

ADAPTER

CLUTCH HOUSING

GASKET

PEDAL ASSEMBLY

CLUTCH DISC

PEDAL PLATE PAD

PEDAL PAD COVER

RELEASE CABLE

RELEASE LEVER SHIELD

RELEASE LEVER

RELEASE HUB AND BEARING ASSEMBLY

PILOT BEARING

PRESSURE PLATE ASSEMBLY

SHIELD RETAINING SPRING

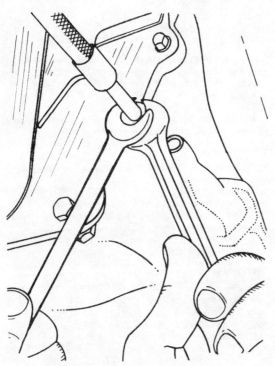

FIG 5:2   Adjusting the clutch cable

Remove the wooden block and fully operate the clutch pedal two or three times, then measure the distance between the lower edge of the pedal and the floor pan with the pedal hard against its back stop. Call this dimension A.

Press the pedal fully down, release it gently and again measure the distance to the floor pan. Call this dimension B.

A–B represents the pedal free play and should be 1.063 + .157 inch (27 + 4 mm).

If this is not correct, readjust the cable as necessary. Make sure that the boot has not been pulled out of the recess in the clutch housing.

5:3 Removing the clutch

In the event of trouble with the clutch, as there is no provision for servicing or adjustment, the complete assembly should be renewed.

Disconnect the battery and raise the car, supporting it securely.

Identify the flanges of the rear axle pinion and the propeller shaft to ensure correct refitting, remove the four retaining bolts and also the two bolts securing the centre bearing carrier to its bracket, lower the rear end of the shaft and slide the front yoke from the gearbox. Insert a dummy yoke or similar plug into the aperture to prevent the oil running out of the box.

Remove the clip and pull out the speedometer cable from the transmission extension housing. Disconnect the exhaust pipe bracket from the gearbox and swing it clear.

Pull back the rubber boot over the clutch release lever and detach the operating cable.

Unclip the spring retainers shown in **FIG 5:4** and disconnect the shifter rods from the gearbox.

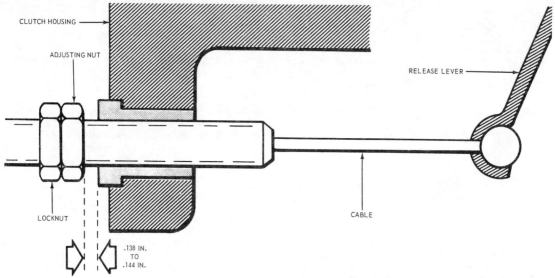

FIG 5:3 Clutch adjustment (early models)

Remove the three securing bolts and move the starter motor to one side.

Remove the six screws securing the clutch housing to the engine and the screws securing the engine rear plate to the front lower portion of the flywheel housing.

Support the gearbox from underneath and remove the four bolts securing the crossmember to the body. Carefully slide the gearbox to the rear, keeping it well supported and square with the engine, ensuring that its weight is not allowed to hang on the hub of the clutch or considerable damage may result.

Remove the four bolts securing the clutch housing to the transmission.

5:4 Servicing the clutch

Clutch disc and pilot bearing

With the clutch housing removed, slacken the six clutch attaching screws progressively and diagonally and then lift off the disc and pressure plate assembly.

To remove the pilot bearing if required, insert the service puller tool behind the bearing and use a slide hammer to extract the bearing.

The new bearing should be fitted by placing it on the service mandrel tool used in conjunction with a spacer tool and then tapped into place in the crankshaft flange.

Place the clutch disc in position after smearing the

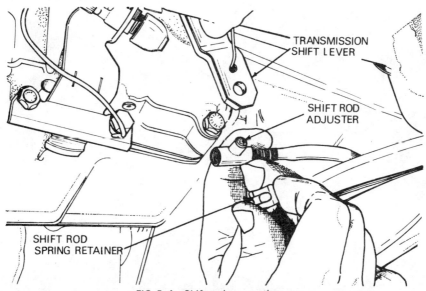

FIG 5:4 Shift rod connection

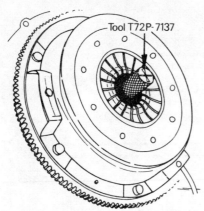

FIG 5:5 Centralising the clutch plate

Tool T72P-7137

splines with a molybdenum grease, noting that the fly-wheel side of the disc is marked near the centre and the raised centre portion is away from the flywheel. Align the plate with the service mandrel tool shown in **FIG 5:5**.

Refit the pressure plate assembly, locating it on the flywheel dowels. Fit the six securing screws and tighten them to 11-14 lb ft.

Remove the centralizing tool and fit the clutch housing as described in **Section 5:5**.

Clutch release bearing:

After removing the clutch housing, withdraw the release lever from the hub and bearing.

To fit a new bearing first apply a smear of molybdenum grease to the hub and release lever and then engage the lever in the slots in the hub and release bearing assembly.

Pass the release lever through the aperture in the clutch housing and slide the release bearing on to the front bearing retainer. See **FIG 5:6**.

Clutch linings:

The driven plate is serviced as an assembly and it is not recommended that the home operator should attempt to rivet on new linings when replacement is due.

Replacement is necessary when the friction material is worn down almost to the level of the rivets or if oil contamination is evident. Normally, the friction material should stand well proud of the rivets and be smoothly polished. It should be of a light colour, with the grain of the material clearly visible through the surface glaze. A dark brown staining is usually the result of oil or grease finding its way on to the linings and of course the cause should be looked for and rectified. To attempt to salvage the linings by washing is rarely successful and a replacement clutch disc is to be recommended in all these cases.

5:5 Re-installing the clutch

The most important part of this operation is the correct centralization of the clutch disc on the flywheel before the pressure plate assembly is fitted. This has already been described in **Section 5:4** and ensures that the hub of the plate lines up with the pilot bearing in the end of the crankshaft and facilitates the correct entry of the gearbox main shaft.

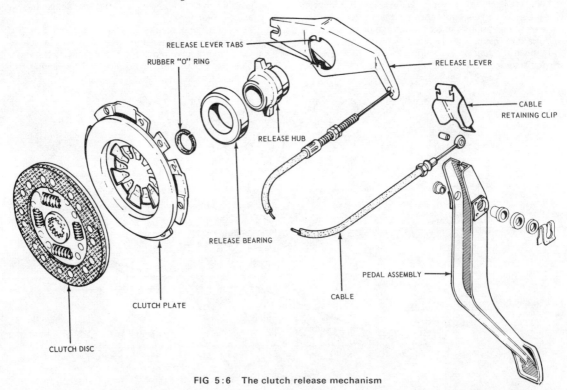

FIG 5:6 The clutch release mechanism

Having located the driven plate fit the pressure plate assembly on the dowels and tighten the six bolts to 11-14 lb ft.

Make sure that the adaptor plate is in position on the rear of the engine then move the gearbox and clutch housing carefully into place until the front end of the input shaft enters the hub of the driven plate. Do not let the weight of the gearbox hang on the hub. Push the gearbox fully home, turning the flywheel a little if necessary to get the splines to mesh. The spigot on the shaft should now be in full engagement with the crankshaft pilot bearing.

Refit the gearbox crossmember to the body, tighten the bolts and remove the transmission support.

Fit the screws securing the clutch housing to the engine. Fit the engine rear plate and secure with the screws.

Fit the starter motor. Fit the gear shift rods, adjust if necessary and secure with clips.

Smear molybdenum grease on the ball end of the clutch operating cable and fit it to the clutch release lever. Fit the rubber boot into the release lever aperture.

Reconnect the exhaust pipe bracket to the gearbox and fit the speedometer cable in the extension housing, retaining it with a clip.

Replace the propeller shaft in the gearbox, line up the marks on the flanges and secure with the four bolts tightened to a torque of 15 to 18 lb ft. Place the centre bearing carrier in position and secure to its bracket with two bolts.

Check the oil level in the gearbox and top up if necessary.

Lower the car and check the gearbox operation.

5:6 Renewing a clutch operating cable

Jack up the front of the car and support it on stands.

Slacken the clutch adjusting nuts, shown in **FIG 5:2** on the clutch housing.

Remove the spring clip securing the clutch cable to the top of the pedal (see **FIG 5:6**) withdraw the pivot pin and pull the cable into the engine compartment.

Move the boot over the clutch release lever and release the cable from the lever. Remove the cable from the car.

Fitting:

Pass the top end of the cable through the engine bulk head and fit it to the top of the pedal. Lubricate and install the pivot pin and secure with the retaining clip.

Connect the lower end of the cable to the release lever, lubricate well and replace the rubber boot.

Adjust the cable as described in **Section 5:2.**

5:7 Fault diagnosis

(a) Dragging clutch

1 Oil on the friction linings
2 Faulty cable
3 Driven plate hub binding on splines
4 Driven plate distorted
5 Warped or damaged pressure plate
6 Broken friction linings

(b) Fierceness or snatch

1 Check 1, 2, 4 and 5 in (a)
2 Worn linings

(c) Slip

1 Check 1 in (a) and 2 in (b)
2 No play in cable adjustment
3 Weak or broken diaphragm spring
4 Outer casing of cable trapped or damaged

(d) Judder

1 Check 1 and 4 in (a)
2 Contact area of linings not evenly distributed
3 Faulty rubber mountings to engine or gearbox

(e) Tick or knock

1 Badly worn splines on driven plates
2 Worn release bearing
3 Faulty pressure plate assembly

NOTES

CHAPTER 6

MANUAL TRANSMISSION

6:1 Description

The manual transmission employed on these cars is a conventional four forward and reverse unit with the four forward gears engaged through block ring type synchromesh. In the interests of silent operation the forward speed gears are helically cut, but the reverse gear on the countershaft has straight cut spur teeth.

Gear selection is by means of a remote control lever mounted on the transmission tunnel which operates three shift levers on the side of the gearbox through the shift rods shown in **FIG 6:1**.

To compensate for manufacturing tolerances and to eliminate excessive end float or backlash in the gears, three of the six snap rings locating the gears are selective and enable close fits to be easily obtained.

6:2 Maintenance and adjustment

After the first 6000 miles the gearbox oil should be drained out and fresh oil of the correct grade poured in through the filler hole on the lefthand side of the casing. When the level is up to the bottom of the filler hole, the plug should be replaced.

At each subsequent 6000 miles the level should be checked and topped up if necessary.

Adjusting the gearshift linkage:

Refer to **FIG 6:2** and fabricate an alignment pin, as shown, out of $\frac{3}{16}$ inch diameter wire and $3\frac{1}{2}$ inches long.

Raise the car to give access to the underside and place the gearshift lever in the neutral position.

Remove the spring retainers and disconnect the shifter rods from the transmission shift levers. See **FIG 5:4**.

Insert the alignment pin in the position shown to ensure that the levers are correctly positioned, place all the shift levers on the transmission in the neutral position and then adjust the length of the shifter rods so that they fit easily into the holes in the shift levers. Replace the spring retainers.

Remove the alignment pin, lower the car and check that all gears can be selected.

6:3 Dismantling the transmission

The removal of the gearbox from the car was described in the previous chapter, **Section 5:3**. Drain the oil from the box. Slide off the clutch release bearing and release fork, take out the four securing screws and carefully remove the clutch housing by tapping it if necessary. Place the gearbox on a suitable stand or fixture.

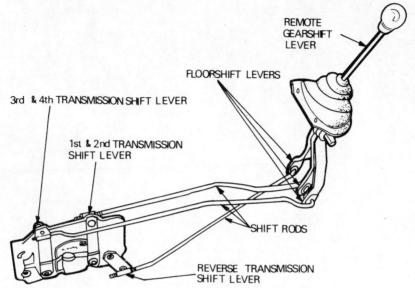

REMOTE GEARSHIFT LEVER

FLOORSHIFT LEVERS

3rd & 4th TRANSMISSION SHIFT LEVER

1st & 2nd TRANSMISSION SHIFT LEVER

SHIFT RODS

REVERSE TRANSMISSION SHIFT LEVER

FIG 6:1   The gearshift mechanism

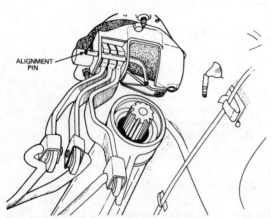

ALIGNMENT PIN

FIG 6:2   Fitting the alignment pin

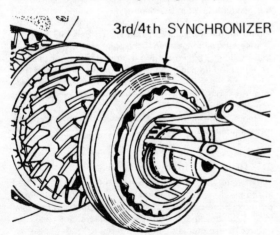

3rd/4th SYNCHRONIZER

FIG 6:3   Removing 3rd gear snap ring

Undo the seven securing screws and remove the top cover. Lift out the shifter forks, then remove the four securing screws and rotate the extension housing until the end of the countershaft is fully revealed.

Using a dummy countershaft drive out the countershaft from the front, taking great care to ensure that the dummy shaft remains in contact with the countershaft at all times so that the needle bearings do not become dislodged. The gear cluster may be lowered into the bottom of the transmission casing.

Tap the input shaft with a soft mallet and pull it out of the casing. Remove the snap ring securing the input shaft bearing and press off the bearing with the special tool.

Remove the extension housing and output shaft assembly from the case. Remove the cluster gear assembly and if necessary dismantle it by withdrawing the dummy shaft. The needle rollers and spacers may now be removed and it may be necessary to retrieve the thrust washers from the casing.

Drive out the reverse idler gear shaft towards the **rear** of the case.

Remove the snap ring in front of the 3rd/4th gear synchroniser on the output shaft (**FIG 6 : 3**) and withdraw the assembly.

Remove the 2nd gear snap ring (**FIG 6 : 4**) and pull off the gear and blocking ring.

Remove the 1st/2nd gear synchroniser sleeve and inserts. Note that the hub is splined to the output shaft and cannot be pressed off.

Unscrew the speedometer drive retainer and remove the driven gear.

Remove the snap ring retaining the output bearing in the extension housing. See **FIG 6 : 5**. Gently tap the output shaft from the housing.

Press out the speedometer drive gear.

Remove the snap ring in front of the output shaft bearing and press out the bearing. Remove the spacer, pull off the 1st gear and blocking ring and remove the insert spring.

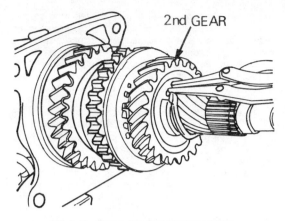

FIG 6:4   Removing 2nd gear snap ring

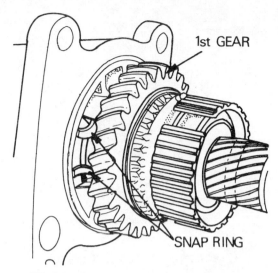

FIG 6:5   Output bearing snap ring location

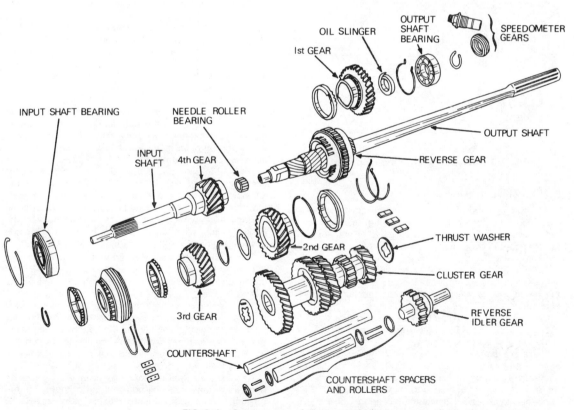

FIG 6:6   Components of the transmission

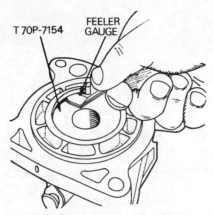

FIG 6:7   Measuring snap ring thickness

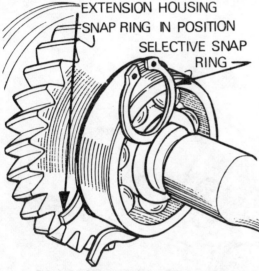

FIG 6:8   Output shaft bearing snap ring

6:4 Assembling the transmission

All components should be carefully cleaned and examined for wear or damage, renewing as necessary. Before assembly dip them all in a specified oil and apply a sealer to those screws which are screwed into the transmission casing. Obtain new circlips throughout.

Refer to **FIG 6:6**. Slide the insert spring, blocking ring, 1st gear and spacer onto the rear of the output shaft with the broad side of the spacer towards the output shaft bearing.

Select a new snap ring for the extension housing output shaft and slide it onto the shaft. The thickness of the new snap ring is selected as follows:

Place the dummy bearing tool T70P-7154 into the extension housing and use feeler gauges to measure the gap between the top face of the tool and the outer edge of the snap ring retaining groove as shown in **FIG 6:7**. The combined thickness of the dummy bearing (.668 inch) and the feeler blades will be the total width between the

bearing stop and the outer edge of the retaining groove. From this measurement subtract the width of the bearing to be used and the result is the thickness of the snap ring required. This must be precisely selected as, when installed, the output shaft must have no end float.

Press the bearing onto the output shaft and secure with the new snap ring which must fit **exactly** in the groove. See **FIG 6:8**.

The speedometer gear is pressed into position using the tool T71P-17271-B, shown in **FIG 6:9**. This is most important as this will locate the gear accurately on the output shaft, there being no locking device for the gear. See **FIG 6:10**.

The springs in the 1st/2nd gear synchroniser are positioned offset to one another by placing one end of each spring into the same insert groove as shown in **FIG 6:11** in order to have their tensions in opposition. The inserts are then placed in their grooves and the 1st/2nd gear synchroniser sleeve slid on to the hub with the selector fork collar facing the front end of the output shaft.

Slide the blocking ring, second gear and thrust washer onto the shaft and fit the snap ring in the position shown by **FIG 6:12**.

In order to obtain a tight fit for the output shaft and bearing in the extension housing, the housing should first be heated in an oven or by immersion in hot water. The shaft and bearing may then be slid into place without using any excessive pressure.

Fit the previously selected snap ring to secure the bearing in the housing.

Fit the 3rd/4th synchroniser springs in the same offset manner as for the 1st/2nd gear, position the inserts in their groove and slide the 3rd/4th gear synchroniser sleeve onto the hub with the narrow shoulder towards the rear. Slide the synchroniser assembly onto the output shaft and fit the retaining snap ring.

Press the input shaft bearing onto the input shaft and secure it with a snap ring selected for thickness to give the minimum end play. Fit the shaft and gear into the transmission case and tap it into place with a brass drift applied to the bearing outer race and then fit the snap ring to the periphery of the bearing.

The seal in the input shaft retainer may be renewed if necessary using tool T71P-7050-B before fitting the retainer to the transmission using a new gasket. Make sure that the oil groove in the retainer lines up with the oil passage in the casing and that it is not covered by the gasket. Secure the retainer with the three screws using a suitable sealer on the threads and new lock washers.

The reverse idler gear is fitted with the collar for the selector fork towards the rear and then the idler gear shaft driven into place until it is flush with the wall of the casing.

The installation of the countershaft assembly is very much a reversal of its removal. Assemble the cluster gear on the dummy shaft and lay it in the bottom of the casing, threading cords underneath it at each end to lift it up into its fork position. The rollers and washers may be held in place by smearing liberally with grease or vaseline.

Replace the extension housing gasket with a sealer on both sides, then slide the housing and output shaft into position being very careful not to damage the caged roller bearing. **FIG 6:13**.

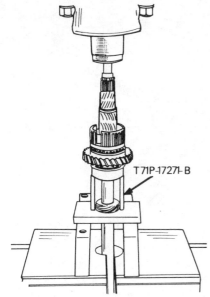

FIG 6:9 Fitting the speedometer gear

T 71P-17271-B

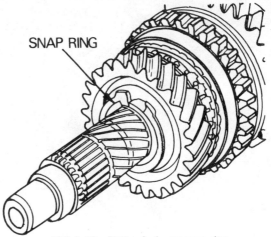

SNAP RING

FIG 6:12 Fitting 2nd gear snap ring

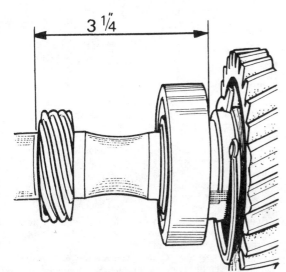

3 1/4"

FIG 6:10 Speedometer gear location

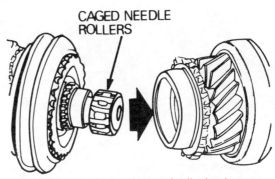

CAGED NEEDLE ROLLERS

FIG 6:13 Fitting the caged roller bearing

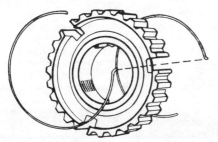

FIG 6:11 Showing typical positions of insert springs

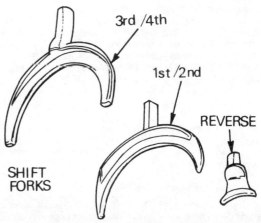

3rd /4th

1st /2nd

REVERSE

SHIFT FORKS

FIG 6:14 Shift fork identification

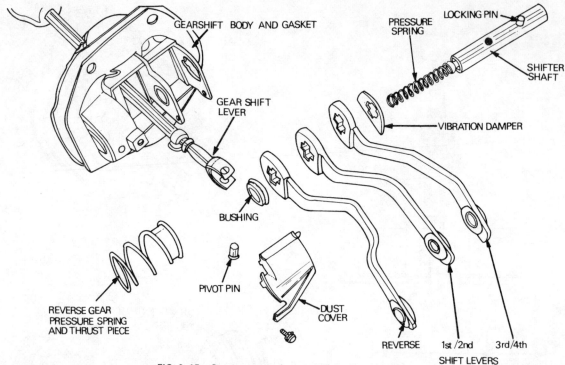

FIG 6:15   Components of gear shift lever assembly

Move the extension housing so as to permit access to the countershaft, then pull the cords to raise the cluster gear into mesh with the main gear train and install the countershaft by pushing it into replace the dummy shaft. Be most careful to see that none of the rollers or washers are displaced during this operation, and ensure that the offset lug on the rear end of the countershaft is correctly located to allow the final installation of the extension housing.

Secure the extension housing, tightening the screws to a torque of 30 to 35 lb ft and using sealer on the screw threads.

Fit the speedometer driven gear.

Refer to **FIG 6:14** to assist in identification and install the shift forks. 1st/2nd and 3rd/4th forks are fitted with the number stamped on them facing to the front, while the reverse fork has its stamped number towards the rear. Note that the short leg of the 1st/2nd fork is towards the bottom of the casing.

Fit the gearshift housing on the transmission using a new gasket and sealer and then check that all gears can be selected.

Position the reversing light switch and secure the gearshift housing with its screws. Fit the clutch housing and tighten the screws to 40 to 47 lb ft. Fit the clutch release lever, hub and bearing.

6:5 The gearshift mechanism

The adjustment of the shift linkage was described in **Section 6:2**, but if further work is necessary, proceed as follows.

Removal:

Raise the car and disconnect the three shift rods from the levers by removing the clips as described earlier. Lever out the panel (wood grain) at the rear of the console.

Undo the two screws and slide the plastic cross panel forward and remove it.

Remove the two screws which will be found underneath the rear corners of the handbrake boot. Lever up the rear edge of the front wood grain panel and remove the centre retaining screw.

Remove one screw from each side of the lower front edge of the console, unscrew the knob of the gearlever and move the console to one side.

Take out the three securing screws and remove the gear shift assembly from the floor pan.

Refitting is a reversal of the above procedure.

Dismantling (see **FIG 6:15**):

Drive out the pivot pin from the shift lever fork and pull the gearshift lever out of the assembly.

Move all three shift levers rearwards into a horizontal position until it is possible to move the grooved pin through the respective cut-outs in the levers and shaft retainers. Pull out the shifter shaft and drive out the locking pin.

Remove the levers and the vibration damper, also the pressure springs, thrust piece and bushings.

Before commencing to reassemble, give all moving surfaces a smear of a suitable lubricant.

56

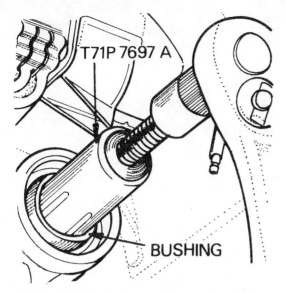

FIG 6:16   Removing the extension housing bushing

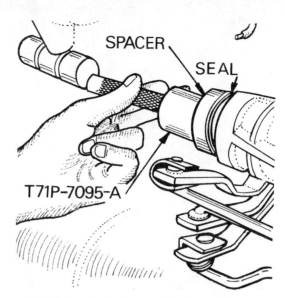

FIG 6:17   Replacing extension housing oil seal

Fit the reverse gear pressure spring on the thrust piece and slide into the gearshift body.

Fit the bushing with the flange towards the levers as shown and then assemble the three levers and vibration damper.

Slide the shifter shaft complete with locking pin and pressure spring into the shaft retainers and levers and then allow the levers to swing into the vertical position.

Fit the gearshift lever and rubber boot and secure it by driving in the front pin.

After assembly, check that the shift operates smoothly and correctly.

6:6 Installing the gearbox

This operation is described in **Section 5:5**, after which the transmission must be refilled with the specified lubricant and the gearshift linkage adjusted as described in **Section 6:2**.

6:7 Renewing the extension housing oil seal

After long use, wear in the rear end of the extension housing may be indicated by an oil leakage and radial movement of the output shaft.

Remove the four bolts in the flange joint between the drive shaft and the rear axle pinion, being careful to mark the flanges for later assembly.

Remove the bolts securing the centre bearing carrier to its bracket.

Lower the rear end of the drive shaft and slide the front yoke away from the transmission.

To renew, screw the tool T71P-7657-A into the seal and extract the seal by screwing in the centre bolt.

The extension housing bush is removed in a similar manner using the service tool (**FIG 6:16**).

Installation:

Fit a new bush on to the replacer service tool (T71P-7095 without spacer) and drive it into position, making sure that the split in the bush is uppermost.

The new seal is fitted by driving it, being careful to see that it is kept square, into position with the same tool but this time with the spacer (**FIG 6:17**).

Refit the remaining components in the reverse order to removal and top up the gearbox to make good any loss of oil.

6:8 Fault diagnosis

(a) Jumping out of gear

1 Worn gearshift mechanism
2 Worn selector cams or plunger spring
3 Worn synchromesh coupling dogs, sleeve or hub
4 Worn selectors forks or sleeves
5 Excessive end play on shafts

(b) Noisy transmission

1 Insufficient oil
2 Excessive end play on output or countershaft
3 Worn or damaged bearings
4 Worn or damaged gear teeth
5 Excessive running clearances

(c) Difficulty in engaging gear

1 Incorrect clutch adjustment
2 Worn synchromesh cones
3 Worn selector mechanism
4 Selector mechanism out of adjustment

(d) Noisy gearchange

1 Worn or damaged synchromesh cones
2 Blocker bars worn, springs weak
3 Worn or damaged teeth on gears

NOTES

CHAPTER 7

THE AUTOMATIC TRANSMISSION

7:1 Description

In the place of the conventional friction clutch and synchromesh gearbox it is possible to have as an option the Ford C4 automatic transmission. This consists of a fluid torque converter and a three-speed planetary gear train, the principal components of which can be seen in the cut-away drawing in **FIG 7:1**.

The torque converter has three elements: the impeller which is bolted to the engine crankshaft, the turbine which is splined to the gearbox input shaft, and the stator located between the two and mounted on a one-way clutch. The converter casing is filled with fluid and it is this which transmits the drive from one unit to another.

When the impeller turns, the fluid flows from the impeller vanes to those of the turbine, imparting a torque, and returns to the impeller by way of the stator vanes. These latter are so shaped that, when there is a considerable speed difference between impeller and turbine, they direct the fluid flow into the impeller in a manner designed to assist it in its rotation and so impart a degree of torque multiplication which ranges from 1:1 to approximately 2:1.

When the turbine has attained a speed of approximately 90% of the impeller speed, the stator begins to turn in the same direction and the three units rotate as one with only

a very slight degree of slip and the assembly becomes a fluid coupling.

The gearbox component has three forward speeds and a reverse and provides automatic up and down shifts between the three forward ratios and also manual selection of first and second gear. Two epicyclic gear trains are used, controlled by clutches and brake bands to provide the desired combinations of gears. These are applied automatically by hydraulic pressure generated by a built-in pump.

The dismantling and servicing of an automatic transmission requires the use of many special tools and skills beyond the scope of the average owner/driver or indeed many service stations. In the event of a failure in the transmission, the car should be taken to a qualified agent for testing and repair or a new unit fitted in replacement. Instructions will be given for a few items of maintenance and adjustment which can be carried out at home, and also details of the removal and installation of a complete transmission.

7:2 Routine maintenance:

This is a matter of ensuring that the fluid level is maintained and that dirt is not allowed to accumulate on the transmission casing or in the cooling grilles otherwise the unit may quickly overheat.

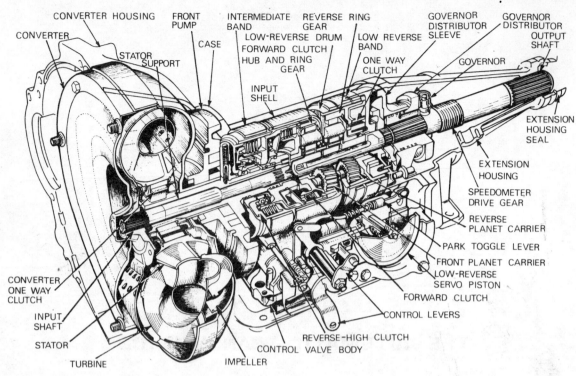

FIG 7:1 A cut-away view of the C4 transmission

Labels in the figure:

CONVERTER HOUSING
FRONT PUMP
INTERMEDIATE BAND
REVERSE RING GEAR
GOVERNOR DISTRIBUTOR SLEEVE
GOVERNOR DISTRIBUTOR
CONVERTER
LOW-REVERSE DRUM
CASE
FORWARD CLUTCH HUB AND RING GEAR
LOW REVERSE BAND
OUTPUT SHAFT
STATOR SUPPORT
ONE WAY CLUTCH
GOVERNOR
INPUT SHELL
EXTENSION HOUSING SEAL
EXTENSION HOUSING
SPEEDOMETER DRIVE GEAR
REVERSE PLANET CARRIER
PARK TOGGLE LEVER
FRONT PLANET CARRIER
LOW-REVERSE SERVO PISTON
FORWARD CLUTCH
CONTROL LEVERS
CONVERTER ONE WAY CLUTCH
INPUT SHAFT
STATOR
TURBINE
IMPELLER
CONTROL VALVE BODY
REVERSE-HIGH CLUTCH

The timing and quality of the gear shifting may be affected, after long periods of use, by wear on the brake bands, and the adjustment of these will be the only adjustment necessary.

All operations on the automatic transmission must be carried out with scrupulous cleanliness. This includes the careful wiping of the filler tube and dipstick before checking the fluid level as dirt may easily enter at this time.

Checking the fluid level:

First make sure that the car is standing on level ground and that the transmission has attained its normal working temperature. Firmly apply the parking brake.

Start the engine and allow it to run at its normal idling speed while moving the selector lever through all its positions, leaving it finally in position P. Do not stop the engine.

Clean all round the dipstick tube, take out the dipstick, wipe it and push it fully back into the tube, making sure that it is properly seated.

Pull out the dipstick and check the fluid level. This should be above the ADD mark. If necessary, pour in sufficient fluid to bring the level between the ADD and FULL marks on the dipstick. Do not overfill.

The specified fluid is Ford Automatic Transmission Fluid, Part No. C1AZ-19582-A.C.D., and approximately one pint is needed to raise the level from ADD to FULL.

Periodic draining and refilling of the transmission is not required, but it must be remembered that if at any time any fluid should be drained out of a hot transmission, it may be sufficiently hot to cause severe scalding if allowed to contact the skin.

Brake band adjustment:

The brake bands should normally require attention only at very long intervals, and to ensure correct adjustment it is most important that the specified tools and procedures are used as follows:

Intermediate band:

Refer to FIG 7:2. Clean all the dirt from around the band adjustment screw. Remove and discard the locknut.

Fit a new locknut onto the adjusting screw and with the tools shown in the illustration, tighten the adjusting screw until the tool handle clicks. The tool is in fact a pre-set torque wrench designed to break when the torque on the screw reaches 10 lb ft. In an emergency, if the special tool is not available, a torque wrench set to the specified value may be used.

Back off the adjusting screw by exactly $1\frac{3}{4}$ turns, hold it in this position and tighten the locknut to 35 to 45 lb ft.

Low-reverse band:

Clean around the adjusting screw shown in FIG 7:3. Remove and discard the locknut.

Fit on a new locknut, and using the tools shown, tighten the adjusting screw until the tool handle clicks, or to a torque of 10 lb ft.

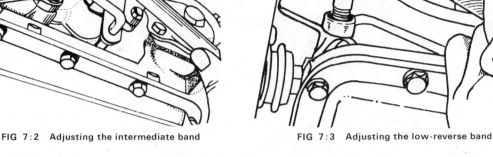

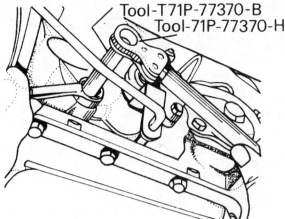

FIG 7:2   Adjusting the intermediate band

FIG 7:3   Adjusting the low-reverse band

Back off the adjusting screw by exactly three full turns and lock it with the locknut tightened to 35 to 45 lb ft.

7:3 Selector positions

The selector lever operates in a quadrant centrally mounted on the transmission tunnel and has six positions indicated by the letters P–R–N–D–2–1 which have the following functions:

P or Park   In this position the engine may be started and run without any drive being transmitted to the road wheels. There is also a mechanical device for locking the transmission which ensures that the car cannot be moved in either direction. Never select P while the car is in motion.

R or Reverse   As the name implies. Do not select R while the car is moving forwards.

N or Neutral   The engine may be started and run without any drive being transmitted to the road wheels. There is no transmission lock.

D or Drive   This position is selected for all normal running. The transmission starts in first or low gear and shifts automatically into second and top or high at speeds dependent upon throttle position and road speed. Down shifts are also made automatically as the road speed drops and at speeds relative to the throttle position.

2   In this position starts are made in low gear and automatic up and down shifts are made as conditions demand, but no shift into high gear occurs. If 2 is selected when in D, an immediate down shift to second gear is effected.

1   This is a lock in low, or first, gear and no shift will occur until the selector lever is moved. If 1 is selected when cruising in D range, there will be an immediate down shift to second and a further shift into low when the speed has dropped sufficiently.

Manual control:

Automatic gear selection may be over-ridden by using the selector lever to engage 1 or 2 as required. If the car is started in 1, second gear will not be engaged until 2, or D, is selected and second can be held until the lever is moved to D to engage high gear.

There is also the 'kick-down' facility whereby a down shift from high to second can be made when in D range simply by depressing the accelerator pedal beyond the normal full throttle position.

Starting:

The system includes an inhibitor device, known as the neutral start switch, which ensures that the engine can be started only when P or N is selected.

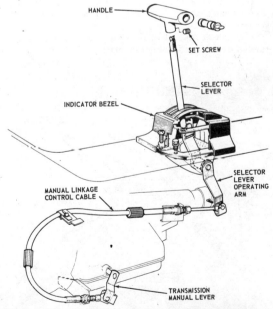

FIG 7:4   The components of a cable selector mechanism

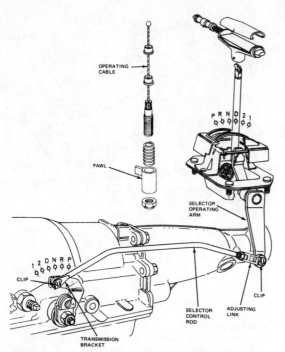

FIG 7:5 The rod-type selector linkage and mechanism

7:4 Shift control linkage

This may be either the cable operated type shown in **FIG 7:4** or the rod operated type shown in **FIG 7:5**. Dismantling and reassembly present no difficulties.

Dismantling:

Raise the car, remove the clevis pin and disconnect the selector control cable and bushing from the selector lever operating arm.

Lower the car and pull out the wood grain panel at the rear of the console. Remove two screws and move the plastic cross panel forward and out.

Remove the two screws which will be seen when the rear corners of the handbrake boot are lifted.

Lever up the rear edge of the front wood grain panel and remove the centre retaining screw.

Remove a screw from each side of the forward lower edge of the console and move the console out of the way.

Lift up the bezel on the selector quadrant (**FIG 7:5**) and remove the three bolts securing the selector lever housing to the floor. Disconnect the indicator light and remove the selector lever and housing.

Refer to **FIG 7:6** and loosen the set screw, depress the push button and remove the handle.

Remove the plug from the side of the selector housing and remove the retaining nut at the base of the selector lever as shown in **FIG 7:7**. Remove the selector lever and bushes by tapping lightly on the shaft.

Tap out the cable retaining pin at the top of the selector lever with a small drift. Remove the cable adjusting nut at the lower end of the lever and remove the detent plunger, spring and bushing (**FIG 7:8**). Slide the cable out of the lever.

Assembly:

Insert the cable through the selector lever and fit the retaining pin.

Replace the bush, spring and detent plunger over the cable and into the lower end of the lever. Push in the plunger and fit the cable adjusting nut.

Fit the lever and its bushings on the operating arm, tightening the retaining nut. Fit the handle and push button on to the lever and tighten the set screw.

With the selector lever in the centre detent, turn the cable adjusting nut to obtain a clearance of .005 to .010 inch between the bottom of the pawl and the detent as shown in **FIG 7:7**. Check the operation and then fit the plug in the side of the selector housing.

The remainder of the installation is carried out by reversing the order of dismantling.

Adjusting the selector cable:

Place the selector lever in the D position. Raise the car and remove the clevis pin to disconnect the cable at the transmission.

Move the transmission selector lever to the D position, which is the third detent from the back of the transmission, then with both levers in the D position adjust the length of the cable until the clevis pin holes in the lever are aligned with the end of the cable as in **FIG 7:9**.

Secure the cable and check the selector operation in each lever position.

Towing:

Provided that the transmission is not damaged and is full of oil the car may safely be towed for short distances, up to about 30 miles, and at speeds of not more than 30 mile/hour. If the transmission is damaged, or high speeds are intended, either the drive shaft must be disconnected or the car lifted and towed on its front wheels.

It should be noted that with this type of transmission tow, or push, starting of the engine is not possible.

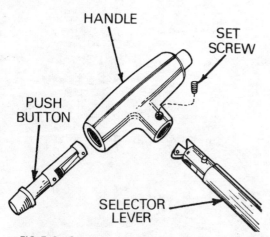

FIG 7:6 Components of the selector lever handle

Throttle linkage:

The correct adjustment of the throttle linkages is most important for the satisfactory operation of an automatic transmission. This is covered in **Chapter 2, Section 2:4**.

Neutral start switch:

Early models:

Before commencing to adjust the neutral start switch, confirm first that the selector mechanism is correctly set, then loosen the two switch securing bolts shown in **FIG 7:10**.

Move the transmission selector lever to neutral and then rotate the body of the switch to a position where a gauge pin (No. 43 drill) can be inserted a full $\frac{31}{64}$ inch into the three holes in the switch as shown.

Tighten the two securing bolts to 55 to 75 lb ft and remove the gauge pin.

Check that the starter operates only in N and P. Should it fail to do so renew the switch.

Later models:

On later models the neutral start switch is in the form of a hexagon bodied cylinder, screwed into the transmission casing just above the selector lever position. It is connected in circuit by means of a five point connecting plug.

In the event of incorrect operation a new switch and 'O' ring must be fitted as no adjustment is possible, but check first that the selector mechanism is correctly set.

A thin walled socket wrench will be required to remove the switch and to tighten it to a torque of 12 to 15 lb ft.

7:5 Removing the transmission

Raise the car and place a pan under the transmission. Starting at the rear of the oil pan loosen the securing bolts and allow the oil to drain into the pan. When all the oil has been drained, hold the pan temporarily in position with two bolts at the front and two at the rear.

Disconnect the starter cable and remove the starter from the converter housing. Remove the access cover from the lower end of the converter housing.

Remove the nuts securing the converter to the flywheel, turning the converter for access by using a wrench on the crankshaft pulley.

Turn the converter also to gain access to its drain plug. Drain off the fluid and replace the plug.

Mark the drive shaft and pinion flanges for correct reassembly and then remove the four securing bolts. Remove the two bolts securing the drive shaft centre bearing to the body, lower the drive shaft assembly and remove it from the transmission.

Disconnect the down shift cable from the transmission lever bracket and the wires for the neutral start switch from the clamps and connectors. Remove the vacuum pipe from the transmission vacuum unit.

Place a jack underneath the transmission to take the weight and then remove the bolt between the insulator and the extension housing bracket.

Remove the securing bolts and remove the crossmember. Unbolt and remove the filler tube. Disconnect the pipes to the oil cooler.

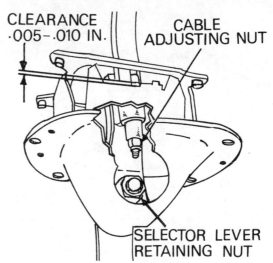

FIG 7:7   Selector lever adjustment

Before removing the bolts securing the converter housing to the engine, secure the transmission to the jack with a safety chain, then remove the transmission downwards and to the rear.

Installing the automatic transmission:

Replace the converter drain plug and fit the converter on the transmission, making sure that the flats on the converter drive are fully engaged in the pump gear. Place the whole assembly on its jack and secure with a chain.

Rotate the converter so that the studs and drain plug line up with their holes in the flywheel.

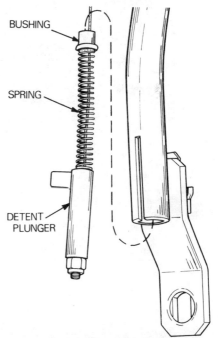

FIG 7:8   The detent plunger

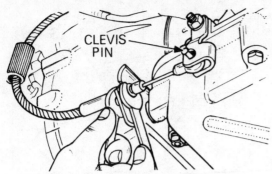

FIG 7:9   Control cable adjustment

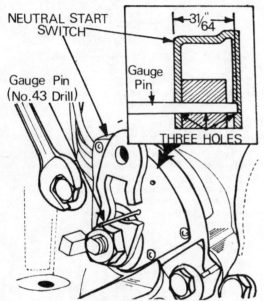

FIG 7:10   Adjusting the neutral start switch

Very carefully move the assembly into position and make sure that the converter fits squarely against the flywheel. Fit the securing bolts to the engine and tighten to 28 to 40 lb ft. Remove the safety chain.

Refit the filler tube to the engine, tightening to 20 to 25 lb ft. Connect the oil cooler pipes.

Raise the transmission sufficiently to install the crossmember, then lower it and fit the insulator to extension housing bracket bolt.

Fit the flywheel securing nuts and tighten to 23 to 28 lb ft.

Remove the transmission jack. Refit the vacuum pipe and the neutral start switch cables. Reconnect the down shift cable to the down shift lever bracket.

Fit the shift cable bracket to the converter housing with the two bolts and connect the cable to the transmission lever. Connect the speedometer cable to the extension housing.

Refit the drive shaft, being careful to see that the mating marks are in line and tighten the bolts to 43 to 47 lb ft.

Refit the centre bearing carrier, tightening the two bolts to 13 to 17 lb ft.

Fit the access cover to the converter housing. Refit the starter and the electric cable.

Lower the car, fill the transmission with the specified fluid (8 US, $6\frac{1}{2}$ Imp. qts) and adjust the linkages as described earlier in this chapter.

7:6 Fault diagnosis

The actual diagnosis of faults may call for many tests, some of them beyond the capabilities and equipment of the average owner. Some of the simpler faults are listed here of which a number may be rectified without calling for professional assistance. As stated earlier, however, in the event of trouble the owner is strongly advised to consult the agent.

(a) Transmission overheats

1 Excessive dirt on outside of unit
2 Oil cooler or lines blocked
3 Stator clutch seized
4 Incorrect brake band adjustment
5 Brakes binding

(b) Noisy operation

1 Incorrect fluid level or incorrect type of fluid
2 Incorrectly adjusted linkage
3 Oil screen to pump intake choked

(c) Incorrect shift speeds

1 Check in (b)
2 Defective vacuum unit
3 Incorrectly adjusted brake bands or defective servos
4 Defective governor assembly

(d) Jumps in engagement or rough engagement

1 Check 4 in (a); 2 in (b) and 2 in (c)
2 Incorrect idling speed

(e) Poor acceleration

1 Check 3 and 4 in (a)
2 Converter stator clutch slipping

(f) Vehicle does not hold in Park selection

1 Check 2 in (b)

(g) Fluid frothing or being forced out of filler tube

1 Too high fluid level
2 Water in system (suspect oil cooler)
3 Air leaks on suction side of pump

CHAPTER 8

FINAL DRIVE, REAR AXLE AND SUSPENSION

8:1 The drive shaft

This can be either a simple one-piece assembly with a universal joint at each end or a two-piece shaft with a third universal joint in the middle. On some later cars this third joint may be of the constant velocity type which is not suitable for dismantling. In these cars the complete shaft must be renewed in the event of excessive wear or damage in the joint.

A two-piece shaft assembly is shown in **FIG 8:1**, together with details of the centre bearing, not of course used on the one piece type, mounted on the body just in front of the centre joint.

The forward end of the shaft in each case is splined to the output shaft of the transmission, the rear end is attached to the differential pinion by a bolted flange.

Removal:

Mark the shaft and the pinion flanges to ensure correct reassembly and then remove the four securing bolts and lockwashers.

Remove the two bolts and washers securing the centre mounting to the body.

Lower the rear end of the shaft and slide the shaft assembly out of its engagement in the transmission. Steps should be taken to catch oil escaping from the transmission when the shaft is removed.

Refitting:

Slide the splined front yoke into the transmission being careful not to damage the oil seal or bearing in the extension housing.

Line up the marks made earlier and fit the four bolts to the rear flange and the differential pinion flange. Tighten to a torque of 43-47 lb ft.

The centre bearing carrier is bolted to its bracket when the car is standing, loaded normally, on its wheels. The bolts should be tightened to 13-17 lb ft.

Check the oil level in the transmission and top up if necessary.

Centre bearing:

Mark the relative positions of the front and centre universal joints for correct reassembly. Bend back the locking tab for the bolt at the rear end of the front shaft, slacken the bolt, remove the U shaped plate and separate the two halves of the drive shaft.

Remove the front shaft and bearing assembly from the rubber insulator and remove the insulator from its carrier by bending back the locating tabs.

Use a suitable puller to remove the bearing and protective caps from the shaft.

Check the bearing for wear and the rubber insulator for deterioration.

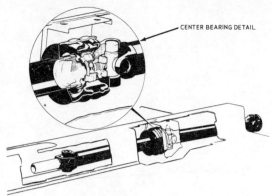

CENTER BEARING DETAIL

FIG 8:1   The two-piece drive shaft assembly

Refitting:

Using a length of suitable tubing, drive the ball bearing and the protective caps on to the shaft.

Insert the rubber insulator into its carrier with the boss upwards and bend the six tabs back over the beaded edge of the insulator.

Slide the carrier and insulator over the bearing assembly.

Fit the securing bolt with a new locking tab on to the shaft, leaving enough space for the insertion of the U plate.

Line up the mating marks on the two universal joints and assemble the shafts. Insert the U plate with its smooth face towards the fork under the retaining bolt head and tighten the bolt to 25-30 lb ft. Bend up the locking tab.

Install the drive shaft as described earlier.

Universal joints:

The components of the early type of universal joint are shown in **FIG 8:2** and these may be dismantled as follows, but on later cars the bearing assemblies are staked into the yokes so that a fault requires the renewal of the complete assembly.

After removing the drive shaft, extract the snap ring from each spider bearing and remove the bearing cups and rollers by gently tapping on the yoke.

Remove the spider and prise off the oil seal and retainer from each spider journal. Kits of spare parts are available to rebuild the joints.

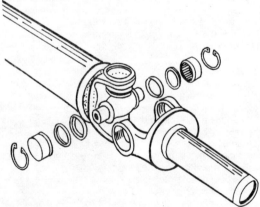

FIG 8:2   Components of a universal joint

Fit new oil seals to the retainers and fit them on the shoulders of the spider journals with the oil seals outwards.

Fit the spider in the drive shaft yoke and assemble the needle rollers in each bearing cup. Pack the bearings with a multi-purpose lithium grease, leaving a certain amount of room for expansion when hot.

Tap the bearings squarely into place, taking care not to displace the rollers. Refit the snap rings and install the drive shaft.

8:2 The rear axle

This is of conventional design with the pinion, differential unit and crown wheel assembled into the axle casing from the rear.

The driving pinion runs in two taper-roller bearings which are pre-loaded by a selective tubular spacer placed between them, the depth of meshing with the crown wheel being controlled by a selective shim between the pinion head and the rear bearing. The crown wheel is bolted to the differential case which is carried in two taper-roller bearings, the sideways location being determined by selective shims on either side which also give a degree of pre-loading on the bearing.

The differential is of the conventional two pinion type with the two axle half shafts being splined to the side gears and supported at the outer ends by ball races with built-in oil seals secured in the outer ends of the axle casing.

It should be noted that all the bolts used in this axle assembly use metric threads. This, of course, makes no difference to the servicing procedure, but does mean that many home operators will need to obtain some extra tools for the procedures outlined in this section.

8:3 Removing and refitting the axle

Jack up the rear end of the car support it on stands and remove the road wheels.

Release the handbrake and disconnect the cable from the lever on the rear of the axle housing. Disconnect the brake hydraulic pipe at the junction on the axle and plug the aperture to prevent fluid loss.

Mark the drive shaft and pinion flanges and remove the four bolts and washers.

Jack up the centre of the axle and remove the bolts securing the lower ends of the shock absorbers. Lower the jack.

On the pre 1973 models remove the bolts to release the rear end of the radius arms from the axle, noting that as these bolts are under load it may be necessary to assist with a screwdriver and C clamp.

Since 1973 the radius arms have been superseded by an anti-roll bar. Remove both anti-roll bar brackets from the rear axle. During the operation pull the anti-roll ball towards the rear axle using a suitable clamp to eliminate the preload from the bolts.

Remove the nuts from the U bolts and detach the bolts and plates. Lift the axle and remove it sideways through a wheel arch.

Refitting:

Slide the axle sideways into position on the springs, making sure that the spring insulators and retainers are correctly located on the spring spigots and the retainers in the holes in the axle pads.

Fit the U bolts over the axle, slide on the lower plates and tighten the locknuts to an initial torque of 5 lb ft.

To refit the anti-roll bar use a suitable clamp to press the bar onto its seating, fit the brackets and bolts and tighten fully.

Jack up the axle and install the lower shock absorber mounting bolts. Lower the jack.

Pull the radius arms into position, using a screwdriver and C clamp as when dismantling, and fit the bolts but do not tighten them at this stage.

Line up and reconnect the drive shaft to the pinion flange, tightening the bolts to 43-47 lb ft.

Remove the plugs and reconnect the brake pipes through the bracket on the axle casing. Reconnect the parking brake cable to the lever on the axle and adjust the cable as necessary.

Adjust the brakes if required by moving the parking brake levers on the brake carrier plates in and out. Bleed the braking system.

Fit the road wheels and lower the car to the ground.

Now that the weight of the car is being carried on its wheels, the rear bolts for the radius arms and the U bolts nuts can be tightened. The specified torques are 22-27 and 18-26 lb ft respectively.

8:4 The axle shafts

1 Jack up the rear of the car, support on stands and remove the road wheels. Release the handbrake.
2 Remove the screw securing the brake drum and lift off.
3 Remove the screws securing the bearing retainer plate to the axle casing. These are accessible through the holes in the axle shaft flange.
4 Pull the axle shaft and bearing assembly out of the axle case using the service tool and sliding hammer.
5 Loosen the inner retaining ring by nicking it deeply with a cold chisel in several places (see FIG 8:3) and slide it off.
6 Press the bearing and seal off the axle shaft.

Installation:

Before replacing the axle shaft it should be inspected for any signs of roughness on the machined surfaces and if these are present they should be carefully removed or, if too severe, the worn or damaged part renewed.

Coat the bearing bores with axle lubricant then place the bearing retainer plate on the axle shaft and press on a new bearing, noting that the shaft journal and the inside of the retainer must be clean and dry.

Press the bearing inner retaining ring on the shaft using the tool shown in FIG 8:4 until the retainer seats firmly against the bearing.

Insert the shaft into the axle casing, engage the splines in the differential side gear and tap it fully home.

Secure the bearing retainer plate with the four bolts and spring washers, tightening to 15-18 lb ft.

Replace the remaining parts in the reverse order of removal.

8:5 Servicing the differential

Before describing the procedure for this operation, the operator is advised that it is not simple and it requires the use of tools and instruments which may not be available. Under these circumstances he may find it preferable to take the assembly to his local service station for attention.

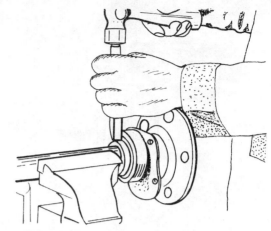

FIG 8:3 Removing a rear wheel retainer ring

Carry out Items 1 through 4 of **Section 8:4** then:

Remove the drive shaft from the pinion flange. Remove the ten retaining bolts and lift off the rear axle cover and gasket, placing a suitable container to catch the oil as it flows out. The gasket should be discarded and the cover cleaned. On axles of German and U.S.A. manufacture the retaining bolts are at the rear of the casing.

Mark the differential bearing caps for later assembly then undo the cap retaining screws and remove the caps.

Use two tapered lengths of wood to lever the differential assembly out of the casing.

Remove the taper roller bearing from each side of the assembly using the tool shown in FIG 8:5 and take the adjusting shims out of the housing.

Unscrew the bolts securing the crown wheel and remove it.

Tap out the locking pin securing the differential pinion shaft in the housing, then remove the differential pinion shaft, the pinion, side gears and adjusting shims.

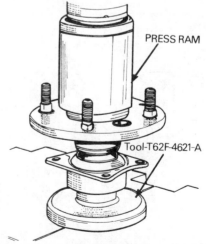

PRESS RAM

Tool-T62F-4621-A

FIG 8:4 Fitting a rear wheel bearing retainer ring

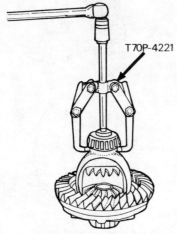

FIG 8:5   Removing differential side bearings

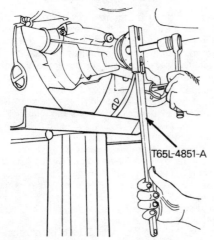

FIG 8:6   Removing the pinion flange

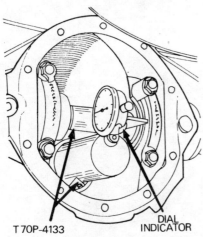

T70P-4133

DIAL INDICATOR

FIG 8:7   Checking pinion depth

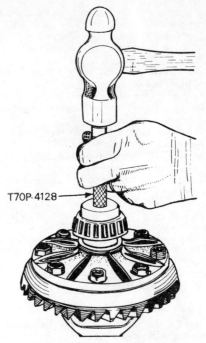

FIG 8:8   Fitting differential side bearings

Hold the drive pinion flange and remove the pinion nut. This self-locking nut may be retained for assembly and checking, but must be renewed on final assembly. Pull off the pinion flange using the tools shown in **FIG 8:6**.

Remove the pinion from the axle casing and pull off the spacer.

Pull the large roller bearing off the pinion shaft with the service tool or other suitable puller and remove the spacing shim from the pinion shaft.

Remove the small taper roller bearing and oil seal from the casing using a suitable drift. Similarly drive out the bearing outer races.

Clean all parts thoroughly and inspect. Renew any worn or damaged parts and any bearings which are rough in action when dry. Renew the oil seal.

Assembling the differential:

Fit first the small then the larger bearing races into the casing using the Ford service tool, being most careful to see that they are squarely and fully positioned.

The next step is to determine the thickness of shimming required for the correct depth of pinion mesh. First position the crossbar of the Ford service tool in the casing together with the side bearings as shown in **FIG 8:7**. Fit the bearing caps (number to number) and tighten the retaining bolts.

Slacken back the bolts and re-tighten with the fingers only.

Hold the bar and rotate the nut by hand. This pre-loads the side bearings by expanding the crossbar. Rotate the crossbar several times to seat the bearings and check that they are still pre-loaded. Do not over expand the bar. Tighten the retaining bolts to a torque of 43 lb ft.

Install the dummy pinion part of the service tool with the bearings but without the shims into the axle case. Lightly lubricate the bearings. Tighten until the correct pinion bearing pre-load of 13 to 19 lb inch is obtained.

Rotate the dummy pinion several times to ensure seating of the bearings. **It is essential that the torque reading be recorded and adhered to for the further adjustment of the drive pinion.** This torque must also be checked after the installation of the actual pinion (with the selected spacer).

Mount a dial indicator on the mounting bracket and position it at zero on the dummy pinion. Slowly rotate the dial indicator over the crossbar and read the total deflection of its pointer. This reading gives the exact thickness of shims to be used. When the pinion gear is marked minus one (1) or minus two (2) this amount must be added to the indicator reading to obtain the correct shim thickness. When the pinion gear is marked plus one (1) or two (2) this amount must be subtracted.

Select a spacer shim of the exact thickness as calculated.

Slide the shim(s) on to the pinion to be installed and press on the large taper roller bearing, wide end towards the gear. Position the side gears with one shim each in the differential case, the grooved side of the shim being towards the gear.

Place both differential pinions and thrustwashers simultaneously between the side gears. Push the pinion shaft into position in the differential case taking care to align the locking pin bores.

Measure the play of each side gear with a feeler gauge and if necessary new shims must be fitted to obtain a clearance between .0004 and .006 inch.

Secure the differential pinion shaft with a locking pin.

Place the crown wheel on the differential case and pull it evenly into position with the four old bolts. Remove the bolts and fit **new bolts** and tighten to 50-54 lb ft. Note that the crown wheel and pinion are supplied only in matched pairs bearing the same number.

To determine end play of differential assembly:

Press the taper roller bearings without shims onto the differential case using the tool shown in **FIG 8:8**.

Fit pressure blocks into the axle tubes on either side of the differential (see **FIG 8:9**) and fit the differential case and bearings into the axle housing.

Fit the bearing caps and tighten the screws. Slacken off the screws and then retighten them finger tight.

Tighten a pressure spindle as shown in **FIG 8:10** in either tube to a torque of 43 lb inch, rotate the differential several times and re-check the torque at the pressure spindle.

Mount a dial indicator on the axle housing so that the stylus contacts the inner side of the crown wheel flange and the pointer is at zero.

Place the pressure spindle into the other housing tube and tighten to 43 lb inch. Read the dial gauge for the total sideways deflection of the differential assembly. Keep a record of this figure. Say, for example, that it is .053 inch (1.35 mm).

To determine thickness of pinion bearing spacer:

Slide the master spacer service tool on to the pinion shaft. Form a ring with soft solder wire of approximately

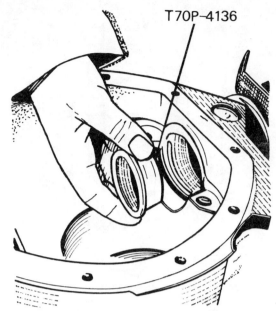

FIG 8:9 Fitting pressure blocks

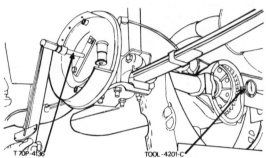

FIG 8:10 Differential set-up spindle and blocks installation

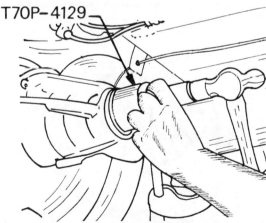

FIG 8:11 Fitting the drive pinion oil seal

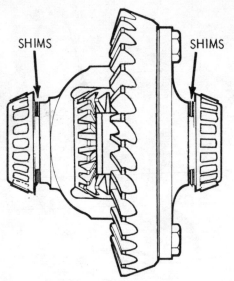

FIG 8:12 Showing location of differential side shims

.08 inch (2 mm) diameter to fit closely round the drive pinion shaft and slide it into place on the gauging tool.

Fit the pinion into the axle casing and slide on the small taper roller bearing and the pinion flange.

Screw on the old self-locking nut which had been retained during dismantling. Hold the drive pinion flange with the special wrench and slowly tighten the nut until the same torque is obtained as that recorded earlier when adjusting the master pinion. If this torque is exceeded the procedure must be repeated with a new piece of solder wire.

Remove the compressed solder ring and measure its thickness at two opposite points and take the mean reading.

Add this value, for example .05 inch (1.21 mm), to the gauge spacer ring, which is .374 inch (9.50 mm), giving the spacer thickness required, i.e. .05 + .374 = .424 inch (1.21 + 9.50 = 10.71 mm). Select a spacer of this thickness from the range of 60 available.

Fit the pinion with the selected spacer, small taper roller bearing, drive pinion flange and the old self-locking nut. Tighten the nut to 72-87 lb ft. Rotate the pinion

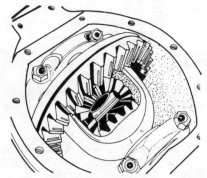

FIG 8:13 Correct gear tooth contact pattern

several times and then carefully check the torque in lbs inch. This must be the same as that recorded on initial assembly with the dummy pinion. Fit a thicker spacer if the torque is exceeded or a thinner one if the specified torque is not reached. Remove the old nut.

Apply some grease between the two sealing lips of a new seal and some sealing compound on the other side and fit the seal as in FIG 8:11. Fit a **new** self locking nut and tighten to 72 to 87 lb ft.

To determine shim thickness for differential bearings:

Replace the pressure blocks back into the axle tubes and place the differential case with the bearing races into the axle casing. Fit the bearing caps and tighten the screws. Loosen the screws and then do them up again finger tight. Using the pressure spindle press the differential case **away** from the drive pinion with a torque of 43 lb inch. Rotate the drive pinion several times.

Set up a dial gauge with the stylus at right angles to a tooth on the crown wheel and measure the backlash. Measure the tooth backlash at three more points at 90 deg. intervals. Deviations of backlash must not exceed .002 inch (.05 mm). Insert the pressure spindle into the other axle tube and screw in slowly until the backlash is .0004 inch (.01 mm).

Set up the dial gauge with the stylus on the flange of the crownwheel. Zero the gauge, insert the spindle into the other axle tube and torque to 43 lb inch. Make a record of the dial reading. For this example let us say .025 inch (.64 mm).

Remove the pressure spindle, differential case and pressure blocks from the axle case.

As an example. If total play is .053 inch (1.35 mm) and .002 inch (.05 mm) is added for pre-load the result would be .055 inch (1.40 mm). The correct pre-load is between .0012 and .0031 inch and a value between these two must be added to the play to give an even figure for the total.

If the shim thickness as measured in the example is .025 inch (.64 mm) subtract from this the desired tooth backlash of .005 inch (.12 mm) and the result is .020 inch (.52 mm). (Note that the backlash value of .005 inch is a constant established as a result of many tests.) This is the thickness of shim required behind the crownwheel.

The remaining shims must be placed on the tooth side of the crownwheel. With total play of .055 inch (1.40 mm), subtract the backside shim thickness of .020 inch (.52 mm) and this thickness is .035 inch (.88 mm).

Remove the differential case bearings as shown in FIG 8:5 and then position the correct shims on the the differential case as shown in FIG 8:12.

Check the contact surfaces and press the taper roller bearings on to the differential case. Insert the case into the axle housing and position the bearing caps as previously marked. Insert the screws with sealing compound and tighten to 43-39 lb ft.

Check the backlash with a dial gauge on one of the crownwheel teeth as before and if it is outside the limits of .005 to .009 inch (.12 to .22 mm) the setting operation must be repeated. If the backlash is too great, remove shims from the crownwheel face (tooth) side and transfer to the rearside. If backlash is too small reverse the procedure. Do not increase or decrease the number of shims, but simply transfer between one side and the other.

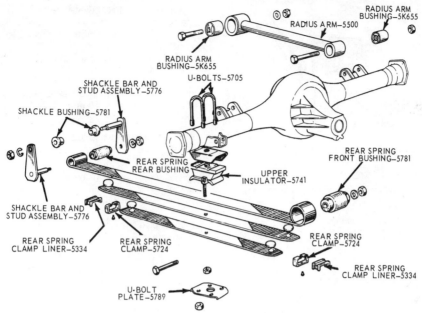

FIG 8:14 Components of the rear suspension

Checking tooth contact pattern:

New crownwheels will show the desired contact pattern from the test run at the factory and should appear as in **FIG 8:13**. If new components have been fitted it will be necessary to check the tooth contact pattern after setting the gears as instructed in the proceding operations.

Coat the teeth of the crownwheel with a marking compound, then, using a wooden wedge as a brake on the crownwheel, turn the drive pinion by a number of turns in both directions corresponding with the number of teeth on the crownwheel.

Backlash has a great effect on the contact pattern, so try altering the backlash between the prescribed limits if the pattern is not satisfactory. The number of shims may not be changed, only moved from one side to another.

When satisfactory, fit a new gasket and the cover and tighten the bolts to 22-29 lb ft.

Fit the parking brake operating lever to the axle casing and connect the return spring to its bracket. Fit the rear brake assemblies on the axle ends.

Connect the parking brake cable to the operating levers on both backplates.

8:6 Servicing the rear springs

The components of the early type rear suspension are shown in **FIG 8:14**. The later system is similar in most respects, but uses an anti-roll, or stabiliser, bar in place of the radius arms. A rear spring assembly is removed from the car as follows:

Chock up the front wheels, jack up the rear end of the car and fit stands under the body jacking points. Take the weight of the rear axle on a trolley jack.

Remove the nuts and washers and detach the combined plate and bolt assemblies. Remove the two rubber bushes.

Unscrew the nut from the front mounting bracket and withdraw the bolt. Remove the U bolt nuts and the attachment plates and lower the spring assembly.

Remove the insulator and retaining plate from the spring.

Using the service tool as shown in **FIG 8:15**, pull the bushes out of the front eye of the springs. The same tool is used for removing the bushes from the spring rear eyes.

Clean all the parts and check for wear or damage, particularly on the rubber bushes and insulators.

Dismantling:

Remove the spring centre bolt and nut. Drill out the rivets securing the spring clips and slide the clips along to the end of the springs thus freeing the two shorter leaves.

Check the condition of the leaves and renew the pads if necessary.

Make sure that the rubber pads are correctly located between the end of the leaves, then assemble and fit the centre bolt and nut. It will be noted that this bolt has a special head.

Replace the clips and rubbers and rivet the clips to the spring.

Installation:

Press new bushes into the spring eyes, being careful to see that they are fitted squarely in the apertures. Assemble the front eye to the mounting bracket, insert the bolt but do not yet tighten up the nut.

Fit the rubber insulating sleeve round the spring and position its retainer plate. Lift the spring up into position and refit the U bolts and retainer plate. Tighten these nuts initially to a torque of 5 lb ft.

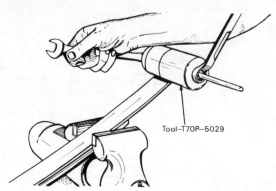

FIG 8:15   Removing the spring bushes

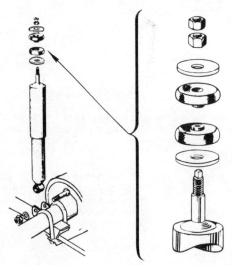

FIG 8:16   Rear shock absorber mounting

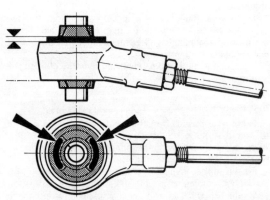

FIG 8:17   Fitting a rubber bush in the end piece

Fit new rubber bushes in the body holes for the rear shackle, hold the spring in place, assemble the bolt and plate assemblies, fit the nuts and washers but do not tighten.

Remove the jack under the axle and lower the car to the ground.

With the weight of the car on its wheels tighten the front and rear attachment bolts and the U bolt nuts to torques of 27-32, 8-10 and 18-26 lb ft respectively.

8:7 The shock absorbers

These are hydraulic, double-acting, telescopic units and are fitted between the rear axle casing and a reinforced mounting point on the floor pan. They are sealed and no periodic attention is required and none is possible. In the event of failure a new unit must be fitted. It is in fact desirable when replacing one shock absorber to replace also the other so as to maintain symmetry in the suspension.

The method of mounting is shown in **FIG 8:16** and removal is as follows:

Chock up the front wheels, jack up the rear of the car and support it on stands under the body jacking points.

From inside the luggage compartment remove the two nuts from the top of the shock absorber, using a second wrench on the flats of the piston rod to prevent it turning. Lift off the top metal washer and the rubber bush.

Remove the nut and bolt from the lower end of the shock absorber and detach it from the bracket on the axle casing. Pull the damper downwards and clear of the body.

Refitting:

Fit the large steel washer and the rubber bush on the top of the unit insert through the hole in the body and then fit the upper bush with the spigot, the washer and the nut, which is not tightened at this stage.

Fit the lower end of the shock absorber into the axle bracket and then insert the bolt. Tighten the nut to a torque of 40-45 lb ft.

Lower the car to the ground and tighten the top mounting nut to 15-20 lb ft. Replace the locknut.

8:8 Anti-roll bar

Removing:

1 Disconnect the handbrake primary cable from the transfer lever at the rear of the axle.
2 Unscrew and remove the securing bolts securing the anti-roll bar to the axle. Use a clamp to secure the anti-roll bar to its lower bracket to eliminate the pre-load on the securing bolts.
3 Disconnect the anti-roll bar from the floor assembly. Withdraw the bar.

Refitting:

4 Locate the anti-roll bar ends into the floor brackets and secure them with the eyebolts. The bolt heads should be on the inside position. Fit the washers and nuts but do not tighten at this stage.
5 Using a suitable clamp, force the anti-roll bar on to the rear axle lower brackets. Fit the saddle and the bolts and tighten fully.
6 Tighten the floor bracket bolts fully.

Renewing bushes:

1 Remove the anti-roll bar, slacken the locking nuts and unscrew the end pieces. Pull off the rubber trunnion bushes.

2 Lubricate the new trunnion bushes with glycerine and slide them on to the bar.

3 To remove the rubber bushes from the eye-pieces, mount the eye-piece on a piece of tube, with sufficient length and ID to accept the old bush. Place them on a press bed. Obtain a piece of tube with a slightly less OD than the bush, place it squarely on the top of the bush and operate the press to force the old bush out of the eye-piece.

4 Refer to **FIG 8:17** and press in the new bush, chamfered side first, noting the final position of the bush recesses.

Adjusting end pieces:

1 Refer to **FIG 8:18** and screw the end pieces on to the bar to obtain dimension 'A' 10.24 inch $\pm$ .10 inch, (262 mm $\pm$ 2.5 mm). B = .39 inch (10 mm). Tighten the locknuts.

2 Refit the anti-roll bar to the car.

8:9 Fault diagnosis

(a) Noisy axle gears

1 Insufficient or incorrect lubricant
2 Worn bearings or gears
3 Incorrect backlash
4 Incorrect meshing of gears
5 Insufficient preload on bearings

(b) Excessive backlash

1 Worn gears, bearings or housings
2 Worn axle shaft splines or side gears
3 Worn universal joints or gearbox splines
4 Loose or broken wheel studs

(c) Oil leakage

1 Defective pinion shaft or axle shaft seals
2 Defective seals on universal joint spiders
3 Faulty gasket or damaged faces of rear cover

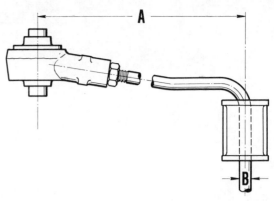

FIG 8:18   Showing correct position of anti-roll bar end pieces

Key to Fig 8:18   A = 10.24 $\pm$ .1 inch (262 $\pm$ 2.5 mm)
B = .39 inch (10 mm)

(d) Vibration

1 Drive shafts out of balance
2 Worn universal joints
3 Rear universal joint flange not mated correctly
4 Yokes on universal joints 90° out of phase
5 Centre bearing carrier defective

(e) Rattles

1 Worn damper mountings
2 Worn radius arm bushes
3 U-bolts or spring clips loose
4 Faulty rubber bushes
5 Broken spring leaf

(f) 'Settling' of suspension

1 Weak or broken spring leaf
2 Badly worn spring eye bush or shackle pin

NOTES

CHAPTER 9

FRONT SUSPENSION AND HUBS

9:1 General description

The arrangement of the front suspension can be seen in **FIG 9:1**. The vertical damper (shock absorber) and spring unit 1 is attached to the body at the top end. The bottom end of the unit is controlled by a track control arm 2 and a stabilizer or anti-roll bar 3. The spring unit carries the front wheel and brake assembly and incorporates a steering arm 5 which is connected to the rack and pinion steering mechanism by track rods 6.

To allow the spring unit to turn for steering purposes, it is connected to the outer end of the track control arm by a ball joint 4. This joint also accommodates the up and down movements due to road shocks and suspension loading. The arrangement is clearly shown in inset 'Y'.

Inset 'X' is a view of the rubber bush 7 which forms the inner pivot of the track control arm.

9:2 Routine maintenance

The suspension and damper units are sealed and do not require topping up. After the first 600 miles (1000 km), at 3000 miles (5000 km) or three months and then at subsequent 6000 mile (10,000 km) or six monthly intervals, do the following:

1 Check the torque of the front suspension crossmember retaining bolts. Correct torque is 25 to 30 lb ft.

2 Check boots or gaiters on steering and suspension joints. Renew if deteriorated or faulty.

At 6000 miles (10,000 km), check and adjust front wheel bearings. Check tracking. At 27,000 and 51,000 miles (45,000 and 85,000 km), repack front wheel bearings with grease and adjust (see **Section 9:8**). Repeat at 24,000 mile (40,000 km) intervals.

9:3 Servicing the track control arm

The bush at the inner end of the arm can be renewed as follows:

1 Jack up the front of the car and fit stands. Refer to **FIG 9:1**.
2 Remove pivot bolt 8 at the inner end. Pull arm 2 downwards and remove bush using a $\frac{3}{4}$ inch bolt.
3 Fit a new bush, using the same tool. Position the arm and fit the pivot bolt, head to the front, flat washer and self-locking nut to the rear. Do not fully tighten nut.
4 Lower the car and tighten nut to a torque of 22 to 27 lb ft.

Removing arm:

With front of car lifted and stands fitted, release stabilizer bar 3 from arm (see inset 'Y'). Remove pivot

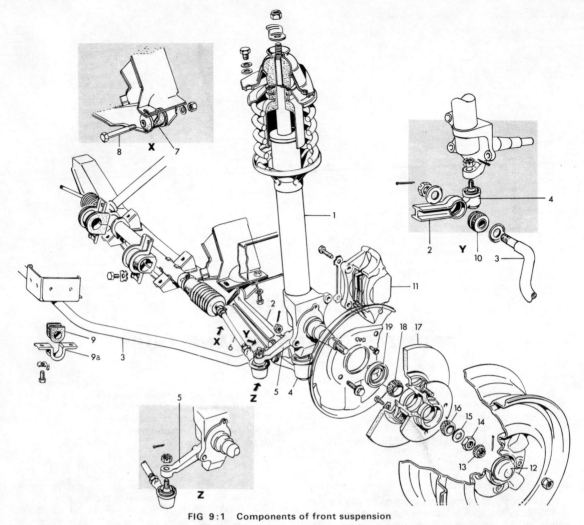

FIG 9:1 Components of front suspension

Key to Fig 9:1   1 Suspension unit   2 Track control arm   3 Stabilizer bar   4 Ball joint   5 Steering arm   6 Steering track rod
7 Pivot bush   8 Pivot bolt   9 Mounting bush   9a Clamp   10 Bush   11 Caliper unit   12 Dust cap   13 Retainer
14 Adjusting nut   15 Thrust washer   16 Outer bearing cone   17 Hub and disc assembly   18 Inner bearing cone   19 Seal

bolt 8. Release ball joint 4 from suspension unit (see inset 'Y').

If track control arm has been damaged in a crash, scrap it. Make no attempt to straighten it. Check condition of ball joint and seal 4 and renew assembly if defective.

Installing arm:

Refit the ball joint stud to the suspension unit, tightening the castellated nut to a torque of 30 to 35 lb ft. Fit a new splitpin. Refit stabilizer bar end to arm and tighten castellated nut to a torque of 15 to 45 lb ft when car is on the ground. Fit the pivot bolt (preceding operations 3 and 4).

9:4 Servicing stabilizer bar

Renewing the bushes (car lifted at front, stands fitted, handbrake applied):

Mounting bushes 9 and control arm bush 10 can be renewed by releasing the stabilizer bar 3 from the arm (see inset 'Y'), after removing clamps 9a (2 bolts each, with locking tabs). Pull stabilizer bar forward and out of arm, removing sleeve and large washer.

Slide mounting bushes off the ends of the bar. Fit the new bushes.

Reassemble bar in reverse order, tightening stabilizer bar clamp bolts to a torque of 15 to 18 lb ft when the car is on the ground. Turn up the lock tabs. Also when the car is on the ground, tighten the bar-to-control-arm nut to a torque of 15 to 45 lb ft then fit a new splitpin.

The bar itself can be renewed while the bushes receive attention. Check for wear due to faulty bushes and look for cracks and bends due to accident damage. Lying the bar on a flat surface will quickly show whether the ends are out of alignment. Do not try to straighten a bent bar.

9:5 Removing and installing suspension unit

Removing:

1 Jack up front of car and fit stands. Remove road wheel(s).

2 Release flexible brake pipe from bracket on unit. Fit plugs to open ends of both unions. Put a jack under the track control arm (2 in **FIG 9:1**) and jack up the suspension unit.

3 Detach track rod end from steering arm 5 (see inset 'Z'). Use tool 3290-C to release the taper pin. Remove the jack. Release ball joint 4 from the bottom end of the unit (see inset 'Y').

4 Release the top end of the unit from the side apron panel (3 bolts) and lift unit away, complete with brake assembly.

Installing:

Fit top end of unit to side apron panel (3 bolts to a torque of 15 to 18 lb ft. At bottom end, fit ball joint stud (castellated nut to a torque of 30 to 35 lb ft). Fit new splitpin.

Fit track rod end to steering arm (castellated nut to a torque of 18 to 22 lb ft). Fit new splitpin.

Remove brake line plugs and connect flexible pipe to bracket on unit. Bleed the brakes (see **Chapter 11**). Fit wheel(s) and lower car to ground.

9:6 Servicing a suspension unit

Removing:

With the unit removed from the car, fit the adjustable spring restrainers, tool P-5045 (see **FIG 9:2**). Refer to **FIG 9:3** and remove top nut and cranked retainer 1. Lift off top mount 6, the dished washer 6a, upper spring seat 10, spring 11 and the bump rubber 3 or 3a.

Remove the brake pads (see **Chapter 11**). Detach the caliper (2 bolts and lockplate). Remove the hub and disc assembly (see **Section 9:7**). Remove the disc shield. Detach the steering arm.

The suspension unit can now be renewed, or overhauled as instructed later.

Refitting:

Refit the steering arm, tightening the nuts to a torque of 30 to 24 lb ft. Fit shield, followed by hub and disc assembly. Adjust hub bearings as instructed in **Section 9:8**. Fit caliper, using new lockplate (bolt torque 45 to 50 lb ft) turn up lock tabs. Refit brake pads (see **Chapter 11**).

Reassemble the spring and other parts in the reverse order to dismantling. The dished washer 6a on top of spring seat 10 has its convex side upwards. The piston rod nut is initially tightened to 5 to 10 lb ft after applying Loctite to threads. Remove spring restrainers. Assemble unit to car and lower to ground.

Now slacken the piston rod nut. Turn the front wheels to the straight-ahead position and set cranked retainer 1 so that it points inwards towards the engine. Retighten the nut to 28 to 32 lb ft.

Overhauling:

Fit restrainers to spring (tool P-5045). Remove top nut, cranked retainer (1 in **FIG 9:3**), top mount 6, dished washer 6a, seat 10, spring 11 and bump rubber 3 or 3a. Check spring.

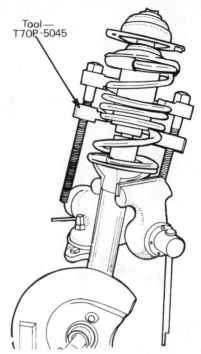

FIG 9:2 Compressing a spring

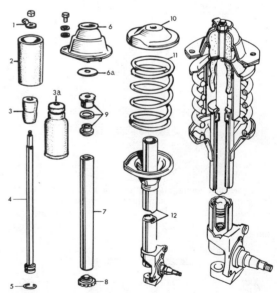

FIG 9:3 Components of front suspension unit

Key to Fig 9:3 1 Cranked retainer   2 Gaiter   3 Bump rubber (early 2000 GT)   3a Later bump rubber   4 Piston rod   5 Piston ring   6 Top mount   6a Dished washer   7 Cylinder   8 Compression valve   9 Bump stop platform   10 Upper spring seat   11 Spring   12 Outer casing

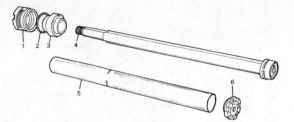

FIG 9:4 Internal parts of suspension unit

Key to Fig 9:4   1 Bump stop platform   2 'O' ring
3 Upper guide bush and gland assembly   4 Piston rod
5 Cylinder   6 Compression valve

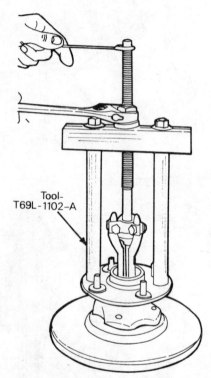

Tool-
T69L-1102-A

FIG 9:5 Removing front wheel bearing cups

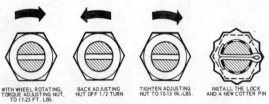

WITH WHEEL ROTATING,   BACK ADJUSTING   TIGHTEN ADJUSTING   INSTALL THE LOCK
TORQUE ADJUSTING NUT,   NUT OFF 1/2 TURN   NUT TO 10-15 IN.-LBS.   AND A NEW COTTER PIN
TO 17-25 FT. LBS.

FIG 9:6 Adjusting front wheel bearing

Refer to **FIG 9:4** and unscrew the bump stop platform 1, using a suitable wrench. Lift platform off unit. Remove O-ring 2. Do not remove the guide bush and gland assembly 3 until the top machined edge of the piston rod 4 has been examined for burrs. Stone off any which may be present. Pull the rod upwards until the bush and gland assembly is clear of the casing and lift off the assembly. Empty the fluid from the casing.

Pull out the piston rod complete with cylinder 5 and compression valve 6. Press on the rod to push out the valve, then withdraw the rod. If necessary, remove the piston ring from the piston.

Clean all the parts and examine for wear or damage. The piston and piston rod are serviced as an assembly. Do not try to dismantle them.

Reassembling:

If the ring was removed, fit a new one to the piston. Insert piston rod into cylinder and fit compression valve into base of cylinder. Carefully fit the assembly into the outer casing. Fill the unit with 326 cc of the correct fluid.

Fit the service tool guide on the end of the piston rod. Slide the gland and bush assembly over the guide and push it down until it enters the cylinder and the complete internal assembly is below the top of the outer casing. Fit the O-ring and locate it correctly round the bore of the outer casing. Screw the bump stop platform into the outer casing using a suitable wrench tightening securely to a torque of 55 to 60 lb ft.

Reassemble the remaining parts and refit according to the instructions in 'Refitting'.

Renew top mount, bump rubber and piston rod gaiter.

These will be readily accessible by following the first paragraphs of instructions in this Section. Renew all rubber parts which show signs of deterioration, softening, or break-up. Reassemble and refit according to the second part of 'Refitting' in this Section.

It is most important to verify that both springs are of the same colour. Never mix springs, as the suspension systems will then be of unequal height, which will upset the handling of the car.

Renewing springs (units out of car):

After the restrainers are fitted to the spring, the top mount is removed, followed by the dished washer and the upper spring set. The spring can then be lifted off.

To fit a new spring, hold the lower end in soft jaws in a vice and fit the spring restrainers. Reassemble in the reverse order.

9:7 Removing and installing front hub

Removing:

With car jacked up and front wheel removed, do the following:

1 Detach brake pipe from bracket on suspension unit and plug both unions.
2 Remove brake caliper 11 (see **FIG 9:1**) from suspension unit (bolts with locking tabs). Remove dust cap 12 from hub. Remove splitpin and items 13, 14, 15 and 16.
3 Pull off the hub and disc assembly 17 to 19.
4 Separate disc from hub (4 bolts with locking tabs).

A new hub will be supplied complete with bearing cups and cones. Check that the cups and cones are of the same make. The name is on the cone and the initial letter of the name is stamped on the hub. For example, T = Timken and S = Skefco.

Installing:

1 Clean mating faces of hub and disc. Align mating marks, fit bolts and new locking plates and tighten to 30 to 34 lb ft. Turn up locking tabs.
2 Pack hub with lithium base grease but do not completely fill, to allow for expansion. Leave space for the spindle. Fit inner bearing cone 18. Fit seal 19 with lip towards bearing using the Ford service tool.
3 Fit assembly to wheel spindle, followed by outer bearing 16, thrust washer 15, and adjusting nut 14. Turn hub while tightening nut to 27 lb ft. Slacken nut by 90 deg. and fit retainer 13 with slot in retainer aligned with spindle hole. Fit new splitpin but do not bend up.
4 Check disc runout with dial gauge. Measured near the periphery of the face, the total runout should not exceed .0035 inch (.089 mm). If excessive, check mating faces of hub and disc. Check bearings and cups for damage.
5 When satisfied, bend up splitpin and fit dust cap. Fit caliper, using new locktabs and tightening bolts to 45 to 50 lb ft. Remove plugs and reconnect brake pipes. Refit road wheel. Torque for wheel nuts is 50 to 55 lb ft. Bleed the brakes (see **Chapter 11**).

9:8 Overhauling front hubs
Renewing wheel stud:

With road wheel removed, drive out defective stud. Locate new stud in splined hole and draw into place using a spacer, such as a short piece of suitable tubing, and the wheel nut reversed.

Lubricating:

At 27,000 and 51,000 miles (45,000 and 85,000 km), pack the front hubs with fresh grease. Remove the hub as described in **Section 9:7** but do not part the hub and disc and do not remove the oil seal unless renewal is required.

Wash the parts free from old grease with a solvent and allow to dry. Pack the hub with fresh lithium base grease but do not fill completely. This will allow for expansion. Leave enough space for the spindle.

Refit the hub and adjust the bearings as instructed in 'Installing' in the same Section. At all times keep grease off the brake discs.

Renewing bearings:

Remove the hub as described in **Section 9:7**. Remove the inner and outer bearing cups, using the Ford service tool as shown in **FIG 9:5**. The same tool is used to fit new cups.

When renewing cones, always fit new cups as well and make sure that cups and cones are of the same make.

If required new hubs may be obtained complete with bearing cones and cups. The cups are already fitted but check that the cones and cups are of the same manufacture. When the cups are fitted the initial letter of the manufacturers name is stamped on the hub. Example T = Timken and S = Skefco.

Refit the hub, after fitting a new seal and packing with grease, as described in the same Section. Adjust the bearings and bleed the brakes.

Front wheel bearing adjustment:

This operation will be necessary if the wheel is loose on the spindle or does not rotate freely.

Raise the car until the appropriate wheel is clear of the ground then lever off the wheel cover and remove the grease cap from the hub.

Wipe any excess grease away and remove the adjusting nut, cotter pin and nut lock.

Loosen the bearing adjusting nut three turns, then rock wheel, hub and brake disc assembly in and out several times to push the brake pads away from the disc (rotor).

Refer to **FIG 9:6**, rotate the wheel and at the same time torque the adjusting nut to 17-25 lb ft to seat the bearings.

Back off the adjusting nut one half turn and then retighten it to 10-15 lb inch or finger tight.

Locate the locknut on the adjusting nut so that the slots in the locknut are in line with the cotter pin hole in the spindle. Fit a new cotter pin and bend over as shown.

Check the front wheel rotation. If it is in order, refit the grease cap and hub cap. If movement is still rough, clean or renew the bearings as necessary.

Before driving the car, pump the brake pedal several times to restore normal brake operation.

9:9 Suspension geometry

The camber, castor, and kingpin angles are given in Technical Data at the end of this manual. All these angles are set during manufacture and they are not adjustable.

Defects in the suspension and steering which affect the handling of the car, particularly if they seem to follow accident damage, may be due to incorrect angles. These must be checked on an alignment gauge. Faults and possible checks are as follows:

Incorrect castor angle:

Check that stabilizer bar is not bent, and that its attachment bolts are tight.

Incorrect camber or kingpin inclination:

If kingpin inclination is correct but camber angle is wrong, check the wheel spindle for distortion. If both angles are wrong, check track control arm for distortion and control arm ball joint for slackness and excessive wear. Also check the inner mounting of the track control arm for wear and distortion.

9:10 Fault diagnosis

(a) Wheel wobble

1 Worn or slack hub bearings
2 Broken or weak front springs
3 Uneven tyre wear
4 Bent stabilizer bar or track control arm
5 Loose suspension mountings, worn bushes
6 Loose wheel nuts

(b) 'Bottoming' of suspension

1 Check 2 in (a)
2 Rebound rubbers defective
3 Dampers not working
4 Broken stabilizer bar

(c) Heavy steering

1 Front tyres under-inflated
2 Wrong suspension geometry

(d) Excessive tyre wear

1 Check 4 and 5 in (a); 3 in (b) and 2 in (c)

(e) Rattles

1 Check 2 and 5 in (a) and 4 in (b)
2 Stabilizer bar clamps loose

(f) Excessive rolling

1 Check 2 in (a); 3 and 4 in (b) and 1 in (c)

CHAPTER 10

THE STEERING SYSTEM

10:1 Description

The layout of the steering system is shown in **FIG 10:1**, from which it will be seen that it is of the rack and pinion type with the steering gear mounted in rubber insulators on brackets attached to the front crossmember.

The components of the steering column and the steering gear assemblies are shown in **FIGS 10:2** and **10:3**. The steering wheel has a bellows type hub which will collapse on impact with the drivers body in the event of a severe frontal impact and so minimize possible injury.

Steering wheel movements are transmitted to the pinion shaft through the steering gear shaft and the flexible coupling and universal joint assembly. At the lower end of the pinion shaft is a helical pinion which meshes with the rack and rotation of the pinion in either direction results in a transverse movement of the rack inside its housing.

The outer ends of the rack carry ball jointed track rods which in turn, are ball jointed to the steering arms on the suspension units. Adjusting the length of the tie rods enables the tracking of the front wheels to be set to the specified values.

Shims are used to set the preload on the pinion bearings. Shims also adjust the degree of damping on the rack exercised by the rack adjusting bearing or slipper. Preload on the track rod inner ball joint is regulated by movement of the ball housing screwed on the end of the rack.

A system of power assistance for the steering is available on later cars, operated by hydraulic pressure from a pump driven by a belt from the crankshaft pulley.

10:2 Routine maintenance

When working on the car with the front wheels clear of the ground, do not move the wheels quickly from lock to lock. Such movement builds up hydraulic pressure that may burst or blow off the bellows, and possibly also damage the gear tooth.

1 At the first 600 miles (1000 km) check the front wheel toe-in.

2 At every 6000 miles (10,000 km) or six-monthly intervals, examine the rack bellows for leaks or damage, and check the gaiters on the track rod outer ball joints for splits or deterioration. Also check the condition of the steering shaft universal joint and the flexible coupling.

Section 10:4 gives details of the method of introducing oil into the rack housing after renewing a bellows in situ. Note the warning which is given to ensure that the housing is not overfilled, otherwise the bellows may be split or blown off due to a build-up in hydraulic pressure.

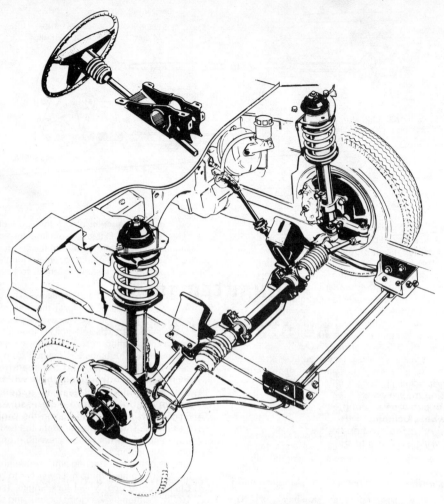

FIG 10:1 Layout of the steering system

10:3 Toe-in and steering angles

The correct figures for toe-in, and wheel lock angles are given in Technical Data. **If either the wheel lock angles or toe-in is adjusted, then both must be re-checked after the adjustment.** As the amateur owner is not equipped to check the wheel lock angles, it is recommended that these, and alignment checks are made by a garage which has accurate gauges for the job.

Before making checks, the tyres must be correctly inflated, the wheels must be running true and the hub bearings correctly adjusted. The stabilizer bar clamps must be tightly secured and there must be no excessive play in the ball joints. Check springs for correct seating. The toe-in can be roughly checked as follows:

1 Bring the car to rest after running forward. Set the front wheels straight-ahead.
2 Measure the distance between the rims at wheel centre height at the front. Mark the points with chalk and roll the car forward for half a turn of the wheels. With the marks now at the rear, measure the distance between them. This dimension should exceed that at the front by .06 to .25 inch (1.5 to 6.4 mm) or by the nominal fraction of $\frac{5}{32}$ inch. The wheels will then toe-in.
3 If adjustment is needed, slacken the locknuts securing the ball joints at the outer ends of the track rods (see **FIG 10:4**). Slacken the small clips at the outer ends of bellows.
4 Turn the track rods until the toe-in is correct, making sure that the rods are approximately equal in length (within $\frac{1}{4}$ inch or 6.35 mm). The number of threads exposed will be a good guide. If necessary, screw one rod into its outer ball joint and unscrew the other rod by an equal amount, remembering that one is a right-hand thread and the other a lefthand. This will rectify any inequality without affecting the toe-in. Screwing both rods into (or out of) the ball joints by equal amounts will then adjust the toe-in correctly.

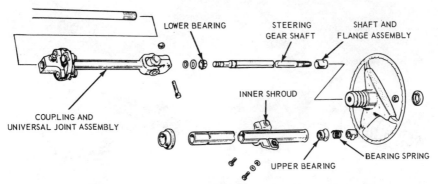

FIG 10:2 Components of steering column assembly

Wheel lock angles:

These must be checked on suitable equipment. When a lock angle of 35 deg. is set on one wheel, the front lock angle of the other must be 32 deg. 15 min. to 33 deg. 45 min. If the steering is turned onto left lock, the back lock angle is taken on the left wheel and the front lock angle on the right, and conversely for a turn on right lock.

Repeat on the other lock. If readings are incorrect or unequal, alter the track rod lengths. To keep toe-in correct, turn the rods equal amounts. If one rod is screwed into its outer ball joint and the other unscrewed by the same amount (or vice versa), the toe-in will not be affected.

Recheck the wheel lock angles and then recheck the toe-in. When satisfied, tighten the outer ball joint locknuts and the clips on the bellows.

Incorrect wheel lock angles:

If the angles are incorrect, comparing one lock with the other, first check the toe-in. If this is correct, check that the track rods are approximately equal in length. Minor differences in length up to a maximum of $\frac{1}{4}$ inch (6.35 mm) are acceptable, to compensate for manufacturing tolerances.

If both toe-in and track rod lengths are satisfactory, examine the steering arms and track rods for distortion. Also check the steering linkage ball joints for wear or slackness.

Checking steering angles:

These must be checked on a suitable wheel alignment gauge. Before starting operations, refer to the figures given in Technical Data for castor angle, camber angle, and kingpin inclination.

Refer to **Section 9:9** of the preceding Chapter for possible faults which may lead to incorrect angles, remembering that there are no adjustments.

10:4 Renewing bellows in situ

These are shown in **FIG 10:3** and they must always be renewed as soon as they are seen to have split or deteriorated. **The entry of road grit and the loss of lubricant will otherwise have a disastrous effect on the rack mechanism.** Renewal is possible without removing the rack from the car, as follows:

1 Apply the handbrake, jack up the front of the car and support it on stands. Remove the splitpin and nut from the ball joint pin on the connecting rod end (see **FIG 10:4**). Extract the pin from the end of the rod.

2 Remove the ball joint end from the connecting (track) rod. Count turns required to remove joint so that it can be replaced in the same location, to keep the toe-in correct.

3 Slacken clips at each end of bellows. There may be soft iron wire instead of a clip at the inner end. Cut this away and use a screw clip as a replacement. Set a container to catch draining oil and pull off the bellows. Move the steering from lock to lock several times to ensure that all lubricant is drained from the steering gear. **If any remains, and the specified quantity of fresh oil is introduced, there will be a chance that overfilling will lead to a bellows being blown off due to hydraulic pressure.**

4 Fit the new bellows and tighten the large inner clip, leaving the small one loose. Refit the ball joint to the outer end of the track rod, screwing it on as far as its original position.

5 Fit ball joint pin to steering arm, tighten nut to 18 to 22 lb ft and fit a new splitpin. Lower car to ground.

6 Check toe-in and wheel lock angles (see **Section 10:3**). Tighten the ball joint locknut and the small clip on the bellows.

7 Refer to **FIG 10:3** and remove housing end coverplate. Withdraw the spring and slipper, taking great care of the joint and shims. Pour in .25 pint (.3 US pint or .15 litre) of SAE.90.EP oil through the damper hole.

8 Refit the slipper, spring, shim pack, joints and coverplate, tightening the bolts to 6 to 8 lb ft.

If both bellows need renewal, the operations remain the same, but make sure the clips on both sides are tightened before introducing the oil.

10:5 Renewing track rod ends

Track rod ball joints at the outer ends are sealed and are not adjustable. Damaged or deteriorated rubber boots will permit the entry of road grit and loss of lubricant. If this has happened, the joint assembly must be renewed. Do this by following the instructions for removal in operations 1 and 2 in the preceding Section. Fit wheel stands (not chassis stands) or raise car on hoist so that wheels are loaded. Fit the new parts according to operations 4, 5 and 6. If adjustment to toe-in is necessary, refer to **Section 10:3**.

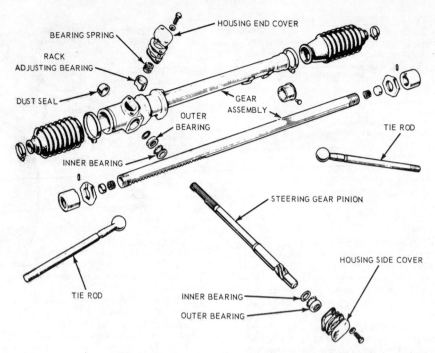

FIG 10:3 Components of the steering gear

10:6 Renewing steering arms

A steering arm can be seen in **FIG 9:1** in the preceding Chapter. If it has been bent in an accident, or if this is suspected because alignment checks prove that something is wrong, the arm must be renewed. **No attempt should be made to straighten it.** Remove as follows:

1 Jack up front of car, fit stands and remove wheel. Detach brake supply pipe from bracket on suspension unit and plug both open pipe ends.
2 Unlock and remove bolts securing brake caliper and lift caliper away.
3 Remove hub and disc assembly (see **Section 9:7** in preceding Chapter).
4 Remove track rod end from steering arm (see operation 1 in **Section 10:4**).
5 Remove splitpins and nuts to detach steering arm from suspension unit.

Installing:

1 Secure the arm to the suspension unit, using a torque of 30 to 34 lb ft on the nuts. Fit new splitpins.
2 Refit track rod end to arm, tightening nut to 18 to 22 lb ft. Fit new splitpin.
3 Refit hub assembly (see **Section 9:7** in preceding Chapter), adjusting the bearings as instructed.
4 Fit the brake caliper. Use new locktabs and tighten bolts to 45 to 50 lb ft. Reconnect brake pipes and tighten securely. Fit road wheel.
5 Bleed the brakes as instructed in **Chapter 11**. Lower car to ground.

10:7 Overhauling steering gear

Removing:

In this operation the wheels must remain loaded, so that it is not practicable to fit chassis stands. Either raise the car on a hoist, fit wheel stands, or block up the wheels when the car is jacked up, lowering the car onto the blocks after making sure the rear wheels are chocked and the handbrake applied. The steering wheel must be straight-ahead. Then proceed as follows:

1 Referring to **FIG 10:2**, look under the bonnet and identify the flexible coupling. Remove the nut and bolt clamping the coupling to pinion shaft.
2 Release the steering gear from the body crossmember. The clamps can be seen just below inset X in **FIG 9:1** in the preceding Chapter. The clamp bolts have lock-plates.
3 Detach the track rod outer ball joints from the steering arms as instructed in operation 1 of **Section 10:4**. Unscrew the joints as in operation 2.
4 Put one wheel on lock to remove steering gear, so that opposite end will clear stabilizer bar.

Overhauling:

Those operations which can be carried out without complete stripping of the steering gear will be covered first.

Renewing bellows:

When pulling off bellows, be ready to catch the oil which will drain out of the gear. Remove the bellows as instructed in operation 3 in **Section 10:4**. Expel all oil by holding rack vertically, then traverse from lock to lock.

To fit new bellows, mount gear vertically in soft jaws in a vice. This assumes that one bellows is already in position and is at the bottom end.

Into the space between the casing and the track rod inner ball joint, pour .25 pint (.3 US pint or .15 litre) of SAE.90.EP oil. Traverse the rack to help the flow of oil. Fit the new bellows, securing both ends with clips and not wire. Refit the outer ball joints.

Renewing track rod inner ball joint:

Each end of the steering rack (see **FIG 10:3**) carries a ball joint assembly for the tie rod and adjustment of this joint is possible by screwing the ball housing along the rack.

To dismantle the joint, drill out the pin shown but be careful not to drill too deeply. Hold the locknut and screw the ball housing off the end of the rack shaft using a suitable wrench. Remove the spring and ball seat from the recess in the rack and discard.

Examine the bearing surfaces of the track rod ball and the ballhousing for wear and damage. Renew the parts if defective, as accurate adjustment will otherwise be impossible.

Reassemble by fitting a new spring and seat into the rack. Smear SAE.90.EP oil on the ball, seat and housing. Fit the parts to the rack and tighten the housing until articulation of the track rod shows signs of stiffness. Effort to articulate joint is measured as in **FIG 10:6**. Before doing this, turn the track rod through at least seven revolutions, so that the reading will be true. A spring pull scale reading up to 10 lb (5.6 kg) will be suitable.

Fit a piece of wire to the scale and hook it round the rod about $\frac{1}{4}$ inch (6.3 mm) from the end. With the rod parallel to the rack as shown, screw the ballhousing either in or out as required until the scale records a pull of 5 lb before the rod begins to move. Tighten the locknut on the housing and check that the effort required to articulate the rod is still 5 lb.

Do not fit a locking pin in the existing hole if it happens to line up. Always drill a fresh hole, half in the locknut and half in the housing. Use a $\frac{1}{8}$ inch (3.18 mm) drill to a depth of $\frac{3}{8}$ inch (9.525 mm). Tap the pin into position and secure it by peening the hole.

Dismantling gear:

Refer to **FIG 10:3** for details of the internal parts. The steering pinion shaft runs in ball bearings in which the balls are fitted loose. There are fourteen balls in each bearing and great care must be taken to see that none fall into the rack during these operations. Dismantle as follows:

1 Remove the pinion dust seal, remove the housing side cover and the bearings and then pull out the pinion shaft.
2 Pull out the rack from the pinion end of the casing in order to avoid damage to the support bush on the rack teeth. Remove the outer and inner bearings.

Clean the parts and inspect for wear or damage. If the teeth of rack or pinion are damaged a complete new gear assembly must be fitted. Renew the rack support bush if worn, as slackness here may lead to rattles. Renew the ballbearings if the races are worn or pitted.

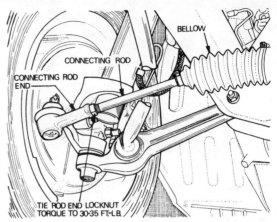

FIG 10:4 Showing the steering connecting (track) rod and ball end

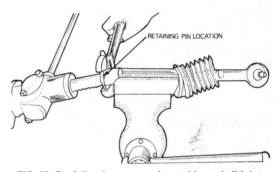

FIG 10:5 Adjusting connecting rod inner ball joint

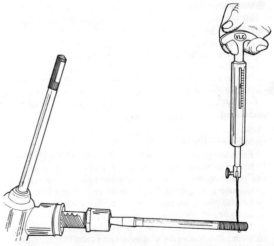

FIG 10:6 Measuring track rod articulation effort

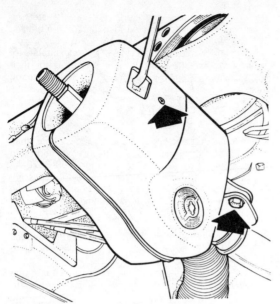

FIG 10:7 Showing location of steering column and shroud mounting screws

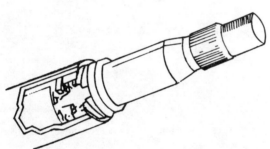

FIG 10:8 Steering column upper bearing

Reassembling:

Fit a new pinion oil seal into the casing, followed by the upper bearing. Stick the balls into place with grease. Fit the rack with its teeth correctly positioned for engagement with the pinion. Set it centrally by checking the length protruding at each end of the casing.

Fit the lower ballbearing to the pinion shaft and slide the shaft into place in the casing with the alignment mark on the pinion vertical (as if seen with the gear assembled in the car). Now do the following:

Pinion bearing preload:

Fit the coverplate without shims or gaskets and tighten the bolts evenly until the plate is just touching the pinion bearing. Use feeler gauges to check the gap between the coverplate and the casing. If the gap varies when measured adjacent to the bolts it shows that they have not been tightened evenly.

The shim pack must include two gaskets, one on each outer face. Make up this assembly so that the total thickness is .002 to .004 inch (.05 to .10 mm) less than the gap measured by the feeler gauges. Steel shims are available in thicknesses of .002, .005 and .010 inch (.051, .127 and .254 mm) and paper gaskets are .005 inch (.127 mm) thick. Fit the shims, gaskets and coverplate and tighten the bolts to 6 to 8 lb ft (.85 to 1.1 kg m). Use sealer on the bolt threads. The pinion bearings should now be correctly preloaded.

Rack damper adjustment:

Correct adjustment is essential to avoid 'knocking' from the steering gear or steering stiffness. Do the following:

Locate slipper in the rack housing so that it fits snugly on the back of the rack, pushing it right home. Place a straightedge across the face of the casing which takes the damper coverplate. Use feeler gauges to measure the distance between the top of the slipper and the underside of the straightedge. Make up a shim pack, sandwiched between paper gaskets so that the total thickness exceeds the feeler gauge dimension ·by .0005 to .0035 inch (.013 to .089 mm). The shims and gaskets are available in the same thicknesses as those for the pinion bearing preload as specified in the preceding instructions.

Fit the spring in the recess in the slipper, position the shim pack, gaskets and coverplate and tighten the bolts to 6 to 8 lb ft (.85 to 1.1 kg m). Put sealer on the bolt threads.

Next measure the torque required to turn the pinion. This should be between 10 and 18 lb inch and if it is not within these limits, the adjustment is incorrect or there is is undue friction somewhere. Check the shimming of the damper cover, and if this is not the cause, look for tight bearings, damaged gear teeth, or lack of lubricant. Continue reassembling by fitting bellows and track rods as described earlier.

Installing steering gear:

Screw the locknuts on the track rods by the number of turns required to remove them. Set the steering wheel in the straight-ahead position. With the steering gear also in the straight-ahead position (the rack should be protruding equally from each end of the rack housing), offer it up to the mounting brackets on the crossmember. Before securing it, check the condition of the mounting rubbers, and align the splines on the pinion shaft and in the flexible coupling. Press the pinion shaft into the coupling and fit the mounting clamps, tightening the bolts to 15 to 18 lb ft. Use new lockplates.

Attach the track rod ends to the steering arms, tightening the slotted nuts to a torque of 18 to 22 lb ft. Fit new splitpins. Tighten the locknuts.

Tighten the flexible coupling clamp bolt to a torque of 12 to 15 lb ft and lower the car to the ground. Check the toe-in and wheel lock angles. Check steering wheel position.

10:8 Removing and installing steering wheel

Set the front wheels straight-ahead. Refer to **FIG 10:2** and prise out the central emblem. Remove retaining nut and pull wheel off splines.

When refitting, make sure that the road wheels are still straight-ahead and then press the steering wheel into place with the spokes correctly set. Tighten the retaining nut to 20 to 25 lb ft. Press the emblem into place with the lug at the bottom.

10:9 Removing and installing column couplings

Disconnect the battery, and the choke cable from the carburetter. Refer to **FIG 10:2** and remove the clamp bolt securing flexible joint to pinion shaft. Remove the clamp bolt from universal joint.

Refer to **FIG 10:7**. Remove the shroud from the column (two cross-head screws, one each side). Remove the two bolts from the column bracket, one of which is indicated by the lower arrow. Disconnect the electrical wiring plugs from their connectors.

Pull the column to the rear enough to permit removal of the joint and coupling assembly.

When reassembling in the reverse order, first check that the steering gear and the steering wheel are both in the straight-ahead position before engaging the coupling splines. Also make sure that the rubber grommet is properly fitted, where the column passes through the floor.

Tighten the coupling clamp bolts to 12 to 15 lb ft, tightening the one for the universal joint first. Reconnect the wiring plugs.

When fitting the two screws for the column shroud, note that one is self-tapping and the other threaded. Secure the column bracket and shroud to the underside of the facia panel. Reconnect choke cable and battery.

10:10 Overhauling steering column

To remove the steering column, repeat the instructions in **Section 10:9** but do not remove the clamp bolt from the lower flexible coupling. An extra item is to lift off the indicator cancelling cam and spring and remove the two screws securing the indicator switch to the top of the column. Remove the wiring loom strap and switch assembly. Withdraw the column.

Dismantling:

Refer to **FIG 10:2**. Pull shaft out of column. Remove lower bearing assembly by prising off the circlip. The upper bearing is shown in **FIG 10:8** and it can be driven out from below with the steering shaft.

Check the shaft splines and the bearings. A new upper bearing can be tapped into place, and a new lower bearing can be fitted to the shaft, using a new washer and circlip.

Before introducing the shaft into the column from the lower end, check that the pin of the steering lock (if fitted) does not protrude into the column. Ensure this by turning the key to 'Ignition' and back to 'Off'. Do not remove the key. Reassemble in the reverse order to dismantling

Installing:

Follow the instructions in **Section 10:9** to refit the column into the car. When the direction indicator switch has been refitted to the top of the column, fit the spring and indicator cancelling cam to the shaft. With road wheels straight-ahead, the 'ear' on the cam must be midway between the cancelling levers of the indicator switch.

10:11 Power steering

A belt driven pump delivers ATF under pressure to a piston mounted on the steering rack and running in the rack tube, the degree of assistance being controlled by a spool valve mounted concentrically with the steering pinion shaft. The fluid reservoir is mounted on a bracket adjacent to the righthand front damper unit.

The components of this system are not suitable for home servicing, but directions will be given for their removal with a view to taking them to a service station for repair or replacement.

Testing:

First check the belt tension. The manufacturers recommend the use of a tension gauge rather than thumb pressure, if accuracy is to be ensured, and specify a tension of 75 to 85 lb using tool T63-8620-A.

Check the fluid level in the reservoir and if necessary top up with Power Steering Fluid D2AZ-19582-A to the maximum level mark. Warm up the engine and allow it to idle.

Increase the engine speed to 1500 rev/min and **slowly** turn the steering wheel five times from one lock to the other, holding it temporarily on lock in order to raise the temperature of the fluid to 158°F.

With the front wheels on a clean dry surface measure the torque at the centre nut of the steering wheel to initiate turning. It should be 6 lb ft.

Bleeding:

This operation should become necessary only if air has entered the system due to a component being disconnected or because the fluid level has dropped too low in the reservoir.

Fill up with the approved fluid, run the engine at 1500 rev/min and slowly turn the steering from lock to lock. At the same time observe the fluid in the reservoir and continue to add fluid until the level is constant and no more air bubbles are seen.

Take this opportunity to check for leaks at all pipe connections, bellows, pump and valve body.

Removing the pump:

Disconnect the battery and raise the front end of the car. Remove the under splash shield if fitted.

Loosen the idler pulley bolts and remove the belt. Disconnect the fluid pipe and drain out the fluid.

The steering pump and its bracket can be removed together and separated as necessary.

Refitting is carried out in the reverse order, but note the tightening torques for the fluid lines: 21 lb ft for pressure lines, 13 lb ft for return lines. Fill the reservoir with fresh fluid and bleed the system as described earlier.

Removing the steering gear assembly:

Disconnect the battery and raise the car to permit working underneath. Drain off the fluid by disconnecting the pipes from the rack.

Remove the lower clamp bolt from the steering shaft coupling. Disconnect the tie rod ends from the steering arms.

The rack assembly is secured by two bolts, remove these and withdraw the rack from the car.

When removing the tie rod ends from the rods, count and record the number of turns required to unscrew them so as to ensure correct reassembly.

Refitting is carried out in the reverse order, but there are a few points to be noted.

Make sure that the tie rod ends are screwed on to their original positions.

Fit the rack into the vehicle and engage the pinion in the steering shaft coupling, with the bolt hole in line with the flat on the shaft.

When fitting the lower clamp bolt, make sure that the coupling segments are all in the same plane. This can be achieved by sliding the coupling up or down on the pinion shaft.

Check, and if necessary, adjust the front wheel alignment as described in **Section 10:3**.

10:12 Fault diagnosis

(a) Wheel wobble

1 Unbalanced wheels and tyres
2 Worn or loose steering connections
3 Incorrect wheel alignment angles
4 Excessive play in steering gear
5 Worn or slack hub bearings
6 Rack damper ineffective, spring broken

(b) Wander

1 Check (a)
2 Uneven tyre pressures or tyre wear
3 Misalignment of suspension unit

(c) Heavy steering

1 Check 2 in (a) and 3 in (b)
2 Very low tyre pressures
3 Lack of oil in rack housing
4 Wrong wheel tracking
5 Pinion preload or rack damping excessive.
6 Steering shaft or column bent, faulty bearings
7 Defective flexible or universal couplings
8 Defective steering ball joints

(d) Lost motion

1 Slack pinion bearings
2 Rack damper not working
3 Loose steering wheel
4 Loose couplings, worn splines
5 Worn or badly adjusted ball joints
6 Rack housing loose in mountings
7 General wear in steering gear

CHAPTER 11

THE BRAKING SYSTEM

11:1 Description

Hydraulically operated brakes are used on all four wheels with disc units on the front and drums at the rear. A dual system is employed in which a tandem type master cylinder supplies pressure through one circuit to the front brakes and another, quite separate, to the rear wheels. These are operated by a pendant type pedal which is coupled directly to a power brake booster (vacuum servo) fitted to the rear bulkhead of the engine compartment. The master cylinder is bolted to the front face of the booster and these two items are replaced as a unit.

The floor mounted handbrake between the front seats operates the rear wheel brakes through a two cable linkage and at the same time causes the self-adjusting mechanism on these brakes to set itself and compensate for any wear on the friction linings.

The layout of the braking system is shown in **FIG 11 : 1**.

11:2 Maintenance and bleeding the system

Very little maintenance is required as both front and rear brakes are self-adjusting, but a regular check should be made on the level of the fluid in the master cylinder reservoir.

Clean the area around it and remove the reservoir filler cap. Fill up with the specified brake fluid, USA reference CZAZ-19542-A (ESA-M6C25-A), UK reference ME-3833-F, making sure that both halves of the container are filled.

At about 6000 mile intervals the following checks should be made:

Check the friction linings and pads for wear and renew as described later in this chapter if necessary.

Lubricate the handbrake linkage.

Check all the pipelines and fittings for possible damage or deterioration. This includes the possibility of chafing on the flexible hoses.

Bleeding the system:

This is not an item of routine maintenance and should be necessary only if air has been admitted into the system after a servicing operation or if the fluid level has been allowed to drop too low in the reservoir. The need for this operation is usually indicated by a spongy feeling or excessive travel on the brake pedal.

It is important to ensure that the piston assembly in the pressure differential valve is held in the central position. This may be done by using a screwdriver with the

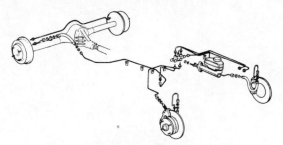

FIG 11:1 Layout of the hydraulic system

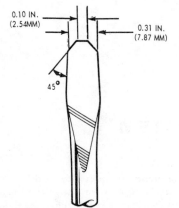

0.10 IN.
(2.54MM)

0.31 IN.
(7.87 MM)

45°

FIG 11:2 Dimensions of tool for centralising the pressure differential valve

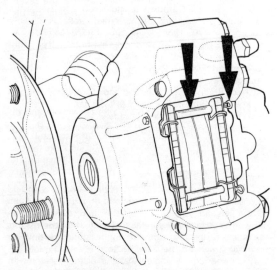

FIG 11:3 Showing the brake pad retaining pins and clips

blade modified as shown in **FIG 11:2**. It should be inserted through the aperture in the base of the assembly after the rubber has been removed.

Fill up the reservoir and be prepared to top up as the operation proceeds in order to replace the fluid as it is used. Do not re-use the fluid expelled in the course of the bleeding.

Remove the dust cap from the righthand front bleed nipple and fit a length of suitable tubing with the free end immersed in a quantity of brake fluid in a clean glass jar.

Unscrew the bleed valve about half a turn and have an assistant to depress the brake pedal fully and allow it to return. Pause for two or three seconds and repeat.

At first the fluid being pumped into the jar will contain bubbles of air and the process should be continued until no air bubbles are present. The bleed valve may then be tightened and the operation repeated on the other front brake and then the lefthand rear brake.

Do not forget to watch the fluid level in the reservoir and top up as necessary.

Replace the bleed nipple covers and the reservoir cap, after seeing that the vent hole is free. Remove the centralizing tool from the differential valve.

Switch on the ignition and depress the brake pedal several times. The warning light should not illuminate.

With the ignition still on, operate the test switch and ensure that the warning light does illuminate.

11:3 Renewing the front brake pads

These should be renewed as soon as they have worn down to a thickness of $\frac{1}{8}$ inch and the procedure is as follows:

Apply the parking brake, jack up the front of the car and support it on stands. Remove the front wheels.

Refer to **FIGS 11:3** and **11:4**. Pull out the retaining clips, withdraw the retaining pins and remove the brake pads, tension springs and shims using, if necessary, a pair of thin nosed pliers.

Before fitting the new pads, check that they are the correct type and colour code and ensure that the disc is undamaged and free from dirt and oil. It will also be necessary to push the pistons back into their bores. This will cause the fluid level in the reservoir to rise and perhaps overflow if some fluid is not siphoned out.

Place the brake pad tension springs on the pads and shims and fit them into the caliper. The pads can go in only one way, but the shims may be fitted either way up. Refit the retaining pins and secure them with the clips, noting that the clips are on the side of the pins away from the piston seal. See also that the tangs of the pad tension springs are underneath the retaining pins.

Operate the brake pedal several times to bring the pads fully into position against the disc, then check that the pads have a little free movement to indicate that the retaining pins are not fouling the pads.

Refit the road wheels and lower the car to the ground.

11:4 Servicing the calipers
Removal:

Raise the front of the car and remove the appropriate road wheel.

Remove the brake pads as described in **Section 11:3**. Piston removal will be facilitated if the brake pedal is now depressed to push them out of their bores.

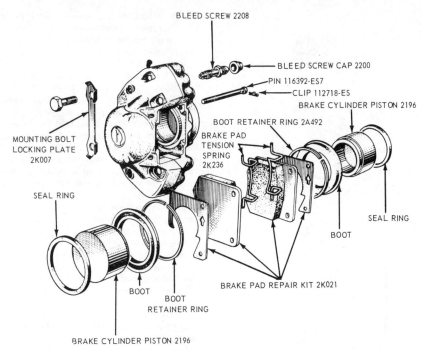

BLEED SCREW 2208

BLEED SCREW CAP 2200

PIN 116392·ES7

CLIP 112718·ES

BRAKE CYLINDER PISTON 2196

BOOT RETAINER RING 2A492

BRAKE PAD TENSION SPRING 2K236

MOUNTING BOLT LOCKING PLATE 2K007

SEAL RING

SEAL RING

BOOT

BRAKE PAD REPAIR KIT 2K021

BOOT

BOOT RETAINER RING

BRAKE CYLINDER PISTON 2196

FIG 11:4   Components of a front brake caliper assembly

Disconnect the fluid supply pipe from the union on the the rear of the caliper and plug each open end to prevent the entry of any foreign matter.

Bend back the locking tabs, remove the two securing bolts and lift away the caliper assembly.

Dismantling:

Under no circumstances should the two halves of the caliper body be separated.

Partially extract one piston and remove the circlip and the sealing bellows from the groove in the piston. The piston may now be withdrawn with the fingers assisted, if necessary, by a little air pressure.

Ease the bellows from the groove in the bore and withdraw the piston sealing ring.

Repeat for the other piston and then clean all the parts in methylated spirit or brake fluid, but do NOT use a mineral base cleaner such as petrol, kerosene or carbon tetrachloride. Check that all the items are fit for further use or renew where necessary. Rubber parts should always be renewed.

Reassembly:

Fit a new piston sealing ring in each cylinder bore and fit the rubber bellows to the cylinder with the out-turned lip firmly in the cylinder groove.

Dip the pistons in clean brake fluid and insert them carefully, crown first, through the bellows into the cylinder Fit the inner edge of the bellows in the annular groove in the piston skirt.

Push the piston as far as possible into the bore and then secure the bellows to the caliper with the circlip.

Reinstallation:

The caliper assembly is refitted using a new locking plate and tightening the bolts to a torque of 45 to 50 lb ft (6.22 to 6.91 Mkg). Bend up the locking tabs.

Reconnect the hydraulic pipe to its union.

Refit the brake pads as described in **Section 11:3**, pushing the pistons back as necessary and ensuring that the piston seals are correctly fitted.

The remainder of the parts are fitted in the reverse order of removal, after which the brakes must be bled as described earlier in **Section 11:2**.

11:5 The hub and disc assembly

Removal:

Remove the grease cap from the end of the hub. Remove the cotterpin and the adjusting nut retainer, then unscrew the adjusting nut and remove the thrust washer and the outer bearing race.

Pull off the hub and disc assembly from the stub axle, make alignment marks on both parts and separate the disc from the hub after bending back the locking tabs and removing the bolts. Both locking plates and bolts should be discarded and new ones obtained.

Refitting:

Clean thoroughly both mating faces, align the mating marks and fit the disc to the hub, tightening the bolts to 30-34 lb ft (4.15 to 4.70 mkg). Secure with the locking tabs.

Replace the assembly on to the stub axle and fit the outer bearing race, thrust washer and adjusting nut, which

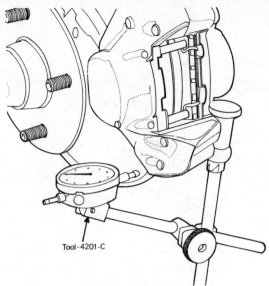

FIG 11 :5   Checking the runout of a brake disc

should be tightened to 27 lb ft (3.73 mkg) while rotating the disc to ensure the correct seating of the bearings.

Slacken the nut back by one quarter of a turn and fit the nut retainer so that one of the castellations lines up with the cotterpin hole in the axle. Fit a new cotterpin.

The disc run-out is now checked as follows:

Disconnect the connecting rod from the steering arm at its outer end, after removing the cotterpin and castellated nut and separating the ball joint.

Mount a dial gauge on the steering arm as shown in **FIG 11 :5**, rotate the disc and check the total indicator reading. It must not be more than .0035 inch (.089 mm).

If, after eliminating the possibility of dirt between the mating surfaces or misalignment of the hub bearings and trying a new location of the disc assembly on the axle, the run-out is still in excess of the specified dimension, a worn or distorted disc is indicated and must be renewed.

Remove the gauge, refit the connecting rod end and tighten to 18-22 lb ft (2.48-3.04 mkg) using a new cotterpin. Replace the grease cap.

Caliper splash shield:

After removing the disc assembly as just described the splash shield is detached by bending back the integral locking tabs and removing the securing screws.

Refitting is a reversal of the removal procedure.

11 :6 Servicing the drum brakes
Dismantling. (See FIG 11 :6):

The shoes should be examined at intervals of about 6000 miles (10,000 km) to see that there is at least $\frac{1}{32}$ inch (.79 mm) of lining material above the rivet heads and that the linings are not contaminated by oil or grease. In either case new shoes should be fitted as it is not possible to satisfactorily remove all traces of the contamination, nor is the home operator likely to be able to reline the old shoes himself.

Chock up the front wheels, raise the rear end of the car and support it on stands. Remove the road wheels, release the handbrake then remove the brake drums by taking out the securing screw.

Remove the hold down springs by giving the top washer a quarter of a turn and pulling outwards.

Pull each shoe out of its slot in the fixed pivot and wheel cylinder. Lift the shoes away and detach the two return springs.

Fit the hold down pins and secure them with a washer, spring and then the second washer, which is turned through 90° to secure it. Check to make sure that the shoes are properly seated and that the springs are not binding on the backplate or wheel cylinder.

Refit the brake drum and secure it with the countersunk screw.

Now bring the shoes into adjustment by operating the parking brake lever behind the backplate for as long as is necessary to cause the clicking to stop.

With the ratchet wheel in the fully off position it is possible for the indexing lever on the parking brake link to over-ride the ratchet and remain in that position. It is necessary, therefore, to ensure that it returns to the fully off position every time.

Refit the road wheel and lower the car to the ground. Operate the handbrake several times to bring the brakes into correct adjustment and check by carrying out a road test.

Rear wheel cylinder:

Having removed the brake shoes, disconnect the hydraulic supply lines, note that there are two on the right handbrake plate, and plug the open ends.

Disconnect the handbrake link on the inside of the plate by removing the spring clip and clevis pin.

Lever off the rubber boot from the rear of the plate and then pull off the two U shaped retainers securing the cylinder to the backplate.

Remove the wheel cylinder and the handbrake link.

Refer to **FIG 11 :7** and remove the boot retainer. Prise off the boot and withdraw the piston complete with seal and spring from the cylinder bore. Detach the seal from the piston.

Remove the ratchet wheel and slot headed bolt from the other end of the cylinder.

Clean all parts as previously detailed, inspect for wear or damage and renew as necessary.

Dip the piston and a new seal in brake fluid and fit the seal on the piston with its flat face next to the rear shoulder of the piston. Insert the spring into the cylinder bore.

Dip in brake fluid and insert the piston assembly into the bore with the seal end innermost and being careful not to damage the seal in the process.

Fit the rubber boot and its retainer.

Rotate the ratchet wheel to the fully off position, abutting on the shoulder of the bolt head, smear with grease and insert into the wheel cylinder.

Apply also a smear of grease to the sliding surfaces of the backplate and the wheel cylinder, then pass the handbrake link and the neck of the wheel cylinder through the aperture in the backplate and secure with the U shaped retainers. Note that the spring retainer is fitted

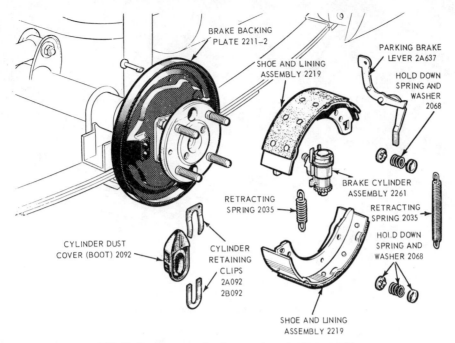

FIG 11:6   Components of a rear drum brake assembly

from the handbrake link end and the flat retainer on top of it from the other end.

Fit the rubber boot over the cylinder and the handbrake link, ensuring that the cylinder is still free to slide in the plate.

Operate the handbrake link to check the self-adjusting action of the ratchet wheel. There is a right handed screw on the righthand wheel cylinder and a left handed screw the lefthand cylinder.

Refit the shoes as described earlier, reconnect the hydraulic supply pipes, fit the drums and the road wheels and bleed the system as described in **Section 11:2**.

11:7 Servicing the master cylinder

Dismantling:

Refer to **FIG 11:8**. Disconnect the hydraulic supply pipes from the cylinder body, taking steps to catch any fluid spillage, and plug the ends of the pipes.

Undo the two securing nuts and lift the master cylinder away from the servo unit.

Lift off the fluid reservoir and remove the rubber plugs. Loosen the stop screw at the centre of the cylinder body (see **FIG 11:9**), push the piston inwards and remove the snap ring using a pair of thin nosed pliers.

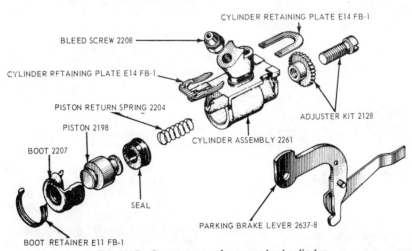

FIG 11:7   Components of a rear wheel cylinder

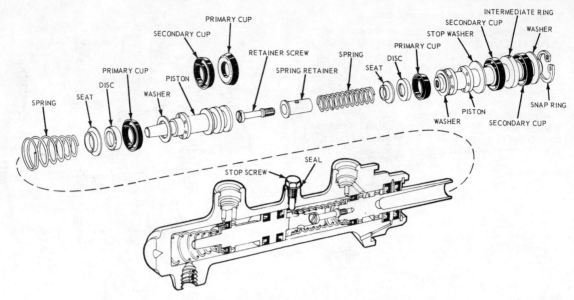

FIG 11:8   Components of the master cylinder

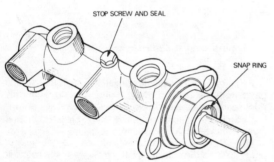

FIG 11:9   Showing the stop screw and piston retaining snap ring

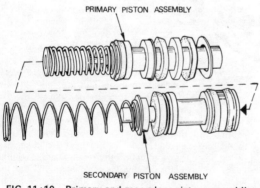

FIG 11:10   Primary and secondary piston assemblies

Withdraw the stop washer and the primary piston assembly, then, using compressed air, carefully press out the secondary piston assembly.

Wash all parts clean in methylated spirit or commercial alcohol and allow to dry. Do not use a cloth from which any fluff might adhere. Renew all parts showing any sign of rust, scoring or other damage or wear. All rubber seals, which will be found in the repair kit, should be renewed.

Reassembly:

Before starting to assemble the master cylinder, immerse all parts in clean brake fluid and study **FIGS 11:8** and **11:10** as it is essential to fit the new cups in the correct directions.

Assemble the secondary piston with filler washer, cups, pressure disc, spring and spring seat and carefully insert it into the cylinder as shown. Push it down to the end of its bore and fit the stop screw and seal. Release the piston and allow it to slowly contact the stop screw. Do not alter the length of the stop screw or the thickness of the seal.

Next assemble the primary piston with filler washer, primary cup, pressure disc and spring, spring seat, retainers and retainer screw. Do not over-tighten this screw.

Assemble the rear end of the piston in the order shown, press it carefully into the cylinder bore and fit the stop washer and snap ring.

Note that the booster unit push rod which operates the master cylinder is of a specific length and is not adjustable.

Place the master cylinder and fluid seal correctly onto the pushrod and hold it in position while screwing in the hydraulic pipe unions by a few turns.

Bolt the master cylinder to the booster unit and tighten the fluid pipe unions.

Refit the rubber plugs and the reservoir. Fill the reservoir with the specified fluid (see **Section 11:2**). Bleed the entire brake system and test on the road.

11:8 The pressure differential valve

This component, which is shown in the exploded view of **FIG 11:11**, is bolted to the rear of the engine compartment. It is connected in series with the fluid supply lines to the front and rear brakes and with normal and equal pressure in each circuit the split piston assembly is maintained in its central position. In the event of a failure in either circuit the pressure will fall and the piston move towards that side and in so doing operate the plunger of the warning switch. This illuminates the light on the instrument panel to warn the driver of the fault and advise him that only one half of his braking potential is available.

Removal:

Disconnect the five hydraulic pipes from the ports on the valve body and plug the ends of the two pipes from the master cylinder.

Disconnect the wiring from the switch terminal.

Unscrew the securing bolt and remove the valve assembly.

Dismantling:

Unscrew the end plug and the adaptor and discard the copper washers. Unscrew the switch.

Very carefully push the two pistons out of the bore, remove and discard the two seals. Pull off the dust cover and discard it.

Clean and inspect all the pieces and renew any that show signs of wear or corrosion.

Assembly:

Fit new seals on the pistons with the larger diameter of each seal towards the slotted end of the piston and dip in clean brake fluid.

Insert the longer piston into the bore with the slotted end towards the outside, as shown in the illustration, until the groove is in line with the hole for the switch plunger and then screw the switch into position and tighten to 2 to 2½ lb ft (.28-.34 mkg).

Insert the shorter piston also with the slotted end outermost.

Using new copper washers, screw in the adaptor and the end plug noting that the adaptor is fitted into the end adjacent to the hole for the mounting bolt. Tighten both to 16-20 lb ft (2.2-2.8 mkg).

Fit a new dust cover.

Testing:

After any of the operations described above or after repairing or disturbing any part of the braking system, it is essential to check the functioning of the system.

Switch on the ignition and momentarily depress the test switch. The warning lamp should light up. If it does not look for an electrical fault in the wiring or connections, or a blown bulb.

Depress the brake pedal several times. The warning light should not illuminate, but if it does there is a fault in the hydraulic system.

Switch off the ignition after making the test.

11:9 The power brake booster

This item, also known as the vacuum servo unit, is mounted on the engine compartment bulkhead and is operated directly by the brake pedal at one end and drives

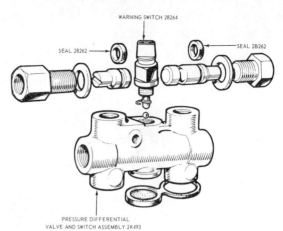

FIG 11:11 Components of the pressure differential valve

the master cylinder at the other. As mentioned earlier, the booster and the master cylinder are replaced as a unit and the home operator is not advised to attempt any servicing on the booster, but to remove it in the event of failure and take it to his service station for attention or renewal.

Removal:

First detach the vacuum supply pipe from the unit and then the fluid pipes from the master cylinder, taking care to avoid fluid spillage or the entry of dirt into the open ends.

Remove the two retaining nuts and lift off the master cylinder, taking care not to damage the fluid seal.

Disconnect the clevis pin from the brake pedal and booster push rod and remove the two bolts securing the booster to the panel bracket. If desired, the bracket can be taken off with the booster and separated after removal from the car.

Fitting:

Fit the booster to its bracket with a new gasket and secure it to the panel. Connect the push rod to the brake pedal with the clevis pin and secure the pin.

Attach the master cylinder to the booster, using a new seal if the old one is in any way damaged, and tighten the two nuts.

Refit the hydraulic pipes to the master cylinder and the vacuum hose to the booster unit. Top up the reservoir and bleed the brake system as described in **Section 11:2**.

11:10 The parking brake

This is hand operated through a cable linkage by a lever mounted on the floor between the two front seats. It also incorporates a mechanism to actuate the self-adjusting devices in the rear brakes as and when necessary. The layout of an early system is shown in **FIG 11:12**.

As mentioned, the wheel brake units are self-adjusting and this automatically maintains the setting for the parking brake also. If, after a long period of use, it is found that excessive travel on the hand lever is required to obtain satisfactory results and it is known that the brakes do not need new linings, the cause may be stretched brake cables.

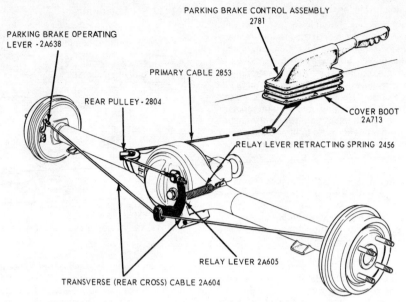

PARKING BRAKE OPERATING
LEVER - 2A638

PARKING BRAKE CONTROL ASSEMBLY
2781

PRIMARY CABLE 2853

REAR PULLEY - 2804

COVER BOOT
2A713

RELAY LEVER RETRACTING SPRING 2456

RELAY LEVER 2A605

TRANSVERSE (REAR CROSS) CABLE 2A604

FIG 11:12 Layout of an early parking brake installation

Adjustment:

The mechanism for adjusting the linkage to compensate for cable wear is shown in **FIG 11 : 13** and is set as follows:

Jack up the rear of the car, chock up the front wheels and release the handbrake. Check that the primary cable follows its correct run and that all cables and guides are well lubricated.

First adjust the effective length of the primary cable by slackening the locknut on the end of the cable at the relay lever on the rear axle and turning the adjusting nut until the primary cable has no slack in it and the relay lever is just clear of the stop on the axle casing.

Next, the effective length of the transverse cable must be adjusted. Slacken the locknut on the end of the cable adjacent to the righthand wheel unit, check that the parking brake operating levers are fully back on the stops in the off position and then adjust so that there is no slack in the cable. Confirm that the operating levers are still against their stops and tighten the locknut.

Lower the car to the ground and remove the jacks.

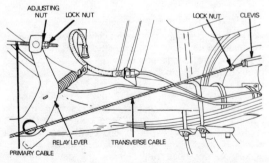

ADJUSTING
NUT   LOCK NUT

LOCK NUT   CLEVIS

RELAY LEVER   TRANSVERSE CABLE

PRIMARY CABLE

FIG 11:13   Adjusting points for handbrake linkage

Capri 2 models:

The layout of the parking brake installation on these cars is a little different and the arrangement at the rear axle is shown in **FIG 11 : 14**. Adjustment on this type is carried out as follows:

Raise the rear end of the car and release the brake lever. Check that the primary cable is correctly fitted.

Engage the keyed sleeve A into the abutment slot B and turn the adjusting nut C until there is no slack in the cable.

Now measure the clearance between the parking brake lever stop and the backplate as shown in the lower inset and, if necessary, carry out any slight further adjustment to obtain a dimension of .039 to .059 inch at this point.

Once this setting has been made, further adjustment should be required only if components are replaced or to take up wear in the linkage.

Handbrake lever:

If it is necessary to remove this, proceed as follows after jacking up the front of the car and chocking the rear wheels.

Release the handbrake and remove the carpet around the brake lever.

Disconnect the primary cable from the end of the handbrake lever under the car by removing the spring clip and clevis pin.

Unscrew the six self-tapping screws and remove the rubber boot, then remove the two securing screws and lift out the handbrake lever assembly.

Replacement is a reversal of the above, after which the cable adjustment should be checked as described earlier. Ensure that all moving parts are well greased.

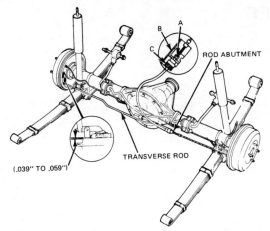

FIG 11:14 Layout of the parking brake linkage on Capri 2 models

11:11 Pipe lines and flexible hoses

Metal pipe lines should be checked at regular intervals for corrosion or accidental damage and renewed if any fault is found. Stocks of pre-fabricated pipe lines are not carried by agents, but replacements are made up from lengths of tubing using the old pipe as a pattern. They are made from Bundy tubing with a wall thickness of .028 inch (.7 mm). Fuel type tubing must not be used as it is not capable of withstanding the much higher pressures used in the braking system.

Flexible hoses should also be inspected and renewed if there is any doubt about their condition. It is recommended that they are renewed after three years use, or 36,000 miles (60,000 km).

Never attempt to remove a flexible hose by turning either end with a spanner. The correct method which avoids strain and twisting the hose, is as follows:

Unscrew the metal pipe line union nut from its connection with the hose. Hold the adjacent hexagon on the hose with a spanner while unscrewing the locknut securing the hose to the bracket. The hose can now be turned without twisting the flexible portion by using a spanner on the hexagon at the other end.

11:12 Fault diagnosis

(a) 'Spongy' brake pedal

1 Leak in hydraulic system
2 Worn master cylinder
3 Leaking wheel cylinder
4 Air in the hydraulic circuit
5 Gaps between rear brakes shoes and linings

(b) Excessive pedal movement

1 Check 1 and 4 in (a)
2 Self-adjusting mechanism not operating
3 Very low fluid level in reservoir

(c) Brakes grab or pull to one side

1 Distorted or badly worn discs or drums
2 Wet or oily friction linings
3 Disc loose on hub
4 Worn suspension or steering connections
5 Mixed linings, wrong grade, differing thicknesses
6 Unequal tyre pressures
7 Broken shoe return springs
8 Wheel cylinder not free on backplate
9 Seized piston in one brake cylinder
10 Loose caliper mountings

(d) Excessive pedal pressure required

1 Defective servo unit
2 Leak in vacuum hose
3 Servo filter blocked
4 Wet brake linings
5 Incorrect friction lining material
6 Glazed linings or excessively worn
7 Defect in one hydraulic circuit

(e) Loss of pedal pressure

1 Defective master cylinder
2 Leaking wheel cylinder or booster unit
3 Leaking brake pipes or connections
4 Empty fluid reservoir

NOTES

CHAPTER 12

THE ELECTRICAL SYSTEM

12:1 Description

The electrical system is 12 volt with the negative side of the battery earthed. Current is supplied by an alternator mounted on the righthand side of the engine and driven by the fan belt from the crankshaft pulley. A separate regulator of the non-adjustable type is used.

A Bosch starter is fitted to the German and USA models and is of the pre-engaged type in which an in-built solenoid engages the drive pinion with the starter ring gear before the main starting current is applied.

A four lamp headlamp system is employed in which all four lamps are illuminated for main beam, but only the dipped filaments in the two outer units for town driving or meeting oncoming traffic.

The standard instrument layout consists of a speedo-meter and a combined fuel and temperature gauge cluster, all fed with a steady 5 volt supply from an instrument voltage regulator. There are also four warning lights for turn indicators (green), main headlamp beam (blue), charge condition (red) and oil pressure (amber). On GT

models there is also a tachometer, odometer, trip meter, oil pressure gauge, and an electric clock. A battery condition indicator gauge is also included.

The wiring for the car's electrical services is mainly carried in three harnesses. The first includes the wiring from the various instruments and switches on the panel and is connected to the engine harness and the front lamp harness by means of multiple connectors. A further loom carries the wiring associated with the fuel tank gauge and the lights at the rear of the car.

In this chapter will be found details of several of the electrical components used in the car, but it is stressed that the instruments and equipment necessary for servicing and adjusting them correctly are unlikely to be available to the private owner and it may be more satis-factory and economical in time and money, to replace defective components with new or reconditioned units.

The following precautions must be observed when working on cars fitted with an alternator.

Strict polarity must be observed at all times when making any connections in the electrical circuit.

When refitting the battery, always connect the positive cable first and then the negative (ground) cable to the battery.

Never run the engine while the battery is disconnected, nor with the main alternator output cable removed.

When arc welding on the car, always isolate the alternator by removing the moulded connectors.

12:2 The battery

In view of the importance of the battery in the operation of any automobile, its correct maintenance is of the first priority, particularly in winter when greater demands are made on the electrical system.

Maintenance:

Always keep the top of the battery clean and dry. If there are any signs of corrosion or acid split on the parts, the areas affected should be washed with a weak solution of ammonia.

A frequent cause of insufficient current to operate the starter motor is a high resistance joint on the battery terminals. These should be kept clean and smeared lightly with petroleum jelly before making the connection, which must be kept tight and also smeared over with vaseline.

At regular intervals the level of the electrolyte in the cells must be checked and if necessary topped up with distilled water to just above the tops of the plate separators. Do not use neat acid to replace loss. If electrolyte is to be used for this purpose, it should be ready mixed to the correct specific gravity before use and remember: NEVER add water to acid, ALWAYS acid to water, when mixing, otherwise the resulting reaction may cause serious injury.

If the car is to stand idle for a long period or the battery removed for storage, the battery should be given a freshening change at about four weekly intervals, otherwise sulphation may occur and the battery ruined.

Testing:

Service stations have a number of instruments for battery testing, but the best method available to the owner driver is the specific gravity test made with a hydrometer.

The end of the hydrometer is inserted into each cell in turn and an adequate sample of electrolyte drawn up to enable the float to swim freely so that a reading may be taken.

Indications are as follows:

For climates below 32°C (90°F)

Cell fully charged	Specific gravity 1.270 to 1.290
Cell half charged	Specific gravity 1.190 to 1.210
Cell discharged	Specific gravity 1.110 to 1.130

Use electrolyte of 1.270 S.G. for topping up.

For climates above 32°C (90°F)

Cell fully charged	Specific gravity 1.210 to 1.230
Cell half charged	Specific gravity 1.130 to 1.150
Cell discharged	Specific gravity 1.050 to 1.070

Use electrolyte of 1.210 S.G. for topping up.

The above figures are given assuming a standard electrolyte temperature of 16°C (60°F). Convert the actual reading to standard by adding .002 for each 3°C (5°F) increase of actual electrolyte temperature above standard. Similarly, subtract .002 for each similar value below the standard temperature.

If the readings are reasonably uniform the battery should be healthy, but if they are low, the need is shown for a bench charge or a long daylight run. If the readings are irregular with one or more cells .050 lower than the rest, the battery is no longer serviceable and should be renewed.

12:3 The alternator

The alternator is mounted low down on the righthand side of the engine and driven at 1.88 times engine speed by the fan belt. If there is any serious fault in the alternator the owner is advised to take it to the service station for repair or replacement but there are a few simple tests he may wish to make himself to locate the trouble before removing the machine from the car.

Continuity test:

Disconnect the terminal plug from the rear of the alternator and connect a voltmeter negative lead to ground.

With the ignition switched ON, connect the voltmeter positive lead to each of the connector wires in turn as shown in **FIG 12:1**.

In each case the voltmeter should show full battery voltage. If it does not do so, trace each wire to locate the fault.

Voltage drop test:

Connect the voltmeter between the negative terminal of the battery and the alternator housing.

Start the engine and run it at about 3000 rev/min. If the voltmeter reading exceeds .25 volts, a high resistance in the negative side of the charging circuit is indicated.

In this event, check for loose, dirty or corroded connections and rectify them.

Output test:

Disconnect the terminal plug from the alternator and connect an ammeter in series between the centre connector terminal on the alternator and the corresponding socket on the plug.

Connect also a wire between the alternator D+ terminal and its corresponding socket on the connector plug. See **FIG 12:2**.

Start the engine and run it at 3000 rev/min, giving an alternator speed of approximately 6000 rev/min. Switch on the headlamps and leave on for about 5 minutes.

The ammeter should give a reading of 35 amps at normal operating temperature.

Regulator control voltage check:

Connect a voltmeter across the battery terminals and an ammeter in series between the B+ terminals on the alternator and the corresponding terminal on the connector plug. Connect also a lead between the alternator D+ terminal and the corresponding terminal on the connector plug.

Run the engine at 3000 rev/min until the indicated charging rate drops below 10 amps. The voltmeter should then read between 14.1 and 14.4 volts.

If these readings cannot be obtained the regulator is faulty and must be renewed.

12:4 Removing the alternator

Disconnect the battery ground cable. Disconnect the clip securing the plug connector to the rear of the alternator and pull out the plug.

Disconnect the wiring from the regulator at the alternator.

Disconnect the heater hose bracket from the alternator.

Loosen the three mounting bolts and swing the alternator in towards the engine so that the driving belt may be removed.

Pull out the mounting bolts and lift off the alternator from the engine.

Refitting is a reversal of the above procedure, noting that the fan belt should be tensioned to give $\frac{1}{2}$ inch free movement at a point mid-way between the alternator and the fan pulley.

12:5 Dismantling the alternator

The alternator is a component for which professional attention is advised, but the following information is given for those who may feel competent to carry out the work at home. Refer to **FIG 12:3** which shows the components of a typical Bosch alternator.

1a (Bosch) Remove the brush and connector plug assembly (see **FIG 12:4**) from the rear housing and mark the front and rear housings to ensure correct alignment when assembling.

1b (Lucas) Remove two screws securing the rear plastic cover. Make a note of the connections and disconnect the leads from the regulator to the brush gear. Remove two screws and take off the regulator.

2 (Both) Undo the pulley retaining nut and remove the lockwasher, pulley and fan. Extract the key from the rotor shaft.

3a (Bosch) Remove four bolts holding the two housings together and pull off the front housing complete with rotor.

3b (Lucas) Remove lead connecting brush gear to rectifier pack and then the two screws securing the brushgear. Lift off the brushgear.

4a (Bosch) Press out the rotor and shaft assembly and remove the front retainer ring from the front housing and the rear spacer from the rotor shaft. The front bearing may be removed if required by taking out the securing screws and removing the bearing retainer plate. Use a puller to extract the bearing.

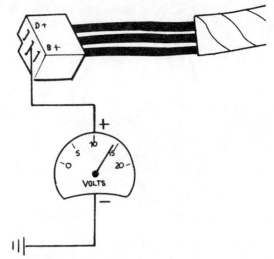

FIG 12:1 Alternator continuity check

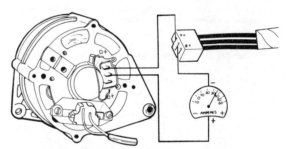

FIG 12:2 Alternator output test

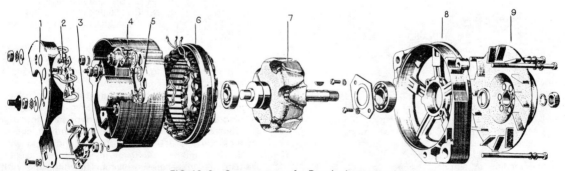

FIG 12:3 Components of a Bosch alternator

Key to Fig 12:3 1 Rectifier and diode plate   2 Rectifier   3 Brush holder   4 Slip ring end shield   5 Rectifier   6 Stator   7 Rotor   8 Drive end shield   9 Fan and pulley

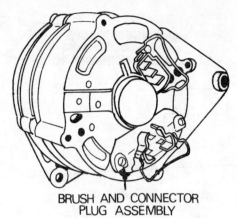

BRUSH AND CONNECTOR PLUG ASSEMBLY

FIG 12:4   Brush and connector plug assembly

4b (Lucas)   Unscrew and withdraw the three through bolts, press the drive end bracket off the rotor shaft and retrieve the spacer. Remove the circlip securing the bearing in the bracket and press the bearing out. Retain the grease seals.

5a (Bosch)   If it is necessary to remove the diode plate, remove the four screws which will release both stator and diode plate. Retrieve the waved washer in the bore of the rear housing.

5b (Lucas)   Loosen the nut securing the rectifier pack and if necessary unsolder the leads on the rectifier pack using a pair of long nosed pliers to act as a heat sink. Note the connections.

6a (Bosch)   If necessary, unsolder the three wires from the diodes using a pair of long nosed pliers as described in item 5b (see also **FIG 12:5**).

6b (Lucas)   To separate the slip ring end bracket from the rotor, slide a 3 inch long metal sleeve over the slip ring moulding, to engage the outer ring of the bearing and drive it out. If necessary unsolder the field winding connections from the slip ring moulding. Slide off the moulding and the bearing. Carefully prise the stator out of the end bracket.

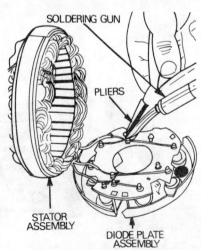

FIG 12:5   Unsoldering the diode plate

7 (Both)   Clean and inspect all components, renewing any worn or damaged bearings. The carbon brushes should be renewed if they are less than .2 inch (5 mm) in length and care taken to see that new brushes slide easily in their holders. The brush springs may be checked for tension which should be 10.6 to 14.1 oz (300 to 400 g) on the Bosch and 7 to 10 oz (198 to 283 g) on the Lucas.

Testing:

Test the rotor windings for a short circuit by connecting an ohmeter between the two slip rings. The resistance indicated should be 3.4 to 3.74 ohms.

Test the rotor insulation with a test lamp (less than 40 volts), by placing one lead on a slip ring and the other on the rotor shaft. The test lamp should not illuminate.

Test the stator windings for short circuit by connecting any two of the three stator wires in series with an ohmmeter. Repeat the test with the third wire. Resistance should be .25 to .275 ohms at 68°F.

Test the stator windings for earthing with the test lamp rig. Place one test lead on the housing and the other in turn with the three winding ends. The lamp should not light up.

Stator continuity is tested by placing the test lamp rig across any two of the three wiring ends and then again using the third wire in place of one of the first two tested. The lamp should light in each case.

Test the diodes with a 1.5 watt test bulb and a 12 volt supply across each diode in turn. Reverse the connections to the diode and note that the lamp should light in one direction only. If the bulb lights in both tests or not in either the diode is faulty. If any one diode is faulty the entire diode plate assembly must be renewed.

Reassembling:

1a (Bosch)   Resolder the stator wires to the diodes and fit the stator/diode assembly into the rear housing and retain with the four screws.

1b (Lucas)   Replace stator in slip ring end bracket ensuring that the slots in the stator line up with the bolt holes.

2 (Both)   Grease the rear bearing and press it onto the rotor shaft with the shielded side of the bearing towards the slip ring.

3a (Bosch)   Fit the front bearing in the front housing with its shielded side forward. Fit the retainer plate.

3b (Lucas)   Re-engage the slip ring moulding with the slot in the rotor shaft. Resolder the field to the slip rings.

4a (Bosch)   Place the spacer ring on the rotor shaft and fix the rotor into the front housing. Place the front bearing retainer ring on the rotor shaft and press into the front housing.

4b (Lucas)   Press the bearing into the slip ring bracket and replace the inner grease seal in the drive end bracket. Grease the bearing and press it into the bracket. Refit the outer grease seal and the circlip. Press the bracket onto the rotor shaft and secure with through bolts.

5a (Bosch)   Coat the bore of the rear housing with grease and fit the waved washer. Fit the front housing, with the rotor, onto the rear housing aligning the marks made earlier and install the four bolts.

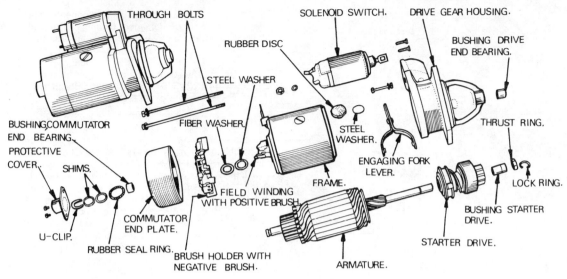

FIG 12:6   Components of a Bosch starter motor

THROUGH BOLTS

SOLENOID SWITCH.

DRIVE GEAR HOUSING.

RUBBER DISC

BUSHING DRIVE
END BEARING.

STEEL WASHER

BUSHINGCOMMUTATOR
END   BEARING.
PROTECTIVE
COVER.

FIBER WASHER.

STEEL
WASHER.

THRUST RING.

SHIMS.

ENGAGING FORK
LEVER.

FIELD WINDING
WITH POSITIVE BRUSH.

FRAME.

LOCK RING.

U-CLIP.

COMMUTATOR
END PLATE.

BUSHING STARTER
DRIVE.

RUBBER SEAL RING.

BRUSH HOLDER WITH
NEGATIVE BRUSH.

ARMATURE.

STARTER DRIVE.

5b (Lucas)   Replace and solder the leads to the rectifier
pack (use long nosed pliers). Tighten the nut which
secures the rectifier pack to the alternator. Refit
the brush gear and secure with the two screws.
Reconnect the brush gear to the rectifier pack.
Refit the regulator and reconnect the leads to the
brush gear. Refit the plastic cover.

6 (Both)   Position the key in the rotor shaft and fit the
fan pulley, lockwasher and nut. Tighten to 25-29 lb ft
(3 to 4 kgm).

12:6   The starter motor

Bosch:

This is a pre-engaged type in which the drive pinion
is engaged with the starter ring gear before the drive
shaft starts to rotate. An exploded view of the component
parts is shown in **FIG 12:6** and any maintenance will be
similar to that required for any other electric motor.

Removal:

Disconnect the battery ground cable and also the
cables from the starter solenoid switch.

Remove the three mounting bolts and lift off the starter.

Fitting is the reverse of the above after cleaning and
checking the ring gear and pinion for wear.

Dismantling:

Disconnect the field winding cable from the solenoid,
unscrew the solenoid retaining screws and lift off.

Unscrew the two screws and remove the small protective cover, U clip, spacer washers and rubber gasket
ring.

Remove the through bolts and the rear end plate.

Use a wire hook to pull the brushes out of their holder,
then remove the brush holder, fibre and steel washers as
shown in **FIG 12:7**.

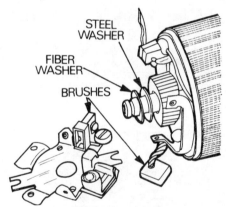

STEEL
WASHER

FIBER
WASHER

BRUSHES

FIG 12:7   Brush removal

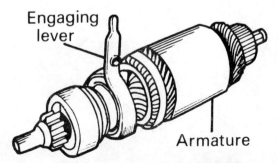

Engaging
lever

Armature

FIG 12:8   Armature with engaging lever

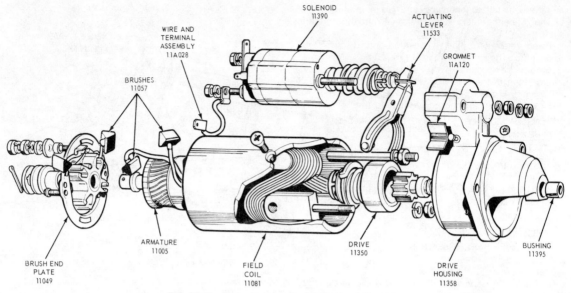

FIG 12:9 Components of a Lucas starter motor

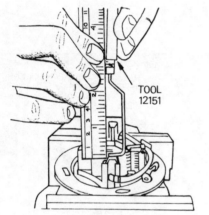

FIG 12:10 Checking the brush spring pressure

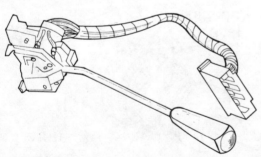

FIG 12:11 Turn signal combination switch

Withdraw the housing from the drive end, unscrew the engaging lever guide screw, remove the rubber and steel washers from the drive end frame and then remove the armature complete with the engaging lever out of the frame.

Use a sleeve to push the thrust ring inwards towards the pinion and remove the lock ring with a pair of suitable pliers.

Check the groove in the armature shaft and remove any roughness with a very fine file. Pull off the thrust ring and pinion.

After cleaning all the parts, replace any that show excess wear or damage and allow any bushings to soak in oil until required. This will impregnate the porous metal to provide its self lubricating properties.

The four carbon brushes should be examined at this time and measured for length. The minimum dimension is .375 inch and the brushes should be renewed if any are worn down to this figure. Check also that the brush springs have a pressure of 42.3 oz, and that the brushes are able to move freely in their bores. If they are not, a fine file may be used to obtain the necessary clearance.

Reassembly:

Smear some silicon grease on the coarse thread of the armature shaft and the engaging ring of the drive gear, and then slide the drive gear, stop ring and snap ring onto the armature shaft.

Press the snap ring into the groove on the armature shaft, then press on the stop ring against the snap ring using a press or claw puller.

Position the engaging lever onto the engaging ring and insert into the drive end plate together with the armature. See **FIG 12:8**. Attach the engaging lever with the guide screw.

Fit the steel washer into the drive end plate and then the rubber washer with the tab pointing towards the armature. Install the housing and place in the rubber washer. Slide the steel and fibre washers onto the armature shaft.

Place the brush holder in position and, using a wire hook, lift up the springs and insert the carbon brushes.

Mount the rear end plate and position the insulator rubber, then fit the rubber washer, shims and U clip. Fit the protective cover and secure with its two screws.

Fit and tighten the through bolts and then check the armature shaft end play. This should be between .004 and .012 inch and may be corrected by using shims if necessary.

Couple up the solenoid to the engaging lever and secure with the two mounting screws. Connect the field winding cable.

Seal all joints and screw heads with lacquer and check the starter operation.

Lucas:

As an alternative to the Bosch starter described in the first part of this section, a similar unit of Lucas manufacture may be fitted. The components of this model are shown in the exploded view of **FIG 12:9** and dismantling and servicing will be carried out similarly to the procedures mentioned earlier. One noticeable point of difference is that the Lucas starter motor has its brushes so disposed that they bear on the end of a face-type commutator.

Two important dimensions to be observed when servicing a well used starter are the armature end float, which must not exceed .010 inch (.25 mm) and the distance between the leading edge of the pinion and the thrust washer on the armature shaft extension when the solenoid is energised. This is done by removing the connection from the solenoid to the starter body and energising the solenoid with an 8-volt supply. The correct clearance should be between .005 and .150 inch (.13 to 3.8 mm).

When reassembling this starter pay attention to the correct operation of the brushes and check the spring tension by pressing them down with a spring scale such as that shown in **FIG 12:10**. With the brushes protruding $\frac{1}{16}$ inch (1.55 mm) the scale should read 28 oz (.81 kg). If these values are not obtained a new end bracket assembly must be fitted.

The armature end float can be adjusted by fitting suitable shims between the thrust plate and the cotter pin.

12:7 The headlights

Four headlights are fitted using sealed beam units. On main, or high, beam all four lights are used, but on dip only the low beam filament of the outboard units is in operation.

The numeral 2 is moulded in the glass lens of the outboard units, which also have locating tabs moulded in the glass to permit their mounting in the outboard position only. The single filament (No. 1) units also have tabs moulded in the glass to allow their mounting only in the inboard support frames.

The headlight dipper switch, which is incorporated with the turn indicator switch and horn button, is shown in **FIG 12:11** and is mounted on the steering column. The switch in the USA 2600 model is on the left of the

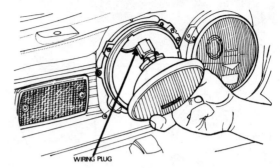
FIG 12:12   Removing a headlight unit

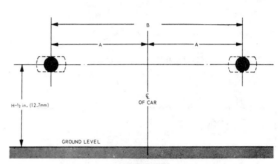
FIG 12:13   Headlight alignment diagram

Key to Fig 12:13   H = centre of headlight height above ground   B = 42.2 inch (1072.4 mm)   A = 21.1 inch (536.2 mm)

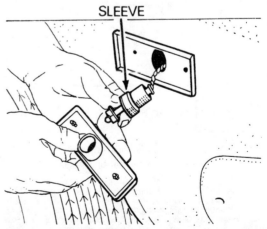
FIG 12:14   Side marker light, front

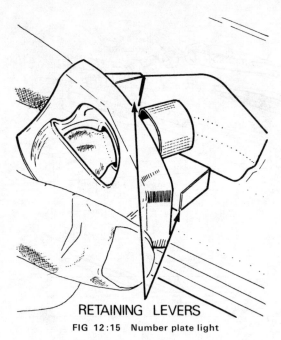

RETAINING LEVERS

FIG 12:15 Number plate light

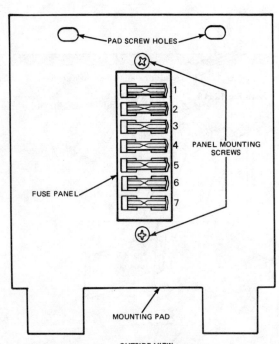

PAD SCREW HOLES

PANEL MOUNTING
SCREWS

FUSE PANEL

MOUNTING PAD

OUTSIDE VIEW
PAD AND PANEL INSTALLED
FIG 12:16 A typical fuse panel

Key to Fig 12:16   1 (8 amp) interior lights, cigar lighter, hazard flasher   2 (8 amp) Left side marker lights, left tail light, instrument panel illumination bulbs   3 (8 amp) Right side marker lights, right tail light, licence plate light   4 (8 amp) Headlights, high beam   5 (8 amp) Headlights, low beam   6 (8 amp) Stop lights, heater, turn signal, gauges and back up lights   7 (8 amp) Windshield wiper

instrument panel has three positions for OFF, headlights and parking, tail and marker lights. The European models may have ON :OFF press switches to operate the head and side lights.

Removal:

Disconnect the battery ground cable.

Remove the four screws securing the headlight bezel and lift it off.

Slacken the three retaining screws, turn the lamp anti-clockwise, and lift out the sealed beam units as shown in **FIG 12 :12**.

Disconnect the wiring plug from the rear of the unit.

The lamp is fitted in the reverse order and the beam setting adjusted if necessary.

Beam setting:

This should preferably be carried out using an optical aiming instrument, but if this is not available the following procedure should give satisfactory results.

With the car at normal curb weight and the tyres correctly inflated, position it square on to a wall at a distance of 10 feet (3 m) and mark on the wall a vertical line as shown in **FIG 12 :13**, corresponding to the centre line of the car and a horizontal line parallel to the ground at a height equal to the height of the headlight centres minus $\frac{1}{2}$ inch (12.7 mm).

Remove each headlight outer bezel and switch on the headlights.

By means of the horizontal and vertical adjusting screws, adjust each lamp so that the centres of brightest illumination lie on the horizontal aiming line 42.2 inch (107.2 cm) apart and equidistant from the centre line.

Switch off the lights and refit the bezels.

12:8 Service lights

Front parking and turn indicator light (USA model):

To replace a lens and/or bulb, remove the two cross headed screws and remove the glass.

To remove the lamp assembly, first remove the radiator opening panel (5 screws) and then remove the bulb socket and the two lamp body retaining nuts.

European:

To renew the turn indicator bulb refer to the USA model.

To remove the lamp assembly, unscrew and remove the two screws securing the lamp to the bumper. Disconnect the feed wire.

Rear, stop and turn indicator lights:

From inside the luggage compartment it is necessary to unscrew two nuts to remove the bracket securing the light assembly to the body.

A bulb can be renewed by pulling off the rear light trim cover, pulling out the spring loaded bulb holder and removing the bulb.

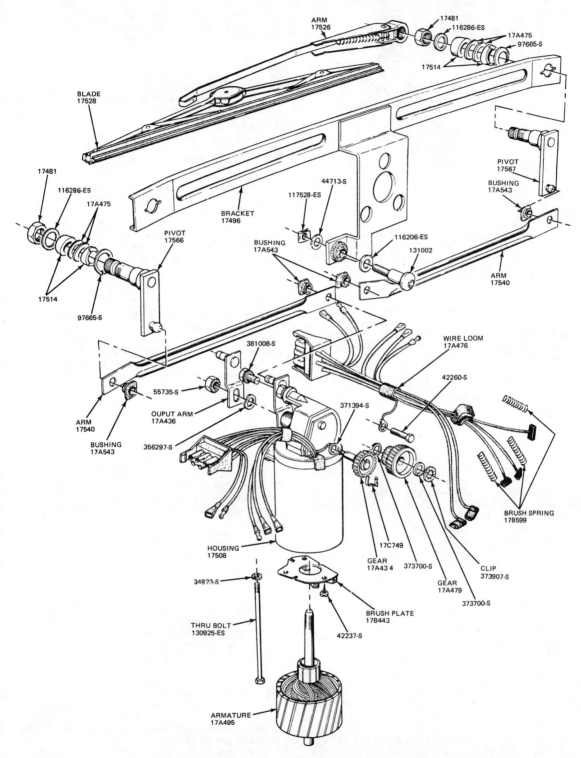

FIG 12:17   Components of the windshield wiper system

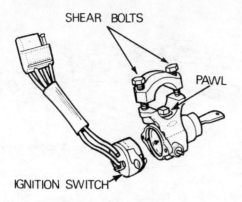

SHEAR BOLTS

PAWL

IGNITION SWITCH

FIG 12:18 Ignition and steering lock

Marker light—front:

From behind the front fender remove the two securing nuts and pull off the unit, pull back the rubber boot over the bulb holder, turn the holder a little anticlockwise and pull out. See **FIG 12:14**.

Marker light—rear:

Access to this is from inside the luggage compartment.

Remove two nuts and lift off the lamp protective bracket, hold the lamp body and turn the bulb holder slightly anticlockwise to remove. The bulb is pulled straight out of the holder.

License light:

This is mounted in the rear bumper and the battery should be disconnected before removing the lamp.

Disconnect the ground and feed cables inside the luggage trunk and pull the wires through the hole in the floor.

From underneath the bumper press the two retaining levers inwards (see **FIG 12:15**) and pull out the lamp body. Remove the bulb from the assembly.

Replacement is carried out in the reverse order, but do not forget the sealing grommet when passing the wires through the trunk floor.

Back-up light:

To replace the bulb, simply undo the lens retaining screws and lift off.

The angular bracket for the back-up light switch is mounted on the gearshift housing and is adjusted as follows:

Loosen the mounting screw and move the gearshift lever into reverse, then move the switch towards the lever until the back-up lights illuminate and then tighten the screw.

12:9 Fuses

The fuse panel may be mounted either on top of the side panel in the engine compartment or to the lower righthand edge of the instrument panel. On early cars the fuse panel contained six fuses of 8 amps, later cars have 7 fuses. A typical installation is shown in **FIG 12:16** for early cars. On 2800 models the fuses are connected as in the table below:

Fuse No.	Rating	Circuits
1	16 amps	Clock, cigar lighter, interior light
2	8 amps	Number plate and panel lamps
3	8 amps	Righthand front and rear lamps
4	8 amps	Lefthand front and rear lamps
5	16 amps	Horn, heater motor
6	16 amps	Reverse lamps, wiper, instruments
7	16 amps	Direction indicators and stop lamps

To obtain access to the fuses it is only necessary to snap off the transparent cover.

12:10 Windshield wipers

The two-speed wiper system is shown in **FIG 12:17**. This is supplemented by a washer system, that is either electrically operated or the footpump which is located on the floor adjacent to the left side trim panel. Exerting a steady pressure on the pump will cause both washer and wiper to operate together. A light pressure on the pump operates just the wipers, while just tapping the pump lightly moves the wipers through one cycle.

Removing the motor:

Disconnect the battery. Remove the two wiper arms and the nuts securing the wiper pivots to the body.

Remove the front parcel tray and the hose from the heater to the windshield defroster vent.

Disconnect the two control cables from the heater and the wiper wires, noting their positions carefully.

Remove the screws securing the motor to its mounting bracket and lift off the motor assembly.

Refitting:

Hold the motor in position behind the instrument panel and secure it to the body with the two wiper pivot nuts.

Reconnect the motor wiring, position the motor and fit the mounting screws.

Reconnect the two heater control cables and complete the operation by reversing the removal procedure.

The linkage:

Carefully prise the short wiper link off the motor output arm and remove the plastic pivot bush.

Separate the motor from the linkage by removing the three securing screws.

Carefully prise the long wiper link from the two plastic pivot bushings which hold the link to the pivots and remove the long link and the bushings.

Prise the short wiper link from the plastic bushing at the lefthand wiper pivot and remove the bushing and spring washer.

Remove two snap rings securing the pivots to the main link frame and remove both pivots.

When reassembling, position both wiper pivots in the main frame and secure with a snap ring.

Fit the spring washer and plastic bush to the lefthand pivot and then fit the short link.

Fit the long link plastic bushes to the pivots and fit the long link. Attach the motor to the linkage.

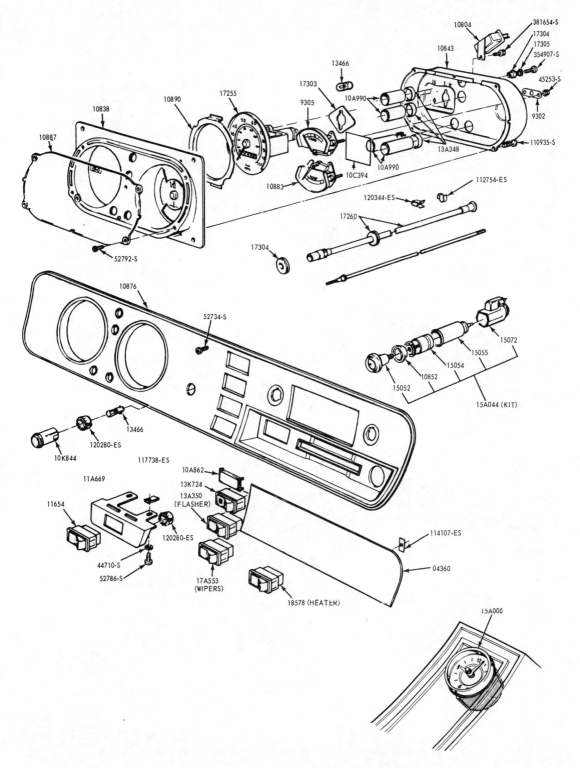

FIG 12:19 Components of a standard instrument panel assembly

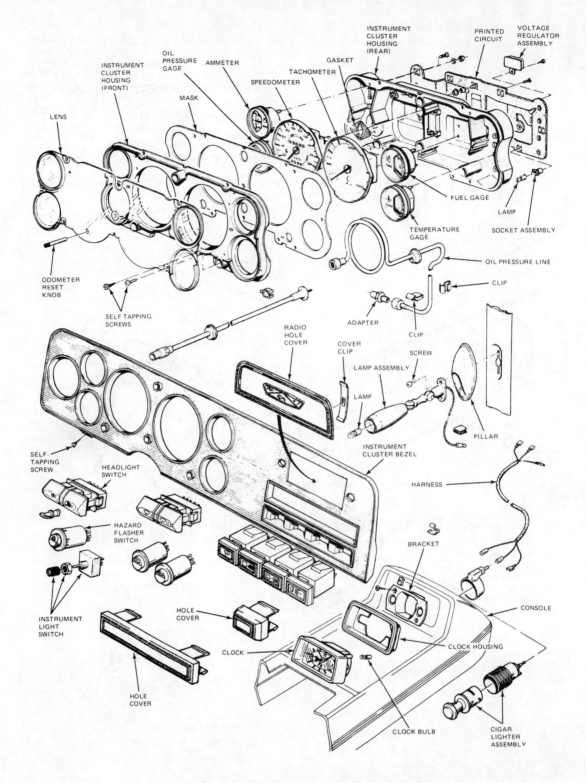

FIG 12:20   The components of a typical 1976 instrument cluster

110

12:11 Turn signals and hazard flasher

The turn signal switch is incorporated with the head-light dipper switch and is shown in **FIG 12:11**. The turn signals operate only when the ignition is switched on.

The hazard flasher switch in the USA model is mounted on the right of the instrument panel and when switched on causes all four of the turn signals to operate simultaneously as a warning to other traffic. The indicator light is to the right of the standard instrument cluster or next to the headlight switch on GT models.

Removing the turn signal switch:

Disconnect the battery.

Disconnect the bolts securing the steering column to the underside of the instrument panel and lower the column.

Remove the steering column shrouds by taking out the two retaining screws. Remove the two screws securing the switch to the column. Disconnect the multi-pin plug and remove the switch.

Refit the switch in the reverse order.

12:12 Ignition switch and steering lock

This anti-theft device has four positions: Lock (0), Accessories (I), Ignition (II) and Start (III). The steering is locked by removing the key at the lock position when a pawl is released and, with a slight rotation of the steering wheel, enters a recess in the steering shaft to prevent any further movement. To unlock the shaft, push the key in and turn to the accessories position.

At (II) the ignition is switched on and the starter operates when the key is moved to (III). If the engine does not start the key must be returned to the off or accessory position before the starter can be operated again. This prevents operation of the starter while the engine is running.

A buzzer mounted on the steering column bracket will sound if the drivers door is opened while the key is in any position in the lock.

Removal. Ignition switch:

Disconnect the battery and remove the steering column shroud.

Turn the ignition key to the 0 position. Mark the leads to the switch and disconnect them.

Remove the two securing screws and withdraw the switch from the lock

Fitting is the reverse of the above, but make sure that the key remains in the 0 position and is the right way up.

Steering lock:

After removing the steering column shroud, remove the upper screws retaining the steering column and turn the column to gain access to the headless bolts.

Disconnect the leads from the ignition switch and lock body, being careful to note their respective positions.

Drill out or use an extractor to remove the headless bolts and lift away the lock assembly.

To refit, position the new lock assembly, with the key in the lock, to the steering column and withdraw the key to allow the pawl to enter the steering shaft. See **FIG 12:18**.

Place the half clamp in position and tighten the shear bolts evenly until the heads shear off. Check for free operation of the pawl while tightening the bolts.

Reconnect all the leads to their respective terminals then turn the steering column back to its correct position and replace the screws securing the column and the shroud. Reconnect the battery cable.

12:13 The instrument clusters

Standard LH steer:

The components of a typical standard instrument panel cluster, LH steer, are shown in **FIG 12:19** and the procedure for its removal is as follows:

Disconnect the battery. Remove the two bolts securing the steering column to the underside of the dashboard and lower the column.

Remove the five crossheaded screws securing the cluster and pad assembly to the instrument panel, then pull the cluster carefully back sufficiently to gain access to the connections at the rear of the panel. Disconnect the cable connections at the rear of the gauges and switches and also the speedometer drive cable.

The cluster and pad assembly may now be removed from the car and separated by taking out the four cluster-to-pad attaching screws.

Later models without air conditioning:

A typical 1976 model instrument panel assembly is shown in **FIG 12:20** and the recommended procedures for removal and refitting are as follows:

Removal:

Disconnect the battery.

Take out the screws securing the shroud on the steering column. Pull off the lower part of the shroud and release the upper part from its retaining clip by pulling it sharply upwards.

Remove the ashtray. Withdraw the hazard warning switch from the panel and disconnect the cable connector.

Remove the screws retaining the turn signal switch and withdraw it; there is no need to disconnect the wiring.

Remove the retaining screws and pull the lower trim panel out to provide access for the disconnection of the cables to the clock and cigar lighter, then remove the trim panel.

Pull off the knob from the instrument light switch, then remove the lower retaining screws for the instrument cluster surround and pull it downwards to release it. Disconnect the seat belt warning light connector and the oil pressure line union.

Remove the screws retaining the instrument cluster to the panel, disconnect the multi-connector at the rear and the speedometer drive and withdraw the cluster assembly.

Refitting:

This is a reversal of the removal procedure.

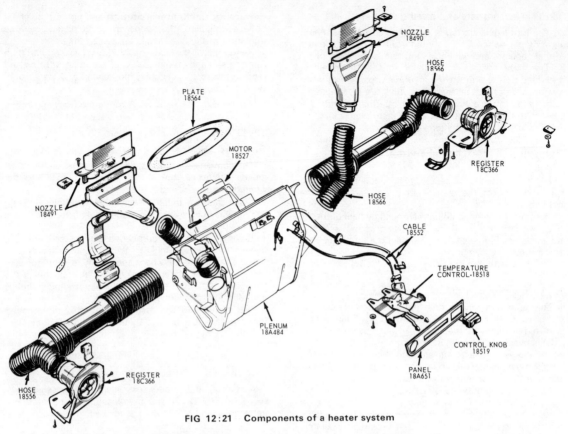

FIG 12:21   Components of a heater system

Labels in figure:
- NOZZLE 18490
- PLATE 18564
- HOSE 18566
- MOTOR 18527
- REGISTER 18C366
- NOZZLE 18491
- HOSE 18566
- CABLE 18552
- TEMPERATURE CONTROL·18518
- PLENUM 18A484
- CONTROL KNOB 18519
- PANEL 18A651
- HOSE 18556
- REGISTER 18C366

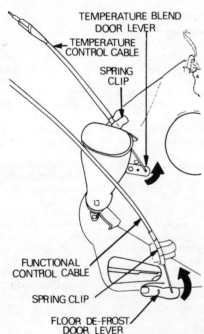

Labels in figure:
- TEMPERATURE BLEND DOOR LEVER
- TEMPERATURE CONTROL CABLE
- SPRING CLIP
- FUNCTIONAL CONTROL CABLE
- SPRING CLIP
- FLOOR DE-FROST DOOR LEVER

FIG 12:22   Heater control cable adjustments

G.T. models LH steer:

The procedure here is similar to that for standard LH steer models, but the two heater control knobs must be removed and also the access cover at the righthand side of the instrument panel by taking out four screws.

Remove three screws and loosen only one nut retaining the cluster and pad assembly to the instrument panel. Release the fuse panel (two screws) and then pull the assembly forward to disconnect all the connections at the rear, being careful not be bend the tube to the oil pressure gauge.

Refitting the instrument cluster is a reversal of the removal procedure.

Reference to the two exploded illustrations should facilitate any further dismantling which may be required.

Control panel RH steer:

The control panel and instrument cluster illustrations of the LH steer are instrumentally identical except that they are positioned the other way round. Removal is very similar in both cases.

1 Open the bonnet and disconnect the battery.
2 Remove two screws and remove the lower half of the steering column shroud. The upper shroud is secured by a pin moulded into the assembly. Push the shroud upwards to remove it.

3 Remove eight screws from the underside panel and after easing over the ignition switch, allow it to hang down.
4 If a radio is fitted pull off the two control knobs.
5 Remove three screws, disconnect the switch mult-plug(s) and detach the facia frame. Remove four screws and ease the cluster forward from its location.
6 Disconnect the speedometer cable, loom, multiplug and oil pressure gauge feed pipe to detach the cluster assembly.

12:14 The heating system

The components of the heating and ventilation system are shown in **FIG 12:21**. Fresh air is drawn in by way of a grille in front of the windshield and, by suitably positioning the two control levers, can be directed in varying ratios to the windshield or the car interior and can either be heated or allowed to pass directly into the interior.

Adjustable vents at either end of the instrument panel allow the amount and direction of face level air to be closely controlled. Stale air is exhausted through a grille below the rear window and ensures a constant flow of fresh or heated air through the car.

Adjusting controls. (See **FIG 12:22**):

These operations should be required only if the cables have been disconnected for any reason.

Directional control:

This is the lower lever and should first be pushed fully to the left or OFF position and then the spring clip securing the cable to the heater removed.

Move the floor/defrost door to the full OFF position by turning its operating lever fully upwards as shown by the arrow.

Slide the end of the cable housing to the lever and secure it with the spring clip.

Temperature control:

Move the upper lever to the extreme left or maximum heat position and then remove its securing spring clip from the heater.

Move the temperature blend door to its max. heat position by turning its operating lever fully anti-clockwise as shown.

Hold it in this position while sliding the cable housing to the lever and secure the cable housing with its clip on the heater.

Removing the controls:

Disconnect the battery, remove the ashtray and pull off the two control lever knobs.

Remove the two screws securing the control quadrant to the panel and pull out the controls from below the panel.

Remove the two cable clips from the quadrant plate and remove the cables from their levers.

The controls are re-installed by reversing the above procedure.

Removing the heater assembly:

Disconnect the battery and drain the cooling system. Disconnect the two heater hoses from the heater core tubes and remove the coverplate and gasket from around the core tubes at the dash panel by taking out two screws.

Inside the car, remove the parcel tray and if a console is fitted it must be removed as follows:

Take out the two screws securing the front end of the console to the floor and also two screws from underneath the rubber boot on the gearshift lever. Remove two screws under the rear panel.

Carefully lift the clock panel and disconnect two electrical connectors and an illumination bulb, then remove the main screw at the back of the area under the clock panel.

Remove the plastic brace under the handbrake lever by sliding it forward then lift the console out of the car.

Disconnect the cables from the control levers, three wire connectors from the terminals on the heater and the bullet connector on the other wire.

Disconnect the two panel vent ducts and the two windshield ducts from the heater.

Remove the four securing screws from the heater and lift it off. It may be necessary to remove the windshield wiper motor to gain access to one of the lefthand mounting screws.

Refitting is a reversal of the removal procedure after which the cooling system must be refilled and bled of any air. Run the engine for a few minutes with the radiator cap removed, check for leaks and top up as necessary. Replace the filler cap and if any air remains in the system it will be necessary to loosen a heater hose at the core until water flows out when the clip may be re-tightened.

12:15 Fault diagnosis

(a) Battery discharged

1 Terminal connections loose or dirty
2 Short circuits in lighting circuits
3 Alternator not charging
4 Regulator faulty
5 Battery internally defective

(b) Insufficient charging current

1 Check 1 and 4 in (a)
2 Drive belt slipping
3 Defective rectifier

(c) Battery will not hold charge

1 Electrolyte level too low
2 Battery plates sulphated
3 Case leaking
4 Plate separators defective

(d) Battery overcharged

1 Defective regulator

(e) Alternator output low or nil

1 Belt broken or slipping
2 Defective regulator
3 Worn bearings
4 Slip rings dirty or worn

5 Armature worn or bent
6 Brushes sticking, springs weak or broken
7 Rotor or stator coils broken, shorted or earthed
8 Rectifier defective

(f) Starter motor lacks power or will not operate

1 Battery discharged, terminals loose or corroded
2 Starter pinion jammed
3 Starter switch or solenoid faulty
4 Brushes worn or sticking
5 Commutator worn or dirty
6 Armature shaft bent

(g) Starter runs but does not turn engine

1 Pinion not engaging
2 Broken teeth on pinion or flywheel gears

(h) Starter inoperative

1 Check 1, 3 and 4 in (f)
2 Broken rotor or stator windings
3 Defective solenoid

(j) Starter motor rough or noisy

1 Worn bearings
2 Mounting bolts loose
3 Damaged teeth on pinion or flywheel

(k) Lamps inoperative or erratic

1 Bulb broken
2 Battery low
3 Faulty earth connection to lamp or battery
4 Faulty switch or bad connections
5 Fuse blown

(l) Wiper motor sluggish

1 Faulty armature
2 Defective brushes, commutator dirty
3 Linkage or spindles binding (lubrication or damage)

CHAPTER 13

THE BODYWORK

13:1 Bodywork finish

The high gloss exterior paintwork of the Capri is produced by an Acrylic resin-based enamel which is stoved on. It is specially formulated so that scratches which do not penetrate to the primer can be removed by rubbing down with a fine cutting compound followed by a polish to restore the original finish.

The finish is a stable one which can be repaired using conventional materials such as cellulose lacquers or air-drying acrylic lacquers which are now readily obtainable in all current standard colours.

Any stopping or priming which may be used to fill minor blemishes should be carefully rubbed down until the surface is smooth and flush with the surrounding area. When spraying keep the central area wet and the outer edges light and dry. Leave to dry for a few hours and then use a fine cutting compound to remove the dry spray. Finish off with polish.

Always remove any traces of wax polish before attempting to apply any paint. Usually a white spirit will be satisfactory, but silicone polishes are best removed with a very fine abrasive.

To maintain the high finish the paintwork should be washed frequently with plenty of water. Never wipe the surface with a dry cloth, this will rub the dust into the surface and have a sandpaper effect on the paint.

To remove stains from the vinyl roof, apply a cleaner to the affected area covering an area of not more than a radius of 12 inches at a time. Brush in circles with a medium hard brush and allow the cleaner to evaporate. If necessary, repeat the procedure and when the stains have been removed, wash the car and wipe the roof with a damp sponge. Always remove immediately any cleaner which may splash on the paintwork.

13:2 Removing door trim panels

Unscrew the knob on the door interior lock and carefully lever out the black plastic handle trim from the chrome escutcheon.

Remove the screw securing the door opening handle escutcheon and lift it off.

Remove the window regulator handle, lever out the plastic cover and undo the retaining screw. Remove two screws and lift off the armrest.

Carefully prise the trim panel away from the door panel to release the spring clips. Remove the panel and the waterproof sheet.

To refit the panel, first apply a coat of adhesive to the inner door panel for a minimum width of 1 inch and stick the waterproof sheet in place, making sure that the edges are sealed all round. Refit all the other pieces in the reverse order of dismantling.

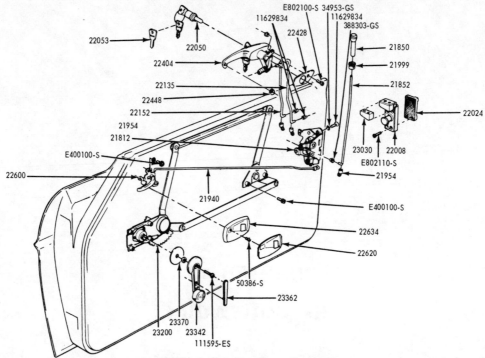

FIG 13:1 Door handles and controls

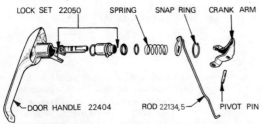

FIG 13:2 Door handle and lock assembly

LOCK SET 22050 SPRING SNAP RING CRANK ARM

DOOR HANDLE 22404 ROD 22134,5 PIVOT PIN

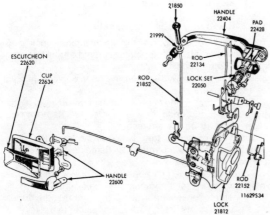

FIG 13:3 Door lock and control mechanism

21850
HANDLE 22404
21999
PAD 22428
ESCUTCHEON 22620
ROD 22134
CUP 22634
ROD 21852
LOCK SET 22050
ROD 22152
HANDLE 22600
ROD 21812
LOCK 21812
11629534

13:3 Door locks and handles

Exterior handle:

Remove the door trim panel as described in **Section 13:2** and then wind the window up. Pull down the waterproof sheet and disconnect the spring clip securing the operating rod to the handle and remove the rod. See **FIG 13:1**.

Disconnect the spring clip and remove the locking rod from the handle.

Through the door access hole remove the front screw securing the exterior handle and slacken the rear screw. Pull the handle forwards to release the rear end and lift it away with the sealing gaskets. See **FIG 13:2**.

Remove the rear screw, gaskets and remote rod clip. Tap out the pivot pin and remove the crankarm and return spring.

Remove the circlip from the end of the barrel to release the locking plate return spring and lock barrel. Pull off the spacer washer and remove the return spring from the end of the cylinder.

Remove the rubber ring from its groove in the handle push button, tap out the pin and remove the lock cylinder from the push button.

The handle is reassembled and refitted in the reverse order to the above.

Door lock assembly:

With the trim panel removed, wind the window up, disconnect the remote control rod from the operating arm on the interior handle as shown in **FIG 13:3**.

Disconnect the push button rod, the exterior operating rod and the locking rod from the lock. Release the window channel by removing two screws.

Remove the three retaining screws and remove the lock assembly.

To refit the lock, first replace the four rod connecting clips on the lock, place the lock in position on the door and secure it with the three screws. Secure the window channel.

Reconnect the four control rods and check the operation of the lock.

Remote control assembly:

Remove the spring clip securing the operating rod to the lock mechanism and disconnect the rod.

Prise out the nylon guide from the door inner panel. Remove the three securing screws securing the remote control to the inner door panel and lift away through the access hole.

Refit in the reverse order.

Door striker plate:

A cranked service tool is used to release the three screws securing the striker plate in position and it may be adjusted as follows:

With the securing screws loosened, press the door outside push button and slowly close the door to the full catch position. Move the door in or out until it is flush with the body panels.

Press in the button and carefully open the door and check that the striker plate is vertical. Tighten the securing screws and check that the door closes correctly and does not rattle, making a further slight adjustment if necessary.

13:4 Window regulators

The window regulating mechanism is shown in **FIG 13:4** and access is gained by removing the interior door trim as described earlier.

Wind down the window and remove the seven screws and washers securing the mechanism to the door.

Carefully pull the assembly towards the rear of the door to release the operating arm from the window glass.

Push the window up and either secure it or take it out of its recess by rotating it through 90 deg. and lifting out, see **FIG 13:5**.

Remove the regulator through the door access aperture.

Window frame:

Remove the chrome door moulding and weatherstrip.

Remove the two bolts securing the front of the frame and one bolt and two screws securing the rear. Lift out the frame and channel assembly from the door and prise out the silent channel strip.

Refit by reversing the above order.

13:5 Replacing a windshield

Cover the adjacent body panels with a sheet to prevent scratching. Remove the wiper arms and blades.

Using a suitable tool push the lip of the rubber weatherstrip under the top and sides of the windshield aperture flange. The glass can now be pushed out from the inside of the car complete with the weatherstrip.

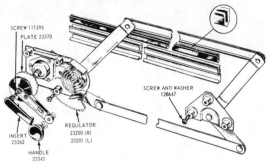

FIG 13:4 Window regulator mechanism

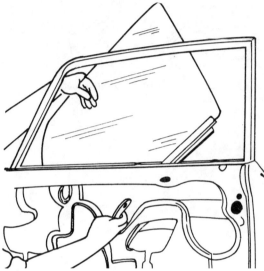

FIG 13:5 Removing a door glass

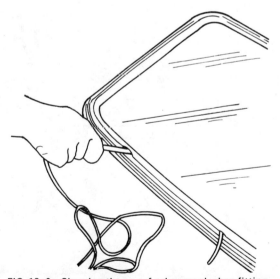

FIG 13:6 Showing the use of a drawcord when fitting windshield

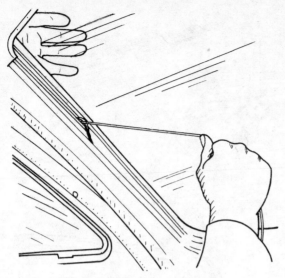

FIG 13:7 Fitting the windshield

Prise out the joint cover clip and pull the finisher strip away from the weatherstrip.

If a glass is being fitted on account of breakage, take great care to see that all traces of broken glass and sealer are removed from the body flanges and the de-mister vents, from which the fragments may be blown when the car heater is switched on.

Fit the weatherstrip around the new glass and with a pressure gun apply a suitable sealing compound (C5AZ-19554-A) in the weatherstrip groove which fits the body flange.

Fit a drawcord in the rubber to body groove as shown in **FIG 13:6** allowing a crossover of about 6 inches at the bottom.

Place the glass in the body aperture with the cord ends inside the car, and while hand pressure is applied to the outside of the glass, lift the rubber lip over the body flange by pulling on the cord as shown in **FIG 13:7**.

Again using the gun, apply sealer to the rubber to glass groove.

Fit the finisher strip in its groove using a lipping tool if necessary and replace the joint cover clip.

Clean off any surplus sealer and refit the wiper arms and blades.

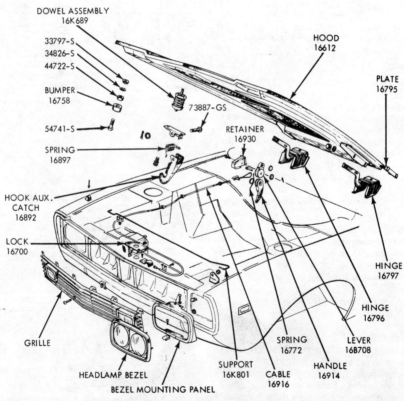

FIG 13:8 Hood and front end assembly

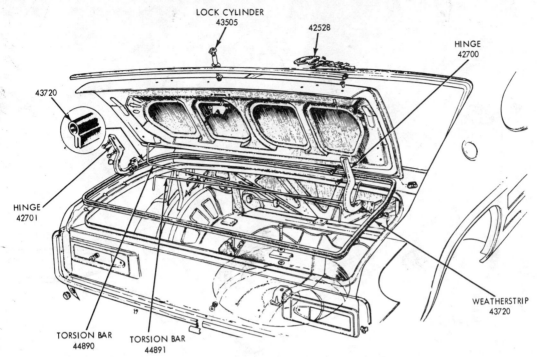

LOCK CYLINDER
43505

42528

HINGE
42700

43720

HINGE
42701

WEATHERSTRIP
43720

TORSION BAR
44890

TORSION BAR
44891

FIG 13:9 Luggage compartment and deck lid

Back window:

A similar procedure is used for removing and replacing a back window.

13:6 The hood

Before starting to remove the hood from the engine compartment it will be advisable to scribe a line around the hinges to ensure their correct location when re-fitting.

Remove the two retaining nuts and washers on each side, remove the two bolt plates and lift off the hood. See **FIG 13:8**.

When refitting, first position the hood on the hinges and replace the two bolt plates and nuts, but do not tighten fully until the hinges have been aligned to the scribed markings made earlier.

Striker:

This is adjustable in order to ensure correct fitting of the hood to the surrounding body panels. Release the locknut and screw the striker in or out as required, then tighten the locknut.

Release cable:

Prise out the clips and remove the radiator trim panel. From inside the car remove both clevis pins and spring and disconnect the cable from the control lever.

Slacken the cable adjuster and release the cable from the hood lock. Remove the body clips and pull the cable through the bulk head.

The hood lock is secured in position by three bolts and is easily removed.

After refitting, adjust the release cable before replacing the radiator cowl panel.

13:7 Luggage compartment deck lid

As with the hood, always mark the position of the hinges before removing the securing screws to ensure correct fitting on re-installation.

The weatherstrip is retained by an internal toothed channel and is removed by carefully prising it off the aperture flanges. See **FIG 13:9**. It is refitted by tapping into place with a rubber mallet and the joint in the weather strip should be sealed with a length of one inch wide body tape.

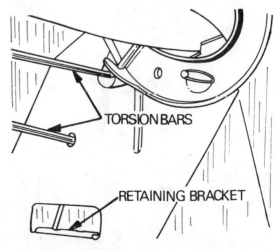

TORSION BARS

RETAINING BRACKET

FIG 13:10 Torsion bar mountings

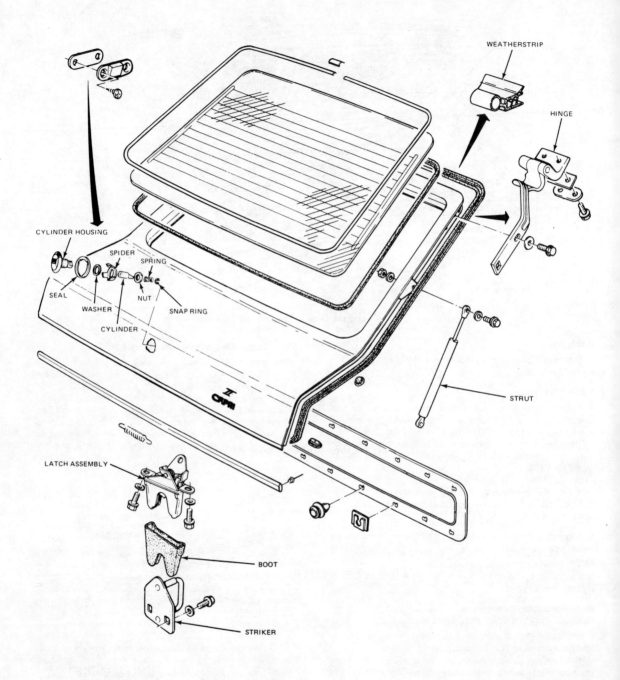

WEATHERSTRIP

HINGE

CYLINDER HOUSING

SPIDER

SPRING

SEAL

NUT

WASHER

CYLINDER

SNAP RING

STRUT

LATCH ASSEMBLY

BOOT

STRIKER

FIG 13:11   The components of the rear hatch on Capri 2 models

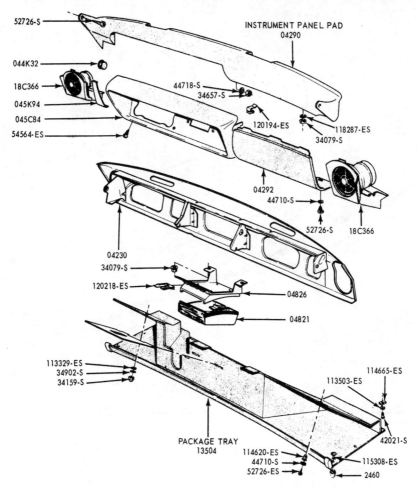

FIG 13:12   Instrument panel pad and parcel tray

Torsion bars:

The mounting for the torsion bars which control the opening of the deck lid is shown in **FIG 13:10**.

To remove them it is necessary to use a pair of adjustable spanners and release the cranked end from its retaining bracket on the body.

Disconnect the double cranked end from the hinge and remove the torsion bar. Repeat for the other torsion bar.

To refit: Engage the double cranked end in the hinge and use a pair of adjustable spanners to locate the other end of the bar in its retaining bracket.

Lock:

With the lid open remove the spring clip from the end of the lock spindle, remove three screws and washers and remove the lock.

Use a pair of long nosed pliers through the hole in the lid to compress the legs of the spring clip retaining the lock cylinder and pull it out.

A new cylinder is simply pressed in until the spring clip engages.

13:8 The rear hatch

This is fitted to later cars in place of the luggage compartment dock lid and is shown in **FIG 13:11**. The removal and refitting are quite straightforward as follows.

Remove the electrical connectors from the supporting struts, then remove the bolts at the upper strut to door mountings.

Mark the hinge locations and then remove the hinge bolts and lift the door away.

The door is refitted in the reverse order and should then be adjusted for conformity with the surrounding body panels.

The upper edge of the door should be parallel and flush with the rear of the roof, the gap at the top being between $\frac{1}{4}$ and $\frac{5}{16}$ inch. Adjustment, when necessary, is made by loosening the hinge-to-door bolts and moving the door as required.

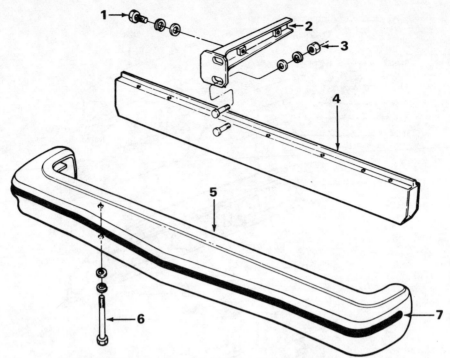

FIG 13:13 Components of the later type front bumper assembly

Key to Fig 13:13   1 Screw   2 Arm   3 Nut   4 Reinforcement   5 Bumper   6 Special bolt   7 Trim strip (replaceable)

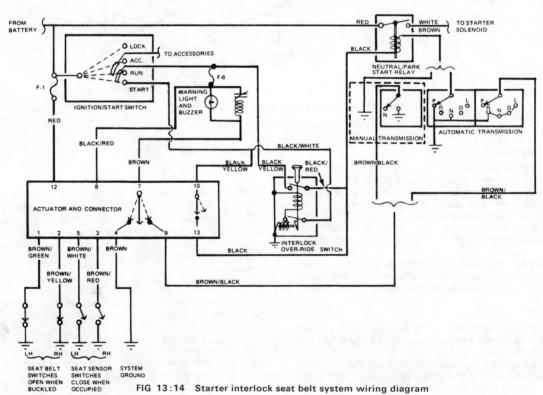

FIG 13:14 Starter interlock seat belt system wiring diagram

The door sides may be repositioned by adding or taking away shims at the mating bumpers screwed on the sides of the C pillars.

The lower edge of the door can be adjusted by suitably moving the lock striker plate which can be moved in all four directions.

The weatherstrip:

This is held in place by an internally toothed channel and can be removed by levering it away from the flanges around the door aperture.

The new weatherstrip is tapped into position with a rubber mallet and the joint should be sealed with a length of inch wide body tape.

13:9 Instrument panel pad

This is shown in **FIG 13:12** together with the parcel tray and removal is effected as follows:

Take out two screws one each side and remove the left and right A post garnish mouldings, then remove each corner screw which is now uncovered.

Remove the instrument cluster panel pad assembly as described in **Chapter 12**.

Remove the two nuts and washers which will be found directly above the opening for the instrument cluster and also the remaining nut on the righthand side of the panel pad.

Lift the panel pad away from the instrument panel.

To refit, first position the pad and retaining clips on the instrument panel assembly—then fit the three retaining nuts and washers.

Fit the left and righthand corner screws and garnish moulding. Refit the instrument panel pad as described earlier.

13:10 The bumpers

The later type of impact absorbing bumper is shown in **FIG 13:13**. Removal is effected as follows:

Unscrew the two bolts (four at the rear) securing the bumper assembly to the two mounting arms. Remove the number plate brackets if applicable.

Remove the bolts retaining the reinforcement member to the bumper and separate them. The trim strip can be pulled off the bumper and a new strip fitted, easing the strip with soapy water.

The bumpers are fitted in the reverse order to the above but care must be taken to see that they are at the correct height from the ground. On front bumpers the bottom edge must be 17 inch above the road surface and on rear bumpers 14.8 inch. Having adjusted the height, check that the two sides of the bumpers are symmetrical with the gap between bumper and body equal on both sides.

13:11 Seat belt/starter interlock system

The components of this system are not suitable for home servicing, but a simplified wiring diagram is given in **FIG 13:14** which will assist in checking the wiring in the event of improper operation.

NOTES

APPENDIX

Inches		Decimals	Milli-metres	Inches to Millimetres		Millimetres to Inches	
				Inches	mm	mm	Inches
	1/64	.015625	.3969	.001	.0254	.01	.00039
1/32		.03125	.7937	.002	.0508	.02	.00079
	3/64	.046875	1.1906	.003	.0762	.03	.00118
1/16		.0625	1.5875	.004	.1016	.04	.00157
	5/64	.078125	1.9844	.005	.1270	.05	.00197
3/32		.09375	2.3812	.006	.1524	.06	.00236
	7/64	.109375	2.7781	.007	.1778	.07	.00276
1/8		.125	3.1750	.008	.2032	.08	.00315
	9/64	.140625	3.5719	.009	.2286	.09	.00354
5/32		.15625	3.9687	.01	.254	.1	.00394
	11/64	.171875	4.3656	.02	.508	.2	.00787
3/16		.1875	4.7625	.03	.762	.3	.01181
	13/64	.203125	5·1594	.04	1.016	.4	.01575
7/32		.21875	5.5562	.05	1.270	.5	.01969
	15/64	.234375	5.9531	.06	1.524	.6	.02362
1/4		.25	6.3500	.07	1.778	.7	.02756
	17/64	.265625	6.7469	.08	2.032	.8	.03150
9/32		.28125	7.1437	.09	2.286	.9	.03543
	19/64	.296875	7.5406	.1	2.54	1	.03937
5/16		.3125	7.9375	.2	5.08	2	.07874
	21/64	.328125	8.3344	.3	7.62	3	.11811
11/32		.34375	8.7312	.4	10.16	4	.15748
	23/64	.359375	9.1281	.5	12.70	5	.19685
3/8		.375	9.5250	.6	15.24	6	.23622
	25/64	.390625	9.9219	.7	17.78	7	.27559
13/32		.40625	10.3187	.8	20.32	8	.31496
	27/64	.421875	10.7156	.9	22.86	9	.35433
7/16		.4375	11.1125	1	25.4	10	.39370
	29/64	.453125	11.5094	2	50.8	11	.43307
15/32		.46875	11.9062	3	76.2	12	.47244
	31/64	.484375	12.3031	4	101.6	13	.51181
1/2		.5	12.7000	5	127.0	14	.55118
	33/64	.515625	13.0969	6	152.4	15	.59055
17/32		.53125	13.4937	7	177.8	16	.62992
	35/64	.546875	13.8906	8	203.2	17	.66929
9/16		.5625	14.2875	9	228.6	18	.70866
	37/64	.578125	14.6844	10	254.0	19	.74803
19/32		.59375	15.0812	11	279.4	20	.78740
	39/64	.609375	15.4781	12	304.8	21	.82677
5/8		.625	15.8750	13	330.2	22	.86614
	41/64	.640625	16.2719	14	355.6	23	.90551
21/32		.65625	16.6687	15	381.0	24	.94488
	43/64	.671875	17.0656	16	406.4	25	.98425
11/16		.6875	17.4625	17	431.8	26	1.02362
	45/64	.703125	17.8594	18	457.2	27	1.06299
23/32		.71875	18.2562	19	482.6	28	1.10236
	47/64	.734375	18.6531	20	508.0	29	1.14173
3/4		.75	19.0500	21	533.4	30	1.18110
	49/64	.765625	19.4469	22	558.8	31	1.22047
25/32		.78125	19.8437	23	584.2	32	1.25984
	51/64	.796875	20.2406	24	609.6	33	1.29921
13/16		.8125	20.6375	25	635.0	34	1.33858
	53/64	.828125	21.0344	26	660.4	35	1.37795
27/32		.84375	21.4312	27	685.8	36	1.41732
	55/64	.859375	21.8281	28	711.2	37	1.4567
7/8		.875	22.2250	29	736.6	38	1.4961
	57/64	.890625	22.6219	30	762.0	39	1.5354
29/32		.90625	23.0187	31	787.4	40	1.5748
	59/64	.921875	23.4156	32	812.8	41	1.6142
15/16		.9375	23.8125	33	838.2	42	1.6535
	61/64	.953125	24.2094	34	863.6	43	1.6929
31/32		.96875	24.6062	35	889.0	44	1.7323
	63/64	.984375	25.0031	36	914.4	45	1.7717

UNITS	Pints to Litres	Gallons to Litres	Litres to Pints	Litres to Gallons	Miles to Kilometres	Kilometres to Miles	Lbs. per sq. In. to Kg. per sq. Cm.	Kg. per sq. Cm. to Lbs. per sq. In.
1	.57	4.55	1.76	.22	1.61	.62	.07	14.22
2	1.14	9.09	3.52	.44	3.22	1.24	.14	28.50
3	1.70	13.64	5.28	.66	4.83	1.86	.21	42.67
4	2.27	18.18	7.04	.88	6.44	2.49	.28	56.89
5	2.84	22.73	8.80	1.10	8.05	3.11	.35	71.12
6	3.41	27.28	10.56	1.32	9.66	3.73	.42	85.34
7	3.98	31.82	12.32	1.54	11.27	4.35	.49	99.56
8	4.55	36.37	14.08	1.76	12.88	4.97	.56	113.79
9		40.91	15.84	1.98	14.48	5.59	.63	128.00
10		45.46	17.60	2.20	16.09	6.21	.70	142.23
20				4.40	32.19	12.43	1.41	284.47
30				6.60	48.28	18.64	2.11	426.70
40				8.80	64.37	24.85		
50					80.47	31.07		
60					96.56	37.28		
70					112.65	43.50		
80					128.75	49.71		
90					144.84	55.92		
100					160.93	62.14		

UNITS	Lb ft to kgm	Kgm to lb ft	UNITS	Lb ft to kgm	Kgm to lb ft
1	.138	7.233	7	.967	50.631
2	.276	14.466	8	1.106	57.864
3	.414	21.699	9	1.244	65.097
4	.553	28.932	10	1.382	72.330
5	.691	36.165	20	2.765	144.660
6	.829	43.398	30	4.147	216.990

TECHNICAL DATA

Dimensions are given in inches, unless otherwise stated

ENGINE (2600)

Type	6 cylinder, 60 deg. V formation
Capacity	2550 cc
Bore	3.545
Stroke	2.630
Compression ratio	8.2 : 1
Firing order	1–4–2–5–3–6
No. 1 cylinder	Righthand bank front
Cylinder block:	
Material	Cast iron
Bore diameter:	
Class 1	3.543
2	3.544
3	3.545
4	3.546
Oversize, .02	3.564
.04	3.584
Main bearing bore:	
Red	2.386
Blue	2.387
Crankshaft:	
Main journal diameter	
Standard, red	2.244
blue	2.243
Undersize, .01	2.234
.02	2.224
.03	2.214
.04	2.204
Clearance	.0005 to .002
End float	.004 to .008
Connecting rod journals:	
Standard, red	2.126
blue	2.125
Undersize, .01	2.116
.02	2.106
.03	2.096
.04	2.086
Connecting rods:	
Bearing insert diameter:	
Standard, red	2.127
blue	2.126
Undersize, .01	2.117
.02	2.107
.03	2.097
.04	2.087
Clearance to journal	.0005 to .002
Pistons:	
Diameter, standard	3.542
oversize, .02	3.562
.04	3.582
Clearance	.007 to .003

Piston rings:
- Number .. .. Three
- Type .. .. 2 compression, 1 oil control
- Gap, compression .. .. .015 to .023
- oil control .. .. .015 to .055

Camshaft:
- Number of bearings .. .. Four
- Diameter, front 1.650
- No. 2 .. .. 1.635
- No. 3 .. .. 1.620
- rear 1.605
- Clearance .. .. .002
- End float .. .. .001 to .004
- Thrust plates:
  - Standard, red .. .. .156
  - blue .. .. .157
  - Oversize, red .. .. .161
  - blue .. .. .162

Valves:
- Seat angle .. .. 45 deg.
- Stem diameter:
  - Inlet, standard .. .. .316
  - oversizes .. .. .008, .016, .024, .032
  - Exhaust, standard .. .. .315
  - oversizes .. .. .008, .016, .024, .032
- Valve guide bore:
  - Standard .. .. .318
  - Oversizes .. .. .326, .334
- Clearance (cold):
  - Inlet .. .. .014
  - Exhaust .. .. .016

Oil pump:
- Type .. .. Eccentric, bi-rotor
- Pressure (hot) .. .. 40 to 55 lb/sq inch at 1500 rev/min

ENGINE (2800)

As 2600 except as specified below

- Capacity .. .. 2792 cc
- Bore 3.66
- Stroke 2.70

Cylinder block:
- Bore diameter:
  - Class 1 .. .. 3.6616
  - Class 2 .. .. 3.6620
  - Class 3 .. .. 3.6624
  - Class 4 .. .. 3.6630
- Oversizes:
  - .020 .. .. 3.6821
  - .040 .. .. 3.7018
- Tolerance .. .. ± .0002

Pistons:
- Diameter:
  - Standard .. .. 3.6605 to 3.6615
  - .020 OS .. .. 3.6802 to 3.6812
  - .040 OS .. .. 3.6999 to 3.7009
- Clearance in bore .. .. .0011 to .0019

FUEL SYSTEM

Fuel pump:
Type	Mechanical
Drive	From eccentric on camshaft
Pressure	3.8 to 5.0 lb/sq inch
Flow (min)	1 pint in 43 seconds at 500 rev/min

Carburetter:
Type	Motorcraft 2-V
Idle speed, manual	800
automatic	670 in D
Fast-idle speed	1500
Fast-idle, choke clearance	$\frac{5}{32}$
Fast-idle, cam clearance	.010 to .020
Float level	.45
Float drop	1.9
Choke plate pull down	.260
Dechoke clearance	.320 at full throttle

IGNITION SYSTEM

Sparking plugs:
Type	Autolite AG22
Gap	.025

Coil:
Type	Oil filled with ballast resistance

Distributor:
Type	Bosch dual diaphragm
Rotation	Clockwise
Gap	.025
Initial advance	12 deg. BTDC
Dwell angle	37 to 41 deg.

COOLING SYSTEM

Type	Pressurised, pump-assisted

Radiator cap:
Release pressure	13 lb/sq inch
Belt tension	$\frac{1}{2}$ inch free play

Thermostat:
New, starts to open	185° to 192°F
fully open	210° to 216°F
Used, starts to open	178° to 199°F
fully open	203° to 223°F

CLUTCH

Type	Single dry plate, diaphragm spring
Actuation	Cable
Diameter	9.5
Free travel	.138 to .144
Pedal free travel	.5 to .75

MANUAL TRANSMISSION

Type	Four-speed forward and reverse
Synchromesh	All forward ratios
Ratios:	
First	3.65:1
Second	1.97:1
Third	1.37:1
Fourth	1.00:1
Reverse	2.66:1
Final drive ratio	3.22:1

AUTOMATIC TRANSMISSION

Type	Three-speed epicyclic with fluid torque converter
Selector	Floor mounted
Fluid	CIAZ-19582-A.C.D. ESW-M2C33-F (type F)

SUSPENSION

Front	Independent with coil springs, single arm and stabiliser bar
Rear	Semi-elliptic twin radius arms
Dampers	Hydraulic, telescopic
Length between spring eye centres	47
Length front eye to axle C/L	19.15
Width of spring levers	2

STEERING

Type	Rack and pinion
Angles:	
Caster	$-\frac{1}{2}$ deg. to $+1\frac{1}{2}$ deg.
Camber	$-\frac{1}{4}$ deg. to $-\frac{3}{4}$ deg.
King pin inclination	7 deg. 30 min to 8 deg. 30 min
Toe-out on turns	Inner 20 deg., outer 18 deg. 15 min to 19 deg. 45 min
Toe-in	0 to .25
Turning circle	31.5 feet

BRAKING SYSTEM

Type	Hydraulic, dual circuit Disc front, drum rear Mechanical handbrake
Front:	
Disc diameter	9.625
Thickness	.50
Run out	.0035
Pad coding	Blue, white, white, white, blue
Rear:	
Drum diameter	9.0
Lining, width	1.75 (later cars 2.70)
thickness (new)	.188
thickness (minimum)	.03 ($\frac{1}{32}$)
Fluid type	ESA-M6C25-A

ELECTRICAL EQUIPMENT

System	12-volt, negative ground
Battery:	
Type	Lead acid
Capacity	66 amp hours
Specific gravity	1.275 to 1.290
Alternator:	
Make and type	Bosch KI
Speed, ratio to engine	1.88 : 1 or 2.2 : 1
Output	35 amps
Brush, min length	.2
spring pressure	10.6 to 14.1 oz
Belt tension	$\frac{1}{2}$ inch total movement
Regulator:	
Type	Bosch, non-adjustable
Starter:	
Make and type	Bosch, pre-engaged
Teeth on pinion	10
Teeth on ring gear	135
Ratio	13.5 : 1
Brush, min length	.375
spring pressure	42.3 oz
Current draw	100 to 130 amps
Light bulbs:	
Outboard headlight	40/50 watts
Inboard headlight	37.5 watts
Side and flasher	4/32 C.P.
Tail and stop	4/32 C.P.
Rear flasher	32 C.P.
Number plate	5 C.P.
Back-up	21 C.P.
Courtez	6 C.P.
Instrument	2.2 watt
Fuses:	
Number	7
Rating	8 or 16 amp, see **Section 12 : 9**

CAPACITIES

Fuel tank	12 gallons ($9\frac{3}{4}$ Imp.)
Engine oil pan	$5\frac{1}{4}$ qts ($4\frac{1}{2}$ Imp.) (including filter)
Cooling	$8\frac{1}{4}$ qts (including heater)
Gearbox	2.8 pts (2.3 Imp.) SAE 80 EP
Automatic transmission	8 qts ($6\frac{1}{2}$ Imp.) ESW-M2C33-F
Steering gear	.3 pts SAE 90 EP
Rear axle	2.3 pts SAE 90 EP

TORQUE WRENCH SETTINGS

Values are in ft lb unless otherwise stated

Engine:

Cylinder head	30-40, 40-50, 65 to 80
Main bearing caps	65 to 75
Connecting rods	22 to 26
Crankshaft gear	32 to 36
Camshaft gear	32 to 36
Flywheel	45 to 50
Front cover	9 to 12
Water pump	6 to 12
Oil pump	10 to 12
Rocker shaft supports	32 to 36
Valve gear covers	2 to 4, 5 to 8
Intake manifold	2 to 4, 15 to 18
Oil pan	2 to 4, 5 to 8

Clutch and gearbox:

Pressure plate to flywheel	11 to 14
Housing to gearbox	40 to 47
Housing to engine	22 to 27
Extension housing to gearbox	20 to 35
Drain and filler plugs	25 to 30
Top cover	12 to 14

Automatic transmission:

Converter to flywheel	23 to 28
Converter to transmission housing	28 to 40
Oil pan	12 to 16
Converter cover	12 to 16
Engine to transmission	23 to 33
Downshift lever to shaft	12 to 16
Filler tube	32 to 42
Neutral switch to case	55 to 75
Cooler line fittings	80 to 120

Rear axle:

Differential bearing cap bolts	43 to 49
Axle shaft bearing retainer	20 to 23
Cover to axle housing	22 to 29
Ring gear to casing	50 to 54
Pinion flange	72 to 87
Axle breather	69 to 102 inch lb

Rear suspension:

Shock absorber to axle	40 to 45
Shock absorber to body	15 to 20 *
Spring U-bolts	18 to 26 *
Spring front hanger	27 to 32 *
Shackle nuts	8 to 10 *
Radius arm to axle body	25 to 30 *

Front suspension:

Stabiliser bar clamp	15 to 18 *
Lower control arm bushing	22 to 27 *
Upper mounting bolts	15 to 18
Ball stud nut	30 to 35
Crossmember to side member	25 to 30
Stabiliser bar to control arm	15 to 45

* To be tightened with weight of car on the wheels

Steering gear:

Steering arm to suspension	..	..	..	30 to 34
Steering gear to crossmember	..	..	..	15 to 18
Coupling to pinion spline	..	..	..	12 to 15
U-joint to steering shaft ..	..	..	..	12 to 15
Steering wheel nut	..	..	..	25 to 30
Connecting rod end	..	..	..	30 to 35

Brakes:

Caliper to suspension	..	..	..	45 to 50
Disc to hub	..	..	..	30 to 34
Road wheel nuts ..	..	..	..	50 to 55
Bleed valves	..	..	..	5 to 7
Hydraulic unions ..	..	..	..	5 to 7
Rear back plate to axle	..	..	..	15 to 18

Electrical:

Starter mounting bolts	..	..	..	20 to 25
Alternator mounting bolts	..	..	..	15 to 18
Alternator bracket	..	..	..	20 to 25
Pulley nut	..	..	..	20 to 25

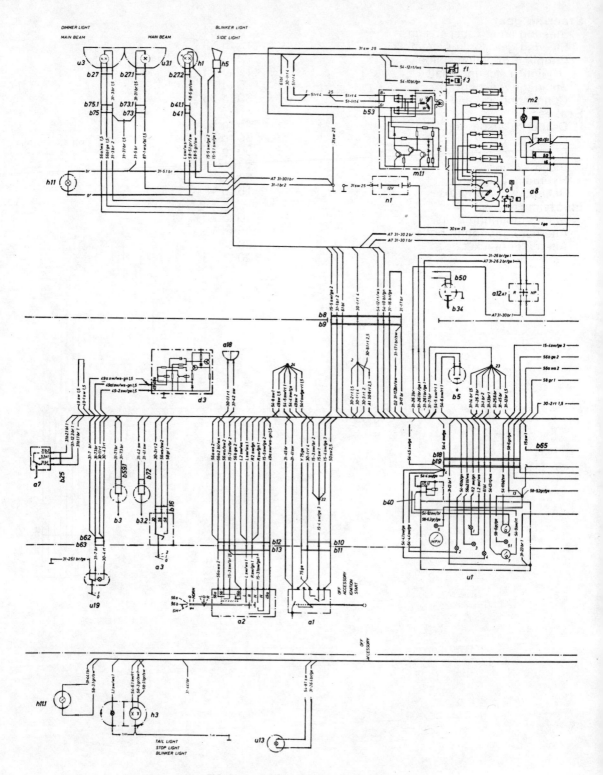

FIG 14:1   Wiring diagram, 2600, part 1

134

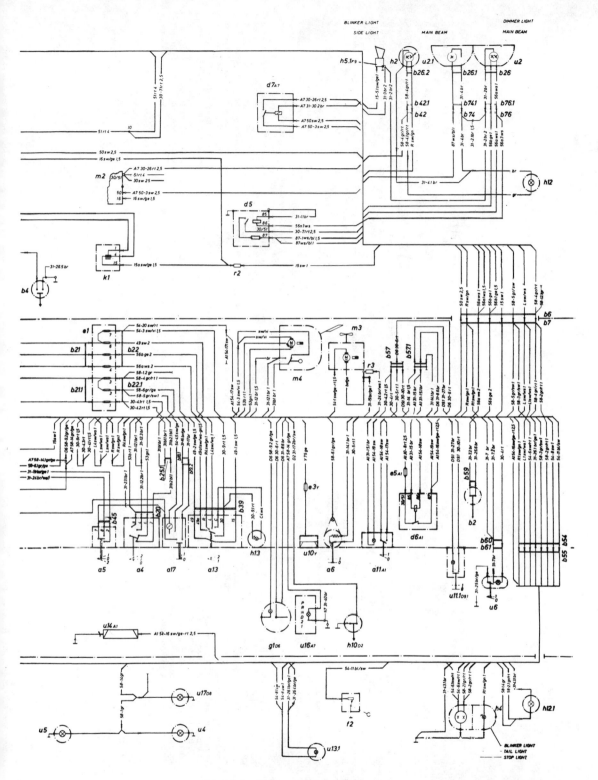

FIG 14:1   Wiring diagram, 2600, part 2

Key to Fig 14:1 a1 Steering/ignition lock a2 Blinker switch a3 Light switch a4 Windshield wiper motor switch, two stage a5 Heating blower switch, two stage a6 Cigar lighter a7 Foot operated switch windshield wiper motor a8 Ignition distributor a13 Blinker switch warning system a17 Switch-control-light, two circuit brake system a18 Buzzer b2 Door contact interruptor righthand interior light b3 Door contact interruptor lefthand interior light b3.2 Door contact interruptor buzzer b4 Back-up light switch b5 Stop light switch b6 Multiple connector, dashboard, right b7 Multiple connector, dashboard, left b8 Multiple connector, dashboard, right b9 Multiple connector, dashboard, left b10 Multiple connector, steering/ignition lock b11 Multiple connector, steering/ignition lock b12 Multiple connector, blinker switch b13 Multiple connector, blinker switch b16 Multiple connector, light switch b18 Multiple connector, instrument cluster b18.1 Multiple connector, switch-control light, two circuit brake system b19 Multiple connector, instrument cluster b19.2 Multiple connector, switch-control light, two circuit brake system b20 Multiple connector, windshield wiper motor switch b21 Multiple connector, fuse box b21.1 Multiple connector, fuse box b22 Multiple connector, fuse box b22.1 Multiple connector, fuse box b25 Multiple connector foot operated switch windshield wiper motor b25.1 Multiple connector wiper wash system b26 Multiple connector main beam headlight, right b26.1 Multiple connector remote headlight, right b26.2 Multiple connector blinker, side light, right b27 Multiple connector main beam headlight, left b27.1 Multiple connector remote headlight, left b41.1 Multiple connector blinker, side light, left b42 Multiple connector blinker, side light, right b42.1 Multiple connector blinker, side light, right b45 Multiple connector heating blower switch b50 Multiple connector warning light switch, two circuit brake system b53 Multiple connector alternator b54 Multiple connector, instrument panel, right b55 Multiple connector, instrument panel, right b57 Multiple connector b57.1 Multiple connector b59 Door contact switch, right b59.1 Door contact switch, left b60 Multiple connector, interior light, right b61 Multiple connector, interior light, right b62 Multiple connector, interior light, left b63 Multiple connector, interior light, left b65 Connector wire 15 b72 Multiple connector buzzer switch b73 Multiple connector remote headlight, right b73.1 Multiple connector remote headlight, left b74 Multiple connector main beam headlight, right b74.1 Multiple connector remote headlight, right b75 Multiple connector main beam headlight, left b75.1 Multiple connector remote headlight, left b76 Multiple connector main beam headlight, right b76.1 Multiple connector main beam headlight, right d3 Blinker unit d5 Relay remote headlights e1 Fuse box f1 Transmitter water temperature gauge f2 Transmitter fuel gauge f3 Oil pressure control switch h1 Blinker, side light, left h2 Blinker, side light, right h3 Combined tail light, left h4 Combined tail light, right h5 Horn, left h11 Side marker front, left h11.1 Side marker back, left h12 Side marker front, right h12.1 Side marker back, right h13 Warning indicator, control light k1 Ignition coil m1.1 Alternator m2 Starter m3 Heating blower motor m4 Windshield wiper motor n1 Battery r2 Series resistance wire ignition r3 Series resistor heating blower u1 Instrument cluster u2 Main beam headlight, right u2.1 Remote headlight, right u3 Main beam headlight, left u3.1 Remote headlight, left u4 Licence plate light, right u5 Licence plate light, left u6 Interior light, right u13 Back up light, left u13.1 Back up light, right u16 Transmission control switch d6 Working current relay heating plate e5 Fuse heating plate a12 Blocking, switch automatic transmission u16 Transmission control selector dial d7 Working current relay automatic transmission h10 Handbrake warning switch g1 Clock u17 Luggage compartment light u11.1 Reading light h5.1 Horn, right e3 Fuse radio u10 Radio b27.2 Multiple connector blinker, side light, left b34 Warning light switch two circuit brake system b39 Multiple connector blinker switch warning system b40 Voltage divider b41 Multiple connector blinker, side light, left 30 Interior lights, reading lights, 4-way hazard flasher, clock, buzzer, cigar lighter 58 Tail light, left, side light front and back, left, illumination, instrument cluster, illumination, cigar lighter, illumination, transmission control selector dial, illumination, clock, tail light, right, side light front and back, right, luggage compartment lights, licence plate lights 56a Main beam, relay remote head lights 56b Low beam 15 Back up lights, heating blower motor, blinker system, stop light, voltage divider, control light, two circuit brake system, control light charging current, control light oil pressure 15 Windshield wiper motor, current circuit heating plate A1 In combination with heating plate A7 In combination with automatic gear D2 In combination with two circuit brake system D6 In combination with clock D8 In combination with luggage compartment light D9 In combination with interior light, left D9.1 In combination with reading light F9 In combination with horn, right Y In combination with radio

Remarks: Interior wiring diagram and symbol according to Din. A. lec.

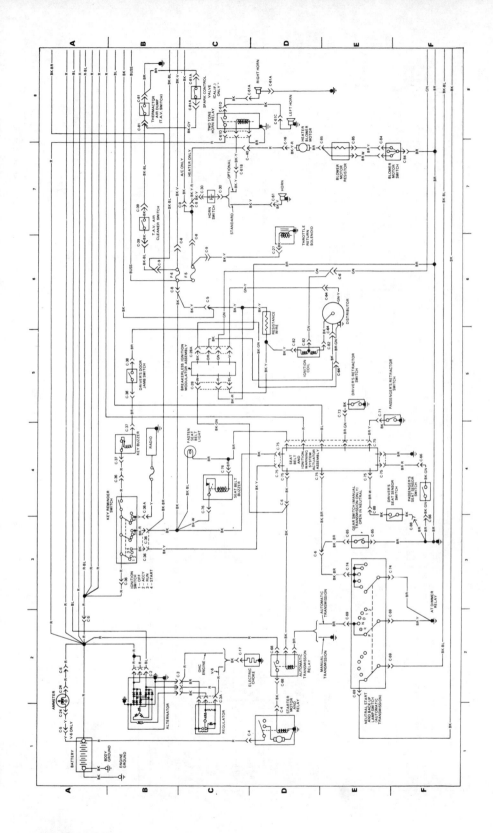

FIG 14:2 Wiring diagram, 2800, part 1

Wiring colour code: BK Black R Red Y Yellow BL Blue W White GN Green GY Grey BR Brown V Violet O Orange

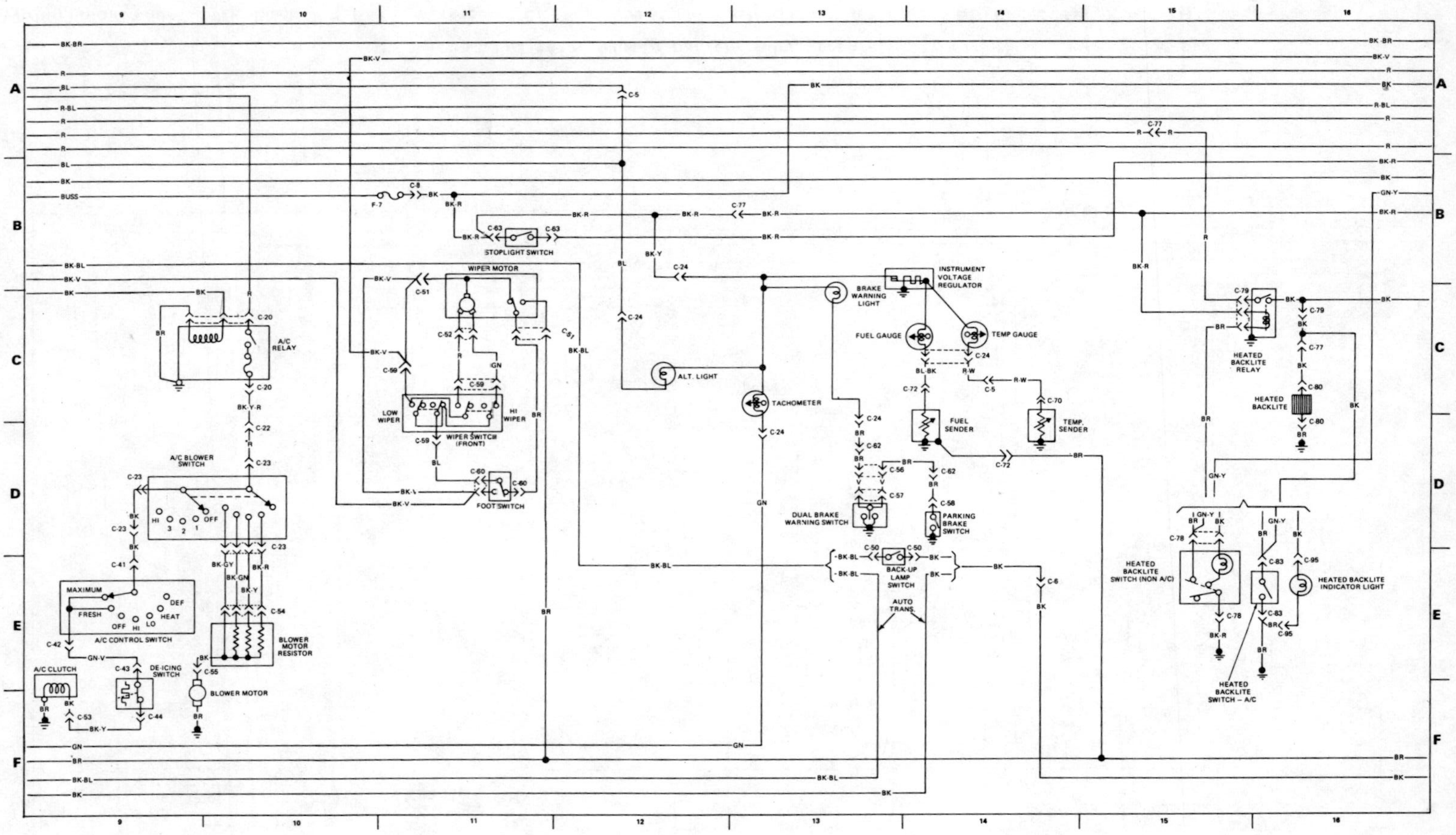

FIG 14:2 Wiring diagram, 2800, part 2

Wiring colour code: **BK** Black **R** Red **Y** Yellow **BL** Blue **W** White **GN** Green **GY** Grey **BR** Brown **V** Violet **O** Orange

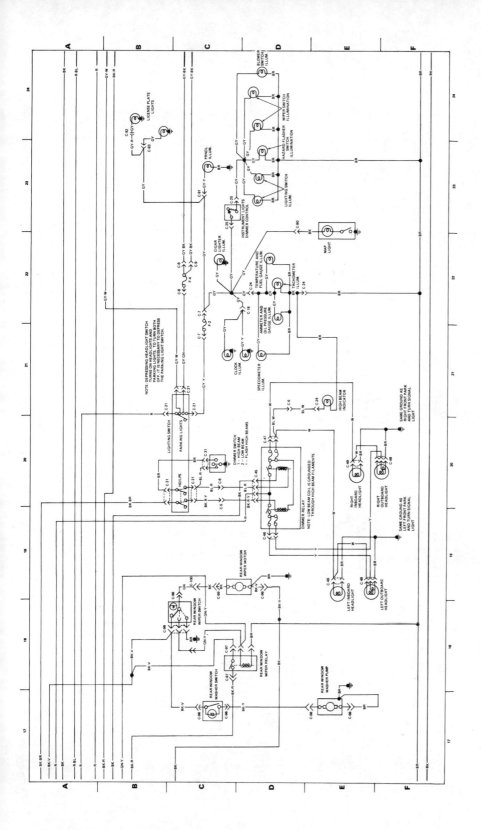

FIG 14:2 Wiring diagram, 2800, part 3

Wiring colour code: **BK** Black   **R** Red   **Y** Yellow   **BL** Blue   **W** White   **GN** Green   **GY** Grey   **BR** Brown   **V** Violet   **O** Orange

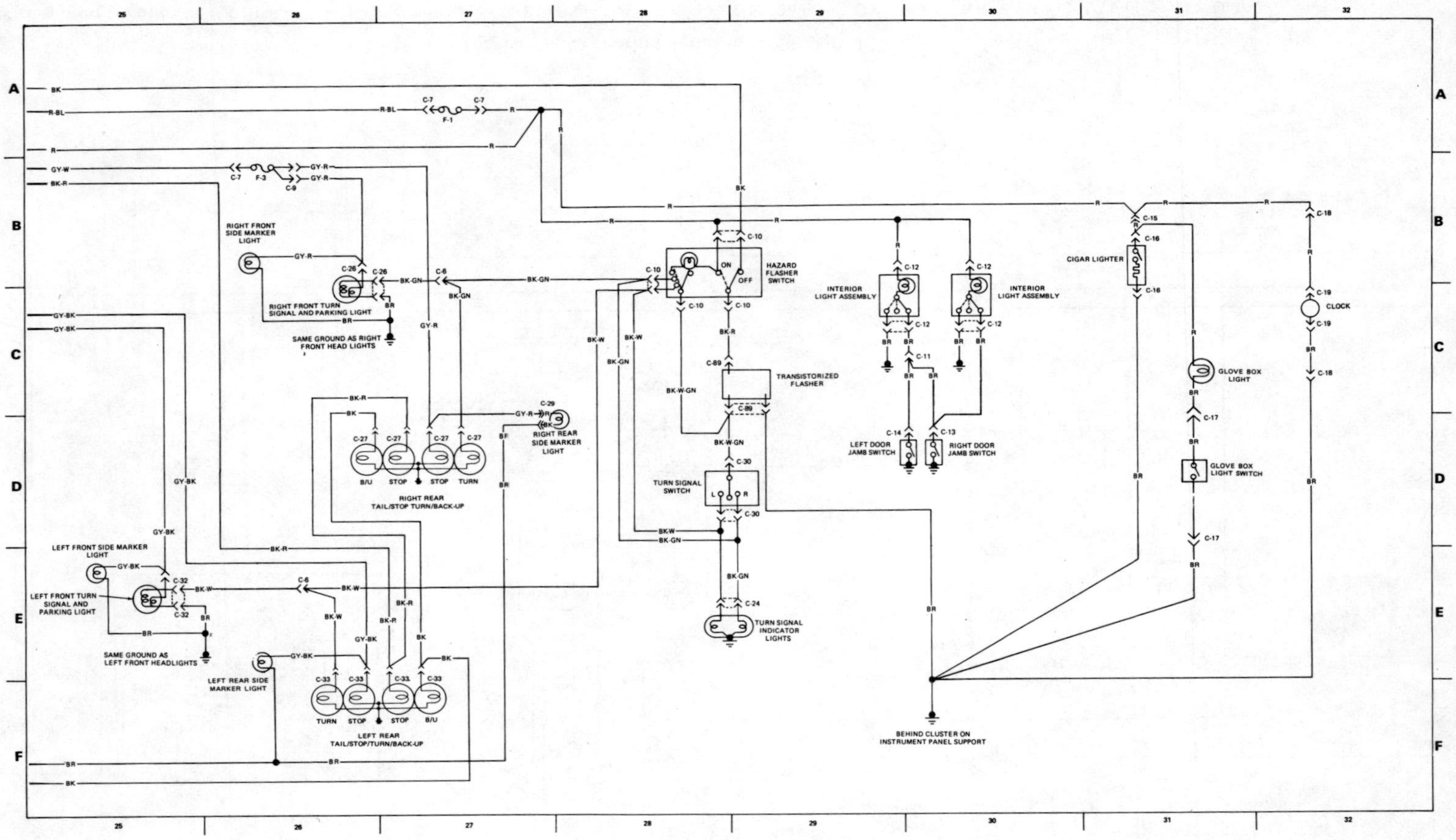

FIG 14:2 Wiring diagram, 2800, part 4

Wiring colour code: **BK** Black **R** Red **Y** Yellow **BL** Blue **W** White **GN** Green **GY** Grey **BR** Brown **V** Violet **O** Orange

140

HINTS ON MAINTENANCE AND OVERHAUL

There are few things more rewarding than the restoration of a vehicle's original peak of efficiency and smooth performance.

The following notes are intended to help the owner to reach that state of perfection. Providing that he possesses the basic manual skills he should have no difficulty in performing most of the operations detailed in this manual. It must be stressed, however, that where recommended in the manual, highly-skilled operations ought to be entrusted to experts, who have the necessary equipment, to carry out the work satisfactorily.

Quality of workmanship:

The hazardous driving conditions on the roads to-day demand that vehicles should be as nearly perfect, mechanically, as possible. It is therefore most important that amateur work be carried out with care, bearing in mind the often inadequate working conditions, and also the inferior tools which may have to be used. It is easy to counsel perfection in all things, and we recognize that it may be setting an impossibly high standard. We do, however, suggest that every care should be taken to ensure that a vehicle is as safe to take on the road as it is humanly possible to make it.

Safe working conditions:

Even though a vehicle may be stationary, it is still potentially dangerous if certain sensible precautions are not taken when working on it while it is supported on jacks or blocks. It is indeed preferable not to use jacks alone, but to supplement them with carefully placed blocks, so that there will be plenty of support if the car rolls off the jacks during a strenuous manoeuvre. Axle stands are an excellent way of providing a rigid base which is not readily disturbed. Piles of bricks are a dangerous substitute. Be careful not to get under heavy loads on lifting tackle, the load could fall. It is preferable not to work alone when lifting an engine, or when working underneath a vehicle which is supported well off the ground. To be trapped, particularly under the vehicle, may have unpleasant results if help is not quickly forthcoming. Make some provision, however humble, to deal with fires. Always disconnect a battery if there is a likelihood of electrical shorts. These may start a fire if there is leaking fuel about. This applies particularly to leads which can carry a heavy current, like those in the starter circuit. While on the subject of electricity, we must also stress the danger of using equipment which is run off the mains and which has no earth or has faulty wiring or connections. So many workshops have damp floors, and electrical shocks are of such a nature that it is sometimes impossible to let go of a live lead or piece of equipment due to the muscular spasms which take place.

Work demanding special care:

This involves the servicing of braking, steering and suspension systems. On the road, failure of the braking system may be disastrous. Make quite sure that there can be no possibility of failure through the bursting of rusty brake pipes or rotten hoses, nor to a sudden loss of pressure due to defective seals or valves.

Problems:

The chief problems which may face an operator are:
1 External dirt.
2 Difficulty in undoing tight fixings
3 Dismantling unfamiliar mechanisms.
4 Deciding in what respect parts are defective.
5 Confusion about the correct order for reassembly.
6 Adjusting running clearances.
7 Road testing.
8 Final tuning.

Practical suggestions to solve the problems:

1 Preliminary cleaning of large parts—engines, transmissions, steering, suspensions, etc.,—should be carried out before removal from the car. Where road dirt and mud alone are present, wash clean with a high-pressure water jet, brushing to remove stubborn adhesions, and allow to drain and dry. Where oil or grease is also present, wash down with a proprietary compound (Gunk, Teepol etc.,) applying with a stiff brush—an old paint brush is suitable—into all crevices. Cover the distributor and ignition coils with a polythene bag and then apply a strong water jet to clear the loosened deposits. Allow to drain and dry. The assemblies will then be sufficiently clean to remove and transfer to the bench for the next stage.

On the bench, further cleaning can be carried out, first wiping the parts as free as possible from grease with old newspaper. Avoid using rag or cotton waste which can leave clogging fibres behind. Any remaining grease can be removed with a brush dipped in paraffin. If necessary, traces of paraffin can be removed by carbon tetrachloride. Avoid using paraffin or petrol in large quantities for cleaning in enclosed areas, such as garages, on account of the high fire risk.

When all exteriors have been cleaned, and not before, dismantling can be commenced. This ensures that dirt will not enter into interiors and orifices revealed by dismantling. In the next phases, where components have to be cleaned, use carbon tetrachloride in preference to petrol and keep the containers covered except when in use. After the components have been cleaned, plug small holes with tapered hard wood plugs cut to size and blank off larger orifices with grease-proof paper and masking tape. Do not use soft wood plugs or matchsticks as they may break.

2 It is not advisable to hammer on the end of a screw thread, but if it must be done, first screw on a nut to protect the thread, and use a lead hammer. This applies particularly to the removal of tapered cotters. Nuts and bolts seem to 'grow' together, especially in exhaust systems. If penetrating oil does not work, try the judicious application of heat, but be careful of starting a fire. Asbestos sheet or cloth is useful to isolate heat.

Tight bushes or pieces of tail-pipe rusted into a silencer can be removed by splitting them with an open-ended hacksaw. Tight screws can sometimes be started by a tap from a hammer on the end of a suitable screwdriver. Many tight fittings will yield to the judicious use of a hammer, but it must be a soft-faced hammer if damage is to be avoided, use a heavy block on the opposite side to absorb shock. Any parts of the steering system which have been damaged should be renewed, as attempts to repair them may lead to cracking and subsequent failure, and steering ball joints should be disconnected using a recommended tool to prevent damage.

3 If often happens that an owner is baffled when trying to dismantle an unfamiliar piece of equipment. So many modern devices are pressed together or assembled by spinning-over flanges, that they must be sawn apart. The intention is that the whole assembly must be renewed. However, parts which appear to be in one piece to the naked eye, may reveal close-fitting joint lines when inspected with a magnifying glass, and, this may provide the necessary clue to dismantling. Left-handed screw threads are used where rotational forces would tend to unscrew a righthanded screw thread.

Be very careful when dismantling mechanisms which may come apart suddenly. Work in an enclosed space where the parts will be contained, and drape a piece of cloth over the device if springs are likely to fly in all directions. Mark everything which might be reassembled in the wrong position, scratched symbols may be used on unstressed parts, or a sequence of tiny dots from a centre punch can be useful. Stressed parts should never be scratched or centre-popped as this may lead to cracking under working conditions. Store parts which look alike in the correct order for reassembly. Never rely upon memory to assist in the assembly of complicated mechanisms, especially when they will be dismantled for a long time, but make notes, and drawings to supplement the diagrams in the manual, and put labels on detached wires. Rust stains may indicate unlubricated wear. This can sometimes be seen round the outside edge of a bearing cup in a universal joint. Look for bright rubbing marks on parts which normally should not make heavy contact. These might prove that something is bent or running out of truth. For example, there might be bright marks on one side of a piston, at the top near the ring grooves, and others at the bottom of the skirt on the other side. This could well be the clue to a bent connecting rod. Suspected cracks can be proved by heating the component in a light oil to approximately 100°C, removing, drying off, and dusting with french chalk, if a crack is present the oil retained in the crack will stain the french chalk.

4 In determining wear, and the degree, against the permissible limits set in the manual, accurate measurement can only be achieved by the use of a micrometer. In many cases, the wear is given to the fourth place of decimals; that is in ten-thousandths of an inch. This can be read by the vernier scale on the barrel of a good micrometer. Bore diameters are more difficult to determine. If, however, the matching shaft is accurately measured, the degree of play in the bore can be felt as a guide to its suitability. In other cases, the shank of a twist drill of known diameter is a handy check.

Many methods have been devised for determining the clearance between bearing surfaces. To-day the best and simplest is by the use of Plastigage, obtainable from most garages. A thin plastic thread is laid between the two surfaces and the bearing is tightened, flattening the thread. On removal, the width of the thread is compared with a scale supplied with the thread and the clearance is read off directly. Sometimes joint faces leak persistently, even after gasket renewal. The fault will then be traceable to distortion, dirt or burrs. Studs which are screwed into soft metal frequently raise burrs at the point of entry. A quick cure for this is to chamfer the edge of the hole in the part which fits over the stud.

5 **Always check a replacement part with the original one before it is fitted.**

If parts are not marked, and the order for reassembly is not known, a little detective work will help. Look for marks which are due to wear to see if they can be mated. Joint faces may not be identical due to manufacturing errors, and parts which overlap may be stained, giving a clue to the correct position. Most fixings leave identifying marks especially if they were painted over on assembly. It is then easier to decide whether a nut, for instance, has a plain, a spring, or a shakeproof washer under it. All running surfaces become 'bedded' together after long spells of work and tiny imperfections on one part will be found to have left corresponding marks on the other. This is particularly true of shafts and bearings and even a score on a cylinder wall will show on the piston.

6 Checking end float or rocker clearances by feeler gauge may not always give accurate results because of wear. For instance, the rocker tip which bears on a valve stem may be deeply pitted, in which case the feeler will simply be bridging a depression. Thrust washers may also wear depressions in opposing faces to make accurate measurement difficult. End float is then easier to check by using a dial gauge. It is common practice to adjust end play in bearing assemblies, like front hubs with taper rollers, by doing up the axle nut until the hub becomes stiff to turn and then backing it off a little. Do not use this method with ballbearing hubs as the assembly is often preloaded by tightening the axle nut to its fullest extent. If the splitpin hole will not line up, file the base of the nut a little.

Steering assemblies often wear in the straight-ahead position. If any part is adjusted, make sure that it remains free when moved from lock to lock. Do not be surprised if an assembly like a steering gearbox, which is known to be carefully adjusted outside the car, becomes stiff when it is bolted in place. This will be due to distortion of the case by the pull of the mounting bolts, particularly if the mounting points are not all touching together. This problem may be met in other equipment and is cured by careful attention to the alignment of mounting points.

When a spanner is stamped with a size and A/F it means that the dimension is the width between the jaws and has no connection with ANF, which is the designation for the American National Fine thread. Coarse threads like Whitworth are rarely used on cars to-day except for studs which screw into soft aluminium or cast iron. For this reason it might be found that the top end of a cylinder head stud has a fine thread and the lower end a coarse thread to screw into the cylinder block. If the car has mainly UNF threads then it is likely that any coarse threads will be UNC, which are not the same as Whitworth. Small sizes have the same number of threads in Whitworth and UNC, but in the $\frac{1}{2}$ inch size for example, there are twelve threads to the inch in the former and thirteen in the latter.

7 After a major overhaul, particularly if a great deal of work has been done on the braking, steering and suspension systems, it is advisable to approach the problem of testing with care. If the braking system has been overhauled, apply heavy pressure to the brake pedal and get a second operator to check every possible source of leakage. The brakes may work extremely well, but a leak could cause complete failure after a few miles.

Do not fit the hub caps until every wheel nut has been checked for tightness, and make sure the tyre pressures are correct. Check the levels of coolant, lubricants and hydraulic fluids. Being satisfied that all is well, take the car on the road and test the brakes at once. Check the steering and the action of the handbrake. Do all this at moderate speeds on quiet roads, and make sure there is no other vehicle behind you when you try a rapid stop.

Finally, remember that many parts settle down after a time, so check for tightness of all fixings after the car has been on the road for a hundred miles or so.

8 It is useless to tune an engine which has not reached its normal running temperature. In the same way, the tune of an engine which is stiff after a rebore will be different when the engine is again running free. Remember too, that rocker clearances on pushrod operated valve gear will change when the cylinder head nuts are tightened after an initial period of running with a new head gasket.

Trouble may not always be due to what seems the obvious cause. Ignition, carburation and mechanical condition are interdependent and spitting back through the carburetter, which might be attributed to a weak mixture, can be caused by a sticking inlet valve.

For one final hint on tuning, never adjust more than one thing at a time or it will be impossible to tell which adjustment produced the desired result.

NOTES

GLOSSARY OF TERMS

Allen key   Cranked wrench of hexagonal section for use with socket head screws.

Alternator   Electrical generator producing alternating current. Rectified to direct current for battery charging.

Ambient temperature   Surrounding atmospheric temperature.

Annulus   Used in engineering to indicate the outer ring gear of an epicyclic gear train.

Armature   The shaft carrying the windings, which rotates in the magnetic field of a generator or starter motor. That part of a solenoid or relay which is activated by the magnetic field.

Axial   In line with, or pertaining to, an axis.

Backlash   Play in meshing gears.

Balance lever   A bar where force applied at the centre is equally divided between connections at the ends.

Banjo axle   Axle casing with large diameter housing for the crownwheel and differential.

Bendix pinion   A self-engaging and self-disengaging drive on a starter motor shaft.

Bevel pinion   A conical shaped gearwheel, designed to mesh with a similar gear with an axis usually at 90 deg. to its own.

bhp   Brake horse power, measured on a dynamometer.

bmep   Brake mean effective pressure. Average pressure on a piston during the working stroke.

Brake cylinder   Cylinder with hydraulically operated piston(s) acting on brake shoes or pad(s).

Brake regulator   Control valve fitted in hydraulic braking system which limits brake pressure to rear brakes during heavy braking to prevent rear wheel locking.

Camber   Angle at which a wheel is tilted from the vertical.

Capacitor   Modern term for an electrical condenser. Part of distributor assembly, connected across contact breaker points, acts as an interference suppressor.

Castellated   Top face of a nut, slotted across the flats, to take a locking splitpin.

Castor   Angle at which the kingpin or swivel pin is tilted when viewed from the side.

cc   Cubic centimetres. Engine capacity is arrived at by multiplying the area of the bore in sq cm by the stroke in cm by the number of cylinders.

Clevis   U-shaped forked connector used with a clevis pin, usually at handbrake connections.

Collet   A type of collar, usually split and located in a groove in a shaft, and held in place by a retainer. The arrangement used to retain the spring(s) on a valve stem in most cases.

Commutator   Rotating segmented current distributor between armature windings and brushes in generator or motor.

Compression ratio   The ratio, or quantitative relation, of the total volume (piston at bottom of stroke) to the unswept volume (piston at top of stroke) in an engine cylinder.

Condenser   See capacitor.

Core plug   Plug for blanking off a manufacturing hole in a casting.

Crownwheel   Large bevel gear in rear axle, driven by a bevel pinion attached to the propeller shaft. Sometimes called a 'ring gear'.

'C'-spanner   Like a 'C' with a handle. For use on screwed collars without flats, but with slots or holes.

Damper   Modern term for shock-absorber, used in vehicle suspension systems to damp out spring oscillations.

Depression   The lowering of atmospheric pressure as in the inlet manifold and carburetter.

Dowel   Close tolerance pin, peg, tube, or bolt, which accurately locates mating parts.

Drag link   Rod connecting steering box drop arm (pitman arm) to nearest front wheel steering arm in certain types of steering systems.

Dry liner   Thinwall tube pressed into cylinder bore

Dry sump   Lubrication system where all oil is scavenged from the sump, and returned to a separate tank.

Dynamo   See Generator.

Electrode   Terminal, part of an electrical component, such as the points or 'Electrodes' of a sparking plug.

Electrolyte   In lead-acid car batteries a solution of sulphuric acid and distilled water.

End float   The axial movement between associated parts, end play.

EP   Extreme pressure. In lubricants, special grades for heavily loaded bearing surfaces, such as gear teeth in a gearbox, or crownwheel and pinion in a rear axle.

Fade	Of brakes. Reduced efficiency due to overheating.
Field coils	Windings on the polepieces of motors and generators.
Fillets	Narrow finishing strips usually applied to interior bodywork.
First motion shaft	Input shaft from clutch to gearbox.
Fullflow filter	Filters in which all the oil is pumped to the engine. If the element becomes clogged, a bypass valve operates to pass unfiltered oil to the engine.
FWD	Front wheel drive.
Gear pump	Two meshing gears in a close fitting casing. Oil is carried from the inlet round the outside of both gears in the spaces between the gear teeth and casing to the outlet, the meshing gear teeth prevent oil passing back to the inlet, and the oil is forced through the outlet port.
Generator	Modern term for 'Dynamo'. When rotated produces electrical current.
Grommet	A ring of protective or sealing material. Can be used to protect pipes or leads passing through bulkheads.
Grubscrew	Fully threaded headless screw with screwdriver slot. Used for locking, or alignment purposes.
Gudgeon pin	Shaft which connects a piston to its connecting rod. Sometimes called 'wrist pin', or 'piston pin'.
Halfshaft	One of a pair transmitting drive from the differential.
Helical	In spiral form. The teeth of helical gears are cut at a spiral angle to the side faces of the gearwheel.
Hot spot	Hot area that assists vapourisation of fuel on its way to cylinders. Often provided by close contact between inlet and exhaust manifolds.
HT	High Tension. Applied to electrical current produced by the ignition coil for the sparking plugs.
Hydrometer	A device for checking specific gravity of liquids. Used to check specific gravity of electrolyte.
Hypoid bevel gears	A form of bevel gear used in the rear axle drive gears. The bevel pinion meshes below the centre line of the crownwheel, giving a lower propeller shaft line.
Idler	A device for passing on movement. A free running gear between driving and driven gears. A lever transmitting track rod movement to a side rod in steering gear.
Impeller	A centrifugal pumping element. Used in water pumps to stimulate flow.
Journals	Those parts of a shaft that are in contact with the bearings.
Kingpin	The main vertical pin which carries the front wheel spindle, and permits steering movement. May be called 'steering pin' or 'swivel pin'.
Layshaft	The shaft which carries the laygear in the gearbox. The laygear is driven by the first motion shaft and drives the third motion shaft according to the gear selected. Sometimes called the 'countershaft' or 'second motion shaft.'
lb ft	A measure of twist or torque. A pull of 10 lb at a radius of 1 ft is a torque of 10 lb ft.
lb/sq in	Pounds per square inch.
Little-end	The small, or piston end of a connecting rod. Sometimes called the 'small-end'.
LT	Low Tension. The current output from the battery.
Mandrel	Accurately manufactured bar or rod used for test or centring purposes.
Manifold	A pipe, duct, or chamber, with several branches.
Needle rollers	Bearing rollers with a length many times their diameter.
Oil bath	Reservoir which lubricates parts by immersion. In air filters, a separate oil supply for wetting a wire mesh element to hold the dust.
Oil wetted	In air filters, a wire mesh element lightly oiled to trap and hold airborne dust.
Overlap	Period during which inlet and exhaust valves are open together.
Panhard rod	Bar connected between fixed point on chassis and another on axle to control sideways movement.
Pawl	Pivoted catch which engages in the teeth of a ratchet to permit movement in one direction only.
Peg spanner	Tool with pegs, or pins, to engage in holes or slots in the part to be turned.
Pendant pedals	Pedals with levers that are pivoted at the top end.
Phillips screwdriver	A cross-point screwdriver for use with the cross-slotted heads of Phillips screws.
Pinion	A small gear, usually in relation to another gear.
Piston-type damper	Shock absorber in which damping is controlled by a piston working in a closed oil-filled cylinder.
Preloading	Preset static pressure on ball or roller bearings not due to working loads.
Radial	Radiating from a centre, like the spokes of a wheel.

Radius rod	Pivoted arm confining movement of a part to an arc of fixed radius.
Ratchet	Toothed wheel or rack which can move in one direction only, movement in the other being prevented by a pawl.
Ring gear	A gear tooth ring attached to outer periphery of flywheel. Starter pinion engages with it during starting.
Runout	Amount by which rotating part is out of true.
Semi-floating axle	Outer end of rear axle halfshaft is carried on bearing inside axle casing. Wheel hub is secured to end of shaft.
Servo	A hydraulic or pneumatic system for assisting, or, augmenting a physical effort. See 'Vacuum Servo'.
Setscrew	One which is threaded for the full length of the shank.
Shackle	A coupling link, used in the form of two parallel pins connected by side plates to secure the end of the master suspension spring and absorb the effects of deflection.
Shell bearing	Thinwalled steel shell lined with anti-friction metal. Usually semi-circular and used in pairs for main and big-end bearings.
Shock absorber	See 'Damper'.
Silentbloc	Rubber bush bonded to inner and outer metal sleeves.
Socket-head screw	Screw with hexagonal socket for an Allen key.
Solenoid	A coil of wire creating a magnetic field when electric current passes through it. Used with a soft iron core to operate contacts or a mechanical device.
Spur gear	A gear with teeth cut axially across the periphery.
Stub axle	Short axle fixed at one end only.
Tachometer	An instrument for accurate measurement of rotating speed. Usually indicates in revolutions per minute.

TDC	Top Dead Centre. The highest point reached by a piston in a cylinder, with the crank and connecting rod in line.
Thermostat	Automatic device for regulating temperature. Used in vehicle coolant systems to open a valve which restricts circulation at low temperature.
Third motion shaft	Output shaft of gearbox.
Threequarter floating axle	Outer end of rear axle halfshaft flanged and bolted to wheel hub, which runs on bearing mounted on outside of axle casing. Vehicle weight is not carried by the axle shaft.
Thrust bearing or washer	Used to reduce friction in rotating parts subject to axial loads.
Torque	Turning or twisting effort. See 'lb ft'.
Track rod	The bar(s) across the vehicle which connect the steering arms and maintain the front wheels in their correct alignment.
UJ	Universal joint. A coupling between shafts which permits angular movement.
UNF	Unified National Fine screw thread.
Vacuum servo	Device used in brake system, using difference between atmospheric pressure and inlet manifold depression to operate a piston which acts to augment brake pressure as required. See 'Servo'.
Venturi	A restriction or 'choke' in a tube, as in a carburetter, used to increase velocity to obtain a reduction in pressure.
Vernier	A sliding scale for obtaining fractional readings of the graduations of an adjacent scale.
Welch plug	A domed thin metal disc which is partially flattened to lock in a recess. Used to plug core holes in castings.
Wet liner	Removable cylinder barrel, sealed against coolant leakage, where the coolant is in direct contact with the outer surface.
Wet sump	A reservoir attached to the crankcase to hold the lubricating oil.

NOTES

INDEX

NOTES

Alfa Romeo Giulia 1600,
    1750, 2000 1962 on
Aston Martin 1921-58
Auto Union Audi 70, 80,
    Super 90, 1966-72
Audi 100 1969 on
Austin, Morris etc.
    1100 Mk. 1 1962-67
Austin, Morris etc. 1100
    Mk. 2, 3, 1300 Mk. 1, 2, 3
    America 1968 on
Austin A30, A35, A40
    Farina 1951-69
Austin A55 Mk. 2, A60
    1958-69
Austin A99, A110 1959-68
Austin J4 1960 on
Austin Allegro 1973 on
Austin Maxi 1969 on
Austin, Morris 1800
    1964 on
Austin, Morris 2200 1972 on
Austin Kimberley, Tasman
    1970 on
Austin, Morris 1300, 1500
    Nomad 1969 on
BMC 3 (Austin A50, A55
    Mk. 1, Morris Oxford
    2, 3 1954-59)
Austin Healey 100/6,
    3000 1956-68
Austin Healey, MG
    Sprite, Midget 1958 on
Bedford CA Mk. 2 1964-69
Bedford CF Vans 1969 on
Bedford Beagle HA Vans
    1964 on
BMW 1600 1966 on
BMW 1800 1964-71
BMW 2000, 2002 1966 on
Chevrolet Corvair 1960-69
Chevrolet Corvette V8
    1957-65
Chevrolet Corvette V8
    1965 on
Chevrolet Vega 2300
    1970 on
Chrysler Valiant V8
    1965 on
Chrysler Valiant Straight
    Six 1963 on
Citroen DS 19, ID 19
    1955-66
Citroen ID 19, DS 19, 20,
    21 1966 on
Citroen Dyane Ami 1964 on
Daf 31, 32, 33, 44, 55
    1961 on
Datsun Bluebird 610 series
    1972 on
Datsun Cherry 100A, 120A
    1971 on
Datsun 1000, 1200 1968 on
Datsun 1300, 1400, 1600
    1968 on
Datsun 240C 1971 on

Datsun 240Z Sport 1970 on
Fiat 124 1966 on
Fiat 124 Sport 1966 on
Fiat 125 1967-72
Fiat 127 1971 on
Fiat 128 1969 on
Fiat 500 1957 on
Fiat 600, 600D 1955-69
Fiat 850 1964 on
Fiat 1100 1957-69
Fiat 1300, 1500 1961-67
Ford Anglia Prefect 100E
    1953-62
Ford Anglia 105E, Prefect
    107E 1959-67
Ford Capri 1300, 1600 OHV
    1968 on
Ford Capri 1300, 1600,
    2000 OHC 1972 on
Ford Capri 2000 V4, 3000 V6
    1969 on
Ford Classic, Capri
    1961-64
Ford Consul, Zephyr,
    Zodiac, 1, 2 1950-62
Ford Corsair Straight
    Four 1963-65
Ford Corsair V4 1965-68
Ford Corsair V4 2000
    1969-70
Ford Cortina 1962-66
Ford Cortina 1967-68
Ford Cortina 1969-70
Ford Cortina Mk. 3
    1970 on
Ford Escort 1967 on
Ford Falcon 6 1964-70
Ford Falcon XK, XL
    1960-63
Ford Falcon 6 XR/XA
    1966 on
Ford Falcon V8 (U.S.A.)
    1965-71
Ford Falcon V8 (Aust.)
    1966 on
Ford Pinto 1970 on
Ford Maverick 6 1969 on
Ford Maverick V8 1970 on
Ford Mustang 6 1965 on
Ford Mustang V8 1965 on
Ford Thames 10, 12,
    15 cwt 1957-65
Ford Transit V4 1965 on
Ford Zephyr Zodiac Mk. 3
    1962-66
Ford Zephyr Zodiac V4,
    V6, Mk. 4 1966-72
Ford Consul, Granada
    1972 on
Hillman Avenger 1970 on
Hillman Hunter 1966 on
Hillman Imp 1963-68
Hillman Imp 1969 on
Hillman Minx 1 to 5
    1956-65
Hillman Minx 1965-67

Hillman Minx 1966-70
Hillman Super Minx
    1961-65
Jaguar XK120, 140, 150,
    Mk. 7, 8, 9 1948-61
Jaguar 2.4, 3.4, 3.8 Mk.
    1, 2 1955-69
Jaguar 'E' Type 1961-72
Jaguar 'S' Type 420
    1963-68
Jaguar XJ6 1968 on
Jowett Javelin Jupiter
    1947-53
Landrover 1, 2 1948-61
Landrover 2, 2a, 3 1959 on
Mazda 616 1970 on
Mazda 808, 818 1972 on
Mazda 1200, 1300 1969 on
Mazda 1500, 1800 1967 on
Mazda RX-2 1971 on
Mazda R100, RX-3 1970 on
Mercedes-Benz 190b,
    190c, 200 1959-68
Mercedes-Benz 220
    1959-65
Mercedes-Benz 220/8
    1968 on
Mercedes-Benz 230
    1963-68
Mercedes-Benz 250
    1965-67
Mercedes-Benz 250
    1968 on
Mercedes-Benz 280
    1968 on
MG TA to TF 1936-55
MGA MGB 1955-68
MGB 1969 on
Mini 1959 on
Mini Cooper 1961-72
Morgan Four 1936-72
Morris Marina 1971 on
Morris (Aust) Marina
    1972 on
Morris Minor 2, 1000
    1952-71
Morris Oxford 5, 6 1959-71
NSU 1000 1963-72
NSU Prinz 1 to 4 1957-72
Opel Ascona, Manta
    1970 on
Opel GT 1900 1968 on
Opel Kadett, Olympia 993 cc
    1078 cc 1962 on
Opel Kadett, Olympia 1492,
    1698, 1897 cc 1967 on
Opel Rekord C 1966-72
Peugeot 204 1965 on
Peugeot 304 1970 on
Peugeot 404 1960 on
Peugeot 504 1968 on
Porsche 356A, B, C 1957-65
Porsche 911 1964 on
Porsche 912 1965-69
Porsche 914 S 1969 on
Reliant Regal 1952-73

Renault R4, R4L, 4 1961 on
Renault 5 1972 on
Renault 6 1968 on
Renault 8, 10, 1100 1962-71
Renault 12, 1969 on
Renault 15, 17 1971 on
Renault R16 1965 on
Renault Dauphine
    Floride 1957-67
Renault Caravelle 1962-68
Rover 60 to 110 1953-64
Rover 2000 1963-73
Rover 3 Litre 1958-67
Rover 3500, 3500S 1968 on
Saab 95, 96, Sport
    1960-68
Saab 99 1969 on
Saab V4 1966 on
Simca 1000 1961 on
Simca 1100 1967 on
Simca 1300, 1301, 1500,
    1501 1963 on
Skoda One (440, 445, 450)
    1955-70
Sunbeam Rapier Alpine
    1955-65
Toyota Carina, Celica
    1971 on
Toyota Corolla 1100,
    1200 1967 on
Toyota Corona 1500 Mk. 1
    1965-70
Toyota Corona Mk. 2
    1969 on
Triumph TR2, TR3, TR3A
    1952-62
Triumph TR4, TR4A
    1961-67
Triumph TR5, TR250,
    TR6 1967 on
Triumph 1300, 1500
    1965-73
Triumph 2000 Mk. 1, 2.5 PI
    Mk. 1 1963-69
Triumph 2000 Mk. 2, 2.5 PI
    Mk. 2 1969 on
Triumph Dolomite 1972 on
Triumph Herald 1959-68
Triumph Herald 1969-71
Triumph Spitfire, Vitesse
    1962-68
Triumph Spitfire Mk. 3, 4
    1969 on
Triumph GT6, Vitesse
    2 Litre 1969 on
Triumph Stag 1970 on
Triumph Toledo 1970 on
Vauxhall Velox, Cresta
    1957-72
Vauxhall Victor 1, 2, FB
    1957-64
Vauxhall Victor 101
    1964-67
Vauxhall Victor FD 1600,
    2000 1967-72

Continued on following page

Vauxhall Victor 3300,
   Ventora 1968-72
Vauxhall Victor FE
   Ventora 1972 on
Vauxhall Viva HA 1963-66
Vauxhall Viva HB 1966-70

Vauxhall Viva, HC Firenza
   1971 on
Volkswagen Beetle 1954-67
Volkswagen Beetle 1968 on
Volkswagen 1500 1961-66

Volkswagen 1600 Fastback
   1965-73
Volkswagen Transporter
   1954-67
Volkswagen Transporter
   1968 on

Volkswagen 411 1968-72
Volvo 120 series 1961-70
Volvo 140 series 1966 on
Volvo 160 series 1968 on
Volvo 1800 1960-73